80541

795 DD

The *Earthquake* at **Port-Royal**

Tuesday the 7th. of

Port Roya

D0984627

Port Royal
Rediscovered

Port Royal
Rediscovered

BY ROBERT F. MARX

DOUBLEDAY & COMPANY, INC.
GARDEN CITY, NEW YORK
1973

ISBN: 0-385-08296-7
Library of Congress Catalog Card Number 72–89330

To Milt Machlin

Port Royal
Rediscovered

Chapter One

On the southern coast of Jamaica, overshadowed by the lush Blue Mountains, a long, low sandspit curves south and then west away from the island. Called the Palisadoes, it forms Kingston Harbour, considered one of the best natural seaports in the Western Hemisphere, the size of which was thus described by a seventeenth-century visitor: "This harbour is one of the marvels of the World for it is capable of holding all the ships of Christendom." Originally there was a small island, or cay, laying off the western tip of the Palisadoes sandspit, separated by a marshy area of mangrove trees. A less auspicious site for a settlement can scarcely be imagined: the cay had no fresh water, no crops grew on its barren sand, and it was a breeding ground for pestilential insects. Yet, in the closing years of the seventeenth century, that cay, having been connected to the Palisadoes through the herculean efforts of the English settlers and named Port Royal, ranked as the most flourishing seaport in the Caribbean and one of the richest cities in the world. A resident in 1683 wrote:

> The town of Port Royal, being as it were the Store House or Treasury of the West Indies, is always like a

continual Mart or Fair, where all sorts of choice merchandises are daily imported, not only to furnish the island, but vast quantities are thence again transported to supply the Spaniards, Indians and other Nations, who in exchange return us bars and cakes of Gold, wedges and pigs of silver, Pistoles, Pieces of Eight and several other coins of both metals, with store of wrought Plate, Jewels, rich pearl necklaces, and of Pearl unsorted or undrilled several bushels; besides which, we are furnished with the purest and most fine sorts of Dust Gold from Guiney, by the Negroe Ships, who first come to Jamaica to deliver their Blacks, and there usually refit and stay to reload three or four months; in which time (though the Companies Gold may be partly sent home) yet the Merchants, Masters of Ships, and almost every Mariner (having private Cargoes) take occasion to sell or exchange great quantities; some of which our Goldsmiths there work up, who being yet few grow very wealthy, for almost every House hath a rich cupboard of Plate, which they carelessly expose, scarce shutting their doors in the night, being in no apprehension of Thieves for want of receivers as aforesaid. And whereas most other Plantations ever did and now do keep their accounts in Sugar, or the proper Commodities of the place, for want of Money, it is otherwise in Jamaica, for in Port Royal there is more plenty of running Cash (proportionally to the number of its inhabitants) than is in London.

Port Royal had the distinction of being labeled "the most wicked city in the world." Although the town was dominated by the spires of St. Paul's Church, it had a reputation for godlessness unrivaled in the Caribbean. Tales of the profligacy, drunkenness, and wantonness that flourished there circulated around the world. A newly arrived clergyman returned to England on the same ship he had arrived in, because as he put it: "This town is the Sodom of the New World and since the majority of its population consists of pirates, cutthroats, whores and some of the vilest persons in the whole of the world, I felt my permanence there was of no use and I could better preach the Word of God elsewhere among a better sort of folk." A visitor in 1690 reported that one out of every four or five buildings in the town consisted "of brothels, gaming houses, taverns and grog shops."

During its heyday, more than five hundred ships, some as large as one thousand tons, called annually at Port Royal, and after long months at sea the crews of these vessels were eager for lusty recreation ashore, which the inhabitants were happy to provide—for a price.

Geographically situated at the center of the Caribbean, Port Royal was ideally located for trading and privateering voyages all over the West Indies and served as a base for merchants, smugglers, pirates, privateers, and other adventurers keen to make money quickly—as many of them did. Often it was a case of easy come, easy go, and more than one fortune was made in a day and lost in a night. Port Royal was a boom town where gold, silver, and precious gems flowed through the bawdyhouses and taverns, across the gaming tables, and through the hands of even the most ordinary shopkeepers and tradesmen—and everyone thought it would last forever.

Port Royal was comparable to many European trade towns of its size, but visitors to the Caribbean port were struck at once by how incredibly crowded the place was. More than two thousand buildings stood crammed together in what appeared to be a solid mass, its edge reaching out into the harbor, where houses had even been built on pilings driven into the soft sand. Approximately half the buildings were built of brick and the others of wood. All had red tile roofs and no chimneys. Owing to the excessive heat of the place, all cooking was done in small brick buildings, called cookhouses, which were built adjacent to the main houses. The average dwelling was two stories high, but there was also a large number of three- and four-story buildings, the ground floor of each generally serving as a shop of some sort.

The highest and most impressive building was St. Paul's Church, the pride and joy of those upstanding citizens in town.

Richly ornamented and well maintained, the church's only inadequacy was the bell in its tower; a document dated 1688 states that the people judged it too small, and there were plans afoot to have a larger one sent from England. Although most of the contemporary accounts affirm that the vast majority of the inhabitants were "Godless Men," the town was the only settlement in the New World, at that time, where there was free toleration of all sects and religions. In addition to St. Paul's, which was Anglican, the Baptists and Presbyterians also had churches; and there were a Quaker meetinghouse, a Roman Catholic chapel, and a Jewish synagogue.

The most palatial brick structure was the Governor's House, where the governors of Jamaica resided and entertained the rich and important people of the town. Other notable buildings were the King's Warehouse, or Custom House, which the governor also used as his place of business and where the courts of chancery were held; the Audencia, or Court House, where the courts of judicature were held; the Exchange, which served as the center for the town's main business transactions; and the two prisons—the Marshallsea for men and Bridewell for women.

In shape, the town resembled a skillet almost entirely surrounded by water, except for the eastern tip—or the tip of the skillet handle—which was connected to the Palisadoes sandspit by a dry moat, gate, and bridge. Fort Rupert was also situated on this narrow neck of sand to protect the town from an attack by land. Most of the wharves, warehouses, and the King's Warehouse were located on the harbor, or north, side of the town, where there was six fathoms of water and ships could tie right up to the wharves, unload, and take on cargoes. Off the western side the water was shallower, and the larger ships had to anchor several hundred yards out and use lighters to transfer their cargoes to and from the shore. Here there was a large protective cove known as Chocolata Hole, and generally there were about one hundred small sloops and schooners anchored, belonging to the traders, fishermen, turtlers, and privateers. The seaward, or southern, side of the town was exposed to the open sea and not used for shipping.

The main streets were well paved with cobblestones, most of which, like the bricks used in the buildings, were brought over from England as ballast on the ships. Street names were simple for the most part: Thames, Tower, Queen, Lime, Broad, High, New, Cannon, York, Church, and Fisher's Row.

Port Royal was strategically situated and ringed by six strong forts containing over three hundred large cannon, giving the town an almost impregnable defensive position. Any hostile ships attempting to enter the harbor had to come from the east because of the prevailing winds and hazardous shoals and reefs lying offshore to the south. The channel was quite narrow and located very close to the shore on the south side of the town, and any ship using it would have to pass under the guns of Forts Rupert, Morgan, and Charles; and then, when rounding the point and beating up into the harbor, the guns of Forts Walker, James, and Carlisle would bear on it. In addition to several hundred regular troops garrisoned in these forts, there was also a regiment of twenty-five hundred militiamen, made up from the town's male inhabitants. Without doubt, Port Royal was one of the best defended ports in the West Indies.

In 1688 the population was computed to be at least eight thousand. There were about five thousand whites—English, Scots, Irish, Jews, and a few Spaniards—and three thousand African slaves. In addition, there were generally always between five hundred and two thousand visitors in town, a number that varied with the activity of shipping. The average life span there was between thirty-five and forty years, and the early deaths of many were attributable to unskilled physicians and quacks, who routinely bled their hapless patients for almost every ill. Malaria, smallpox, yaws, pleurisy, and common fevers were endemic and took a high toll. Excessive drinking doubtless accounted for the early demise of many of Port Royal's populace. Although dueling was forbidden, it was a frequent event and added to the workload of the so-called doctors and undertakers.

Ironically the life span of the town was about the same as

that of its average citizen; for when only thirty-six years old, it met with a catastrophic end; it was almost completely wiped from the face of the earth.

Tuesday, June 7, 1692, dawned sultry and breathless with a cloudless sky. The sea was as still as a mirror, save for occasional ripples as sharks and other fish fed on scraps discarded by fishmongers and butchers. Only the turbulence stirred by porpoise feeding on a school of mullet or the splashes of diving man-of-war birds disturbed the oil-slick water. Humidity weighed heavily on the air, as it had throughout the week. The weather had been hot and tinder dry for five months, subjecting the island to a severe drought, which broke at the beginning of May. It had rained heavily throughout the month and disrupted the normal life of the town. Now the rains had ended and the winds abated, but people in Port Royal were still unhappy, for the lack of wind prevented ships from leaving the harbor. To a thriving seaport such as Port Royal such inactivity was intolerable, because it meant a drop in profits. The insect population had greatly increased with the wet weather, and now the threat of increased malaria and fever added to the charged atmosphere.

The still weather was unwelcome to some not only because of its financial implications but also because it made them uneasy. Ever since the founding of the town, earth tremors had occurred almost annually, and in the preceding four decades every one of them had been felt during scorching, windless weather following a squally spell—the longer the calm, the more severe the quake. Although most of the quakes rarely caused serious damage, people had good cause to be apprehensive. For some of the more superstitious, apprehension verged on terror. Shortly before, a visiting astrologer had predicted a cataclysmic earthquake in the near future, and it was recalled that only four years before, a similar prognostication made by another seer had been followed by a quake that knocked down three houses, damaged countless others, and dislodged the guns of ships in the harbor from their gun ports. To make matters worse, for years the town had tolerated its share of self-styled prophets who stalked the streets proclaiming the day was at hand on which Port Royal would be razed as punishment for its wickedness. Only the Sunday before, the minister of St. Paul's had mentioned in his sermon that the wife of John Taylor, a clergyman who had abandoned Port Royal only a few years before because of "the badness of this place," once predicted that the town "could not stand but would sink and be destroyed by the judgment of God." Now the voices of doom were more clamorous than ever, drawing a parallel with the Great Fire of 1666 that had devastated a wicked Restoration London: Port Royal, they prophesied, was destined for a similar catastrophe.

Most of the town's inhabitants, no more superstitious than they were interested in the weather, except in so far as it affected their pocketbooks or comfort, paid little heed to the predictions. For them it was just the start of another sweltering day and business would go on as usual. There was no reason to suppose that June 7 would differ from any other day.

At daybreak, while lamplighters made their rounds extinguishing the street lamps, Port Royal wakened and began to bustle. Smoke issued from the chimneys of cookhouses, where some of the slaves and indentured servants prepared breakfast for their masters; others converged on the town's three markets to buy the food needed for the day. The largest of these was the produce market, which was located in the center of town on High Street, and there an impressive variety of vegetables, fruits, and herbs were offered for sale. Adjacent to the produce market were two bakeries, which also did a thriving early-morning business. The prosperous inhabitants enjoyed fresh white bread, which although more palatable than the hardtack or cassava bread given to slaves and indentured servants, was described by a visitor: "Of all the victuals that Englishmen prefer, the only thing wanting here is a good soft bread, such as we in English plentiful still enjoy, for tho' they make the bread each day with English flour, but for want of yeast, and by reason of the staleness of the flavor, 'tis not comparable to our English bread; and yet they sell but two small rolls thereof for a royal." At the western end of High Street, where it joined with Fisher's Row, the other two markets were located close to the sea. At the meat market they offered a wide selection of beef, mutton, veal, lamb, pork, chickens, turkeys, ducks, and other types of fowl—including parrots, which were considered a delicacy. A visitor at the fish market in 1690 reported "that they had for sale no less than twenty different varieties of fish, plus lobsters, crabs, turtles, and manatee flesh, which is the sweetest meat I have ever tasted." All the visitors to Port Royal reported that there was a good variety of foodstuffs available in the town, providing that one had sufficient money, since the prices for everything were as much as five times what the same items would cost in England.

The lookouts in the forts were at their posts with the first rays of dawn, scanning the glassy sea for approaching ships. That day they were especially vigilant, for it was expected that a French squadron with a stronghold in St. Ann's Bay, on the north coast of the island, might attack Port Royal at any moment. France and England had been at war for two years, but the hostilities had not affected Jamaica, except for several ships captured by French privateers, until mid-May, when the French squadron arrived on the north coast and sacked and burned a number of sugar plantations, causing a large number of planters to abandon their plantations and flee into the hilly interior of the island. The French ships were unable to sail because of the calm, but the people of Port Royal were unaware of this fact. One of the island's two warships, H.M.S. *Guernsey*, was also becalmed, off the eastern end of the island, where it had been sent to cruise in wait for the French ships. The other, H.M.S. *Swan*, was in the process of being careened and was unavailable for action, but everything possible was being done to ready her as quickly as possible. While the invasion scare was on, the gunners of the fort remained on duty around the clock.

At daybreak the harbor was a scene of teeming activity. Ships were very often loaded and unloaded as early as possible; wharfage rates were steep in Port Royal and captains wanted their vessels moored there as short a time as possible. Although it must have been obvious on this particular morning that ships would not get underway that day because of the lack of wind, the crews would have been busy, for there is always a great deal to be done on board ship and they were in the habit of getting an early start. During the night there had been a brief alarm when a small ship had dropped anchor at the eastern end of the channel into the port to await daylight. The commander of Fort Charles had sent a boat out to identify it and was happy to learn that it was an English merchant ship arriving from Bristol after making a stop at Nevis Island to discharge cargo and passengers. At first light, four longboats manned by fishermen were sent out to the ship and they towed it into port, where it dropped anchor under the guns of Fort James.

Its captain came ashore and went straight to the Admiralty Office, where he presented his papers and a list of passengers and the cargo he carried. He then had to swear an oath that none of his crew or passengers were sick, for if any were, the ship would have to be moved farther away from shore and placed under quarantine until the Admiralty officials were satisfied that they were not introducing any epidemics to the island. The passengers were then brought ashore and ordered to make an appearance that same morning at the King's Warehouse to sign the register: those not fulfilling this observation were considered spies or the enemy and immediately imprisoned. Everyone showing a willingness to become a permanent resident of the island was issued a certificate granting each member of a family fifty acres of free land. Meanwhile, customs officers swarmed over the ship searching for contraband and checking the cargo against the cargo manifest, which the captain had turned over to them.

During the night the fishermen had been busy. June was the month when thousands of turtles crawled ashore on the cays and the beaches of the island to lay their eggs and were easily captured by vigilant fishermen. On the beach near the fish and meat markets several fenced areas known as turtle crawls were maintained near the water's edge, and the fishermen were transferring the turtles from small craft to the crawls, where they would be kept alive until needed in the fish market. As night waned, several dozen other small boats belonging to the watermen were plying between Port Royal and the mouth of the Rio Cobre, located on the northwest corner of the harbor. Because there was no fresh water in the town, all of the water was brought in large wooden casks from this river by the watermen, "water with which the citizens diluted the hot hellish liquor known as 'Kill Devil,' that was the main drink sold in the taverns, but occasionally they did drink plain water to slake their thirst."

In the numerous taverns and alehouses it was not a question of an early start, but of a late ending to a night of carousing. Those who were able to move under their own power wound their way through the narrow streets with empty pockets and groggy heads, while others had to be dragged or carried home. Generally the ranks of roisterers were considerably diminished during the course of the night. Brawling and dueling felled some, and the past night had been no exception, with several men wounded in knife fights. Still more revelers were picked up by roving patrols of militiamen for drunk and disorderly behavior and escorted to the "lockup," a small jail located near Fort Charles.

Like their prisoners, the militiamen regarded dawn as an end rather than a beginning. While the majority of the townspeople set about their daily routine, the militia were coming off a twenty-four-hour tour of duty. But before they could go home to breakfast and a well-earned rest, they had to march their prisoners to the Marshallsea and Bridewell and deliver them to the magistrate. After rapid court proceedings (there was seldom any novelty to the offenses) the magistrate meted out punishment—usually whipping, dunking, or imprisonment. Severity depended upon the nature of the crime, and perhaps on whether the magistrate had managed to get a good breakfast under his belt. Apparently he had not, this morning, for he ordered two runaway slaves to be hanged—against the plea of their master, who no doubt preferred a more lenient and less costly punishment. Sentence was carried out at once, and after those who had been ordered imprisoned were deposited with the warders in the Marshallsea and Bridewell, the others were marched to the main square in the center of town and publicly punished. The whippings and dunkings were always well attended: no doubt the enjoyment of many a spectator was heightened by the knowledge that only luck had spared him from the lash or water this time. For prisoners accused of blasphemy against God's name, being whipped or dunked was only the beginning of their ordeal, for they were generally placed in the stocks and kept there throughout the heat of the day, where they suffered further indignities by being pelted by rocks and garbage by the passing populace.

In the houses of the gentry and the well-to-do merchants, the early-morning pace was not quite so hectic, except in the servants' quarters. The master of the house was generally awakened by a slave in livery, who stood ready to bring the morning glass of Madeira or, if necessary, an antidote for a hang-over. After being bathed and shaved and dressed in fine clothes and a wig, there was time for a large and leisurely breakfast before the master left for his shop or for the Exchange. Probably he uttered a few comments on the weather to his wife. On the morning of June 7, 1692, they would have been highly unfavorable, but it is unlikely that he thought much about the weather. The date was too important: John White, the Lieutenant Governor of Jamaica (then acting as governor in place of Lord Inchinquin, who had died earlier in the year) had scheduled a meeting of the Council of Jamaica at the King's House. Among the topics to be debated, the most important was the possibility of the imminent attack by the French. Word had also reached White the previous day that there were several French spies in the town, and means had to be found to discover their identities.

The citizens of less distinction set about business in the normal way on the day that for many of them was to be their last. In addition to the many merchants and shopkeepers, there were a large number of craftsmen: carpenters, cabinetmakers, wigmakers, painters, jewelers, haberdashers, cobblers, combmakers, ropemakers, glaziers, hatters, and tanners, profitably supplying the needs of the prosperous town. As the morning wore on, the heat grew worse. The children of the rich, confined to their houses with tutors or to a schoolroom, must have envied the poorer children, free to roam the town and dip in the sea to cool off. Everyone must have longed for noon, when activity would cease for three hours and they would have dinner and the subsequent siesta, usually taken in a swinging hammock.

Unfortunately, no one in Port Royal, or elsewhere on the island for that matter, took a siesta that day, but a large number of the island's inhabitants did go into a perpetual sleep.

At twenty minutes before noon, disaster struck: the earth opened to swallow the world's most wicked and sinful city.

A number of contemporary accounts of the disaster have survived, including the following by John Uffgress, a merchant of Port Royal:

Betwixt eleven and twelve noon, I being at a tavern, we felt the house shake and saw bricks begin to rise in the floor, and at the same instant heard one in the street cry, "An earthquake!" Immediately we ran out of the house, where we saw all people with lifted up hands begging God's assistance. We continued running up the street whilst on either side of us we saw the houses, some swallowed up, others thrown on heaps; the sand in the streets rise like the waves of the sea, lifting up all persons that stood upon it and immediately dropping into pits; and at the same instant a flood of water breaking in and rolling those poor souls over and over; some catching hold of beams and rafters of houses, others were found in the sand that appeared when the water was drained away, with their legs and arms out. The small piece of ground whereon sixteen or eighteen of us stood (praise be to God) did not sink. As soon as the violent shake was over, every man was desirous to know if any of his family were left alive. I endeavored to go to my house upon the ruins of the houses that were floating upon the water, but could not. At length I got a canoe and rowed upon the great sea towards my house, where I saw several men and women floating upon the wreck [possibly H.M.S. *Swan*] out to sea; and so many of them as I could I took into the boat and still rowed on till I came to where I thought my house stood, but could not hear of either my wife nor family; so returning again to that little part of land remaining above water. But seeing all the people endeavoring to get to the island, I went amongst them in hopes I might hear of my wife or some part of my family, but could not. Next morning I went from one ship to another, till at last it pleased God I met with my wife, and two of my negroes. She told me, when she felt the house shake, she ran out, and called all the house to do the same. She was no sooner out, but the sand lifted up, and her negro woman grasping about her, they both dropped into the earth together, when at the very instant the water came in, rolled them over and over, till at length they caught hold of a beam, where they hung, till a boat came from a Spanish vessel and took them up.

According to most accounts, there were three strong quakes in a matter of several minutes, each one progressively more violent; the last and most severe was followed by a tidal wave that broke the anchor cables of ships riding in the harbor, wrecked the ships near the wharves, and flung H.M.S. *Swan* into the middle of town, where it came to rest on top of some of the submerged houses and served as Noah's Ark for more than two hundred people. They were the lucky ones. The catalogue of horror, of lives lost and property destroyed, was seemingly endless. Another merchant said:

Those houses which but just appeared the fairest and loftiest in these parts were in a moment sunk down into the earth, and nothing to be seen of them; such crying, such shrieking and mourning I never heard, nor could anything in my opinion appear more terrible to the eye of man: Here a company of people swallowed up at once; there a whole street tumbling down; and in another place the trembling earth, opening her ravenous jaws, let in the merciless sea so that this town is becoming a heap of ruins. . . . Dr. Trapham, a physician of this place, was miraculously saved by hanging by his hands upon the rack of a chimney, and one of his children about his neck, were both saved by a boat, but his wife and the rest of his children and family were all lost.

Several people were swallowed up by the earth, when the sea breaking in before the earth could close, were washed up again and miraculously saved from perishing; others the earth received up to their necks and then closed upon them and squeezed them to death with their heads above ground, many of which the dogs eat. Multitudes of people floating up and down, having no burial. The burying place at Palisadoes is quite destroyed, the dead bodies being washed out of their graves, their tombs beat to pieces, and they floating up and down; it is sad to think how we have suffered. Dr. Heath, the minister of the place, has labored very much, being continually employed in burying the dead, christening of children, preaching and praying with the bruised, wounded and dying people.

One of the most detailed accounts was given by Dr. Heath, the rector of St. Paul's Church, in a letter to a friend:

I doubt not but you will both from gazettes and letters hear of the great calamity that hath befallen this island by a terrible earthquake, on the 7th instant, which hath thrown down almost all of the houses, churches, sugarworks, mills, and bridges through the whole country. It tore the rocks and mountains, destroyed some whole plantations, and threw them into the sea. But Port Royal had much the greatest share in this judgment of God: I will therefore be more particular in giving you an account of its proceedings in this place, that you may know what my danger was, and how unexpected my preservation.

I had been at church reading prayers, which I did every day since I was rector of Port Royal, to keep some show of religion among a most ungodly debauched people; and was gone to a place hard by the church, where merchants used to meet, and where the president of the council was, who acts now in chief till we have a new governor. This gentleman came into my company and engaged me to take a glass of wormwood wine with him, as a whet before dinner. He being my very great friend, I stayed with him. Hereupon he lighted a pipe of tobacco, which he was pretty long in taking; and not being willing to leave him before it was out, this detained me from going to dinner to one Captain Ruden's where I was to dine; whose house upon the first concussion sank into the earth, and then into the sea, with his wife and family, and some who were come to dine with him. Had I been there I had been lost. But to return to the president, and his pipe of tobacco. Before that was out, I found the ground rolling and moving under my feet, upon which I said, Lord, sir, what is this? He replied very composedly, being a very grave man, it is an earthquake, be not afraid, it will soon be over. But it increased, and we heard the church and tower fall; upon which, we ran to save ourselves. I quickly lost him, and made towards Morgan's fort, which being a wide open place, I thought to be there securest from the falling houses, but as I made towards it, I saw the earth open and swallow up a multitude of people, and the sea mounting in upon us over the fortifications. I then laid aside all thoughts of escaping, and resolved to make towards my own lodging, there to meet death in as good a posture as I could. From the place where I was, I was forced to cross, and run through two or three very narrow streets. The houses and walls fell on each side of me and some bricks came rolling over my shoes, but none hurt me. When I came to my lodging, I found there all things in the same order I left them; not a picture, of which there were several fair ones in my chamber, being out of its place. I went to my balcony to view the street in which our house stood, and saw never a house down there, nor the ground so much as cracked. The people seeing me, cried out to me to come and pray with them. When I came into the street every one laid hold of my clothes and embraced me, that with their fears and kindness I was almost stifled. I persuaded them at last to kneel down and make a large ring, which they did. I prayed with them near an hour, when I was almost spent with the heat of the sun, and the exercise. They then brought me a chair; the earth working all the while with new motions, and tremblings, like the rolling of the sea; insomuch that sometimes when I was at prayer I could hardly keep myself upon my knees. By that time I had been half an hour longer with them, in setting before them their sins and heinous provocations, and seriously exhorting them to repentance, there came some merchants of the place; who desired me to go aboard some ship in the harbour, and refresh myself, telling me that they had gotten a boat to carry me off. I found the sea had entirely swallowed up the wharf, with all the goodly brick houses upon it, most of them as fine as those in Cheapside [a section of London], and two entire streets beyond that. From the tops of some houses which lay levelled with the surface of water, I got first into a canoe, and then into a long-boat, which put me aboard a ship called the Siam-merchant. There I found the president safe, who was overjoyed to see me; and continued that night, but could not sleep for the returns of the earthquake almost every hour, which made all the guns in the ship to jar and rattle.

Disasters like this bring out the best in some men and the worst in others. In Port Royal the worst prevailed. One account, by William Reide, stated: "that the great disaster had so little effect upon some people here, that the very same night they were at their Old Trade of Drinking, Swearing and Whoreing, and indeed this place has been one of the Ludest in the Christian World, a Sink of all Filthiness, and a meer Sodom."

The lawless inhabitants of the town and many of the sailors from the ships behaved like savages, looting the houses still standing, driving away and even murdering the owners if they dared to protest. Many a man who had not owned the shirt on his back before the catastrophe became rich because of it. Another member of the clergy vividly described this scene:

Immediately upon the cessation of the extremity of the earthquake, your heart would abhor to hear of the depredations, robberies, and violences that were in an instant committed upon the place by the vilest and basest of the people;

no man could call anything his own, for they that were strongest, and most wicked seized what they pleased, and whose they pleased, and where they pleased, without any regard to propriety. Gold and silver, jewels, plate, or goods was all their own that they could or would lay hands on: Nothing but breaking open of houses, rushing into shops, and taking what they pleased before the owners' faces, forcing goods or money from them in the open street, as they were carrying it elsewhere for better security, succeeded the horrors of this dreadful time; while others in canoes, wherries and shipboats were plundering chests, boxes, screwtores, etc. of what they could find in them upon the water, even the very slaves thought it their time of liberty, wherein they committed many barbarous insolencies and robberies, till they were suppressed by the death of some, and punishment of others. The dead were robbed of what they had about them, some stripped, others searched, their pockets picked, their fingers cut off for their rings, their gold buttons taken out of their shirts.

So that the richest are now the poorest, and the meanest of the people are now enriched by the losses of others, which loss duly to estimate and value, is more difficult than to reckon the number of people lost.

Those of the upright survivors who were able took refuge aboard the ships in the harbor, as did Acting Governor White and the Council members, leaving the remains of Port Royal to the despoilers. They represented the law, but, greatly outnumbered, had no way of enforcing it, and they had troubles enough without taking on a cause they knew to be hopeless.

By the time the sun set that evening, all that remained of the infamous town was a mere ten acres out of an estimated twenty-five, once again separated from the Palisadoes by water. Fewer than a tenth of the houses remained standing, and most of these were in no condition for habitation; the rest were all under water or lying in heaps. Of the six forts, all but Charles had sunk into the sea, along with a large number of ships and smaller vessels.

The toll of property destroyed by the upheaval was incalculable, but it was reckoned that more than two thousand people perished at once and a larger number soon followed.

Port Royal was not alone in the suffering, for the entire island was devastated. Spanish Town, Jamaica's second-largest settlement, was virtually leveled and only a few buildings stood intact. Nearby, the tops of two mountains tumbled down with much of the debris damming up the Rio Cobre, or Copper River, and leaving a large segment of it dry for months afterward.

Other settlements and plantations suffered dearly, and scarcely a building on the island was left standing. Near Port Morant, where two merchant ships overset and were lost, a mountain was reported to have been swallowed by the earth, and a lake more than ten miles long to have appeared in its place. On the north coast, at St. Ann's Bay, where the French invaders had their stronghold, the first quake sent the Frenchmen running for their ships, but some were not quick enough and fifty-three were lost when the third quake caused about a thousand acres of woodland to slide into the sea, carrying the unlucky Frenchmen with it. The total loss of life on Jamaica exclusive of Port Royal was about a thousand persons. Those who were fortunate enough to survive were left homeless and destitute and many of them perished during the ensuing months from the epidemics that ravaged the island.

Chapter Two

Today the Caribbean Babylon is a small and sleepy settlement
of fewer than five hundred residents and what seems like an
equal number of skinny, hungry dogs. Although it is about a
half hour's drive from busy downtown Kingston, most of the
inhabitants are too poor to afford automobiles, and rely on a
ferryboat, which plies between Port Royal and Kingston several
times a day, to get them to the city. About half the men are
engaged in fishing, and the others commute to Kingston to work,
since there is very little employment in the village. Many residents of the once notorious town are notably more open and
easy than the other inhabitants of the island and they proudly
refer to themselves as Port Royalists, rather than Jamaicans. They
dislike having too much contact with what they call "the mainland," and I know of one woman who, at sixty-six, claimed she
had never in her whole life been over to "the mainland." They
are fiercely proud of the town's former glory, and many of them
claim to be descended from the famous buccaneer Henry Morgan
or others of the swashbucklers who once lived there. Although
crime is common in nearby Kingston, it is virtually unknown in
Port Royal, where very few houses even have locks on the doors.

After spending a lifetime traveling all over the world, I found the hardy Port Royalists to be the most honest and friendly people I have ever encountered.

Visitors to Port Royal searching for signs of its former prosperity are usually disappointed, and anyone ignorant of its history would probably dismiss the place without a second look. Where once a crowded town buzzed with activity, there now remain only a few historical monuments basking in the Caribbean sun. Fort Charles, which has recently been restored, stands as the only reminder of the old town. The crumbling foundations of a few walls of the old brick buildings can also be seen protruding from the sand in several areas of the village. A small church built early in the eighteenth century, St. Peter's, contains another memento: on display in the vestry are several pieces of church plate, reportedly plunder brought to Port Royal by Morgan and his men after the sack of old Panama City in 1671, and also an enormous silver tankard with a whistle in its handle, which belonged to Morgan himself. Inside the church the walls are covered by plaques commemorating many of those who perished in the town in the eighteenth and nineteenth centuries. In the churchyard is the tombstone of the first warden of St. Peter's, Lewis Galdy, who was one of the fortunate survivors of the 1692 disaster. It reads:

Here lyes the body of Lewis Galdy Esq., who departed this life at Port Royal the 22 December 1739 Aged 80. He was born at Montpelier in France but left that country for his religion & came to settle in this island where he was swallowed up in the great earthquake in the year 1692 & by the providence of God was by another shock thrown into the sea & miraculously saved by swimming until a boat took him up. He lived many years after in great reputation, beloved by all that knew him and much lamented at his death.

Plans have been afoot for years to make Port Royal into an important tourist attraction, but virtually nothing has been done about it, to the satisfaction of most "Port Royalists," who prefer living in tranquillity.

In 1951 Port Royal was leveled by a hurricane, and most of the village had to be rebuilt. In addition to the small bungalows of the residents, there are two small stores, three bars, a primary school, a customs house, a small yacht club and marina, and a police training school—which was a British military base until Jamaica became an independent country in 1962. The most prominent structure is a massive two-story building, which dates from 1817 and formerly served as a Royal Naval Hospital. The port no longer accommodates large ships, only small fishing vessels and the pilot boats that guide ships into Kingston Harbour. Ships calling at Jamaica from foreign ports drop anchor off Port Royal, where they are boarded by customs and immigration officials, and then continue on to Kingston.

The comedown is saddening, but common sense decrees that no town should ever have been built there, on that vulnerable sandspit. The inhabitants must have known that the foundations of their houses did not rest on bedrock, but without modern equipment they could not have known that it lay more than 120 feet below the surface. Such a shaky foundation might have been simply a nuisance in itself, but the people of Port Royal made matters worse by constructing their buildings high and close together. Thus in a severe earthquake like that of June 7, 1692, the results were disastrous and, to a geologist, a foregone conclusion: tall buildings resting on nothing more than loose, waterlogged sand, only a few feet above sea level, at the edge of a steeply sloping sea bed, were bound to slide or topple down the slope and sink beneath the sea.

Port Royal and the Palisadoes sandspit are both recent additions to Jamaica's topography, formed in recent geological times, when mud and gravel from several rivers that empty into Kingston Harbour, plus loose pieces of dead coral and sand from the ocean floor, were deposited in layers on a solid limestone base. This limestone base—probably the remains of an older coral reef from the early Pleistocene period—is a typical karst formation and rises sharply toward the surface under Port Royal and the surrounding area, with the result that the sea bed drops away steeply from the shoreline.

The early inhabitants of Port Royal were ignorant of the fact that the town lies in an earthquake belt that extends from eastern Mexico through Cuba, Jamaica, Hispaniola, and Puerto Rico. The land masses along this belt are constantly under elastic stress from movements of the earth's crust, which eventually causes the stored energy to be released in the form of seismic waves—tectonic earthquakes, which differ from those caused by volcanic action. The Spanish colonies also suffered from frequent earthquakes and soon learned to build their houses on solid ground and only one story high. However, with the possible exception of an earthquake in 1907, when more than fourteen hundred lives were lost and hundreds of buildings left in ruin in Kingston and Spanish Town, no earthquake in Jamaica, either before or since, has ever caused such severe damage to property and such a great loss of life as that of 1692.

The life span of old Port Royal was not long as cities go. Until the arrival of the English it had little importance, and the date when people first began to live there is a mystery. Since Jamaica, like the rest of the West Indies, does not enter into written history until the arrival of the Europeans, we can only make educated guesses about what happened there before Columbus discovered Jamaica.

When Columbus first reached the island, in May of 1494, he found it inhabited by the Arawak Indians, who numbered over sixty thousand and were scattered throughout the island in more than one hundred settlements. Virtually nothing is known about the origin of the Arawaks; some scholars believe that they came from either Florida or Venezuela, while others conjecture they might have come from the Old World. Unlike the majority of the other Indian cultures of the New World, the Arawak were quite primitive, with no system of writing, and since they died out within a couple of decades after the arrival of the Spaniards, very little is known about them. Our only clues to their existence on Jamaica and most of the other Caribbean islands are derived from a relatively small number of documents written by the early explorers and settlers and an insufficient number of modern-day archaeological excavations. In Jamaica, for example, where at least one hundred Arawak sites are known, excavations have been undertaken on only a very small number of sites, and several of these by untrained persons. We are not certain if they ever inhabited the sandy cay that was to become Port Royal, but we do know that they called it Cagua.

Since they had a name for it, the place must have been of some importance to them and they must have visited it often. Sea food was a staple in their diet, and the calm waters around Port Royal abounded in fish, crustaceans, and mollusks. Previous to my work at Port Royal it was believed that they had never had a settlement on the cay. However, during my excavation of the sunken city a number of discoveries were made that suggest the contrary. Deep in the sediment on the sea floor, below the stratigraphical level of the English occupation of the site, we found hundreds of shards of Arawak pottery and several complete earthenware pots. These artifacts are by no means conclusive proof that the Arawak actually lived on the cay. Some of the local Arawak experts think it more likely that the clay pots were dropped or thrown from the dugout canoes of fishermen and that the shards, some of which had holes drilled through them, were used as fishing sinkers. However, another artifact we discovered certainly indicates a better possibility that they did indeed have a settlement on the cay: one half of a metate (a stone object with short legs, resembling a small stool, on which corn was ground into meal). Grinding corn was always woman's work among the Arawak, and it is hard to imagine the men setting out on a fishing trip, even on an overnight one, with a metate, unless it was a faulty one used as an anchor. If a settlement had existed on the cay, very few traces of it would have survived over the centuries, since Arawak dwellings were built of wood and thatch. There is a possibility that future underwater or land excavations may turn up more clues to the early history of the site, but for the present we are not certain who were the first inhabitants of Port Royal.

Nor are we certain that the Spaniards were the first Europeans to set eyes on the cay. About fifteen years ago a carved marble pedestal bearing a Latin inscription was snagged in the net of a Port Royal fisherman and sold to the owner of a local tavern for a bottle of rum. There it remained for several years as a place for the thirsty customers to scrape the mud off the bottom of their shoes, until it was noticed by a visiting archaeologist. It has since been identified as Roman, dating from the first century A.D. Was it brought over aboard a Roman galley that was accidentally blown across the Atlantic by a storm many centuries ago, or by Roman explorers searching for new lands to conquer and rule? In view of a great deal of recent archaeological and documentary evidence which supports the theory of pre-Columbian voyages made by Old World mariners to the New World, both explanations are possible. Yet, unless more conclusive evidence is found, such as other Roman artifacts or even the remains of a Roman shipwreck in Jamaican waters, we can more safely speculate that the pedestal was brought over as ballast on a Spanish or an English ship and thrown overboard.

In recorded sources the history of Jamaica begins with the discovery of the fertile island by Columbus during his second voyage of exploration, in 1494. With three small caravels he first sighted the long, lush island with its backbone of jagged mountains on May 5. He named it Santa Gloria, "on account of the extreme beauty of its country." He entered St. Ann's Bay, and even before he could drop anchor, hundreds of hostile Arawaks in sixty or seventy large canoes put out from shore and approached his ships, but were quickly repelled by the Spaniards firing their cannon without shot. Unlike his next trip to this bay, his stay was brief: after sending some gifts ashore to the Indians, he sailed the following morning to another bay a few hours' sail to the west, where he hoped to obtain firewood and water. Again the Indians made a big show of force, and only after his men killed and wounded a few of them with their crossbows did they become friendlier and permit the strangers to land. Columbus was disappointed that no gold or other treasure was found, and several days later set sail for the south coast of Cuba. A month later he returned again to continue his exploration of the island and an-

chored in a large shallow bay, known today as Portland Bight, on
the south coast of the island, about twenty miles west of Port
Royal. Word must have spread of the fire-and-thunder-spitting
weapons his men carried, for the Arawaks of that area were quite
pacific and came out to greet him in their canoes, bringing fresh
provisions and water. Several of them were wearing trinkets
made of gold, in which the Spaniards showed great interest. After
a brief stay there, Columbus set sail, heading eastward along the
coast, and passed close to Port Royal. As an experienced mariner,
he probably realized that an excellent harbor lay inside, behind
Port Royal and the Palisadoes, but because he was short of
victuals and his ships were in need of repairs, he used the favorable west winds to head directly for his base in Hispaniola and
did not stop anywhere else on Jamaica.

His next visit to the island occurred nine years later, during
his fourth and last voyage of exploration, but it was not by choice.
After months of exploring along the coast of Central America,
having failed to make any significant discoveries and forced to
abandon two of the four vessels of his fleet because they were
so badly riddled by shipworms, he finally started back for his
base in Hispaniola. His two remaining ships—*Capitana* and
Santiago—soon proved to be in as bad, or even worse, condition
than the two that had been abandoned, and his men had to work
the pumps around the clock to keep them afloat. In addition, the
victuals and water were almost exhausted and many of the men
were sick. After brief stops at the Cayman Islands and on the
south shore of Cuba, where only water was obtained, they continued on their voyage, but then contrary winds and currents
forced them to put in at Jamaica. After another brief stop, at Dry
Harbour, where neither fresh water nor provisions could be
found, they fought their way to the east and entered St. Ann's
Bay, where both vessels were run aground to prevent them from
sinking, for they both were so full of water that their decks were
nearly awash. Fortunately the Arawaks were friendly this time
and they were able to obtain supplies. Unable to repair the
vessels, they were stranded there, and Columbus and his men
lived in the fore and stern castles of the vessels for a year and

five days before a ship arrived from Hispaniola to rescue them. Suffering from the gout and no doubt brokenhearted over the dismal failure of the voyage, Columbus returned to Spain and died soon afterward. However, before his death he extracted a promise from his son, Diego, to return to Jamaica and build a settlement there.

Most likely owing to the scarcity of precious metals found on Jamaica, it was five years before Spain showed any interest in the island that Columbus had thought the most beautiful he had seen in the West Indies. The Spanish Crown granted Diego, Columbus' son and heir, the right to establish settlements on the island, and 1509 he sent a group of colonists from Hispaniola to build a town on the site of his father's enforced residence at St. Ann's Bay. Sevilla la Nueva, or New Seville, grew rapidly, and two similar settlements—Melilla, also on the north coast, and Oristán, on the southwest coast—were also founded. Large tracts of land were granted to the colonists, and the Arawaks were set to work clearing ground, planting crops, and hunting the wild boar that abounded there. Soon they were not only growing provisions to sustain themselves but others for export as well: cocoa, sugar, pepper, cotton, and indigo. Livestock was introduced and multiplied on the fruitful island, providing the settlers with large amounts of hides for export.

Despite this promising start, Jamaica, called the Land of Wood and Water by the Arawaks, soon went into decline. The beauty and fertility of the island were not enough to attract many colonists, particularly when the quick accumulation of wealth was the main object of most of the Spaniards braving the New World. Following the conquests of Peru, Mexico, and other mainland regions—where fabulous riches beckoned—thousands left Jamaica and soon there were very few settlers left to work the land. The indigenous labor force, the benevolent Arawaks, were rapidly exterminated: some succumbed to diseases introduced by the white men; others, accustomed to an easy life of hunting, fishing, and fruit gathering, could not adjust to the enforced agricultural toil and either died from overwork or committed suicide; but the largest percentage were massacred by the Spaniards, ostensibly for religious motives. By the middle of the seventeenth century the Spanish governor reported that the last Arawak had died long before. Some African slaves, brought over by Portuguese slave traders, were imported to fill the gap, but though they throve, there were never enough to satisfy the settlers. The demand for slaves throughout the Spanish colonies always exceeded the supply, and the Crown preferred sending them to the wealthier, mainland colonies rather than to a poor agricultural colony such as Jamaica.

New Seville was surrounded by mangrove swamps in which malaria and yellow-fever-bearing mosquitoes bred, contributing to the town's unhealthful environment. Because of the noxious climate and because there were larger fertile plains, better suited for agriculture than on the north coast, the settlers decided to vacate New Seville in 1532 and establish a new capital in the South. The site of the new town, Villa de la Vega, or Town of the Plain, was six miles inland from Kingston Harbour on the banks of the Rio Cobre, or Copper River, so named because of the color of the river's water. The new capital, like the first, did not flourish. Its population never exceeded 1,500, and at one point in its history, in 1582, the total population, including Negro slaves, was well under five hundred. After many of Jamaica's original settlers had left to join in the conquest of the mainland, the Crown issued a number of decrees forbidding people to abandon the island, but still this failed to deter people from leaving. For a while, those who remained behind fared well enough from the conquests: supplying the expeditions, most of which departed from nearby Cuba, with meats and other provisions. But as soon as the mainland territories were pacified and became self-sufficient, there was no longer a market for Jamaica's products.

In contrast to the grandeur of other Spanish colonial cities, such as Lima and Cartagena, with their opulent palaces, cathedrals, and public buildings, Villa de la Vega could boast only a collegiate church, two monasteries, and a governor's residence, built of stone; while the rest of the town consisted of humble wood and stucco dwellings. Insignificant as the town was, it was the only one Jamaica had (the other two towns had been abandoned along with New Seville) and the only one Jamaica appeared to need. Gentlemen who fell into disfavor with the King were often banished to Jamaica to serve as royal officials for the remainder of their days, to be forgotten, as hundreds of letters, preserved today in the Spanish archives, from these unfortunate officials attest—some complaining that they had not been paid for years and were destitute.

Jamaica, throughout the Spanish occupation of the island, was the only New World settlement from which the kings of Spain failed to reap a profit; thus they were reluctant to expend much in developing or sustaining the island. The backbone of the Spanish monarchy was the treasure fleets, or flotas, which annually carried European products to the New World and returned to Spain laden with treasure. The ships of these fleets generally bypassed Jamaica, although the inhabitants of the island constantly petitioned the Crown to have the island better fortified and to use it as a possible refuge for the treasure fleets in the event of bad weather—but nothing came of this. Actually only once, during almost a century and a half of Spanish rule, did it serve this purpose: In 1605 two richly laden galleons on their way from Cartagena to Havana lost their masts in a hurricane and were forced to make repairs in Jamaica.

Occasionally a ship was sent to Jamaica from Spain or one of the other colonies, but there were periods of up to ten years when no ships came to the island other than small craft. When ships came they called at Puerto de Caguaya, a small port at the mouth of the Rio Cobre, on the northwestern corner of Kingston Harbour, where the water was so shallow and so full of treacherous sandbanks that large ships had to anchor far from shore and unload onto small boats. Not that there was ever much to unload: Jamaica had little money to buy European products, and in what it had to sell, the mother country displayed little interest. Consequently the colony stagnated and the inhabitants lost all incentive to do much more than feed and clothe themselves.

Yet Spain might well have been interested in what Jamaica had to offer. There were great unexploited agricultural resources: sugar cane, tobacco, many types of spices, timber, wild boar, and the semi-wild cattle that had multiplied rapidly since the early settlers introduced the stock. There was the harbor, one of the finest in the Indies, going to waste. Port Royal, then called Cayo de Carena, or Careening Cay, with its advantageous location at the entrance of the harbor, was used for little more than careening (a process that consists of cleaning and repitching a ship's bottom) and refitting the few ships that visited Jamaica. Above all, Spain should have been interested in Jamaica's strategic value because of its position at the very center of the Caribbean. Within sight of its tall mountain peaks passed virtually all the wealth of Spain's vast overseas empire. The governors and royal officials of Jamaica repeatedly petitioned the Spanish Crown to build fortifications and garrison troops there to protect the island against enemy attack. To these please the Crown, always short of funds because of expensive European wars, turned a deaf ear.

The island was all but defenseless and could have been captured and most likely held by any nation that wanted it. There were no regular troops, few weapons of any worth, and in an emergency they could only call out a rag, tag, and bobtail citizens' militia. The only fortification on the whole island was a small wooden stockade surrounded by earthworks at Puerto de Caguaya, which boasted only a few cannon and often was without powder or shot. The inhabitants relied chiefly on a lookout station on top of a hill (known today as Henderson Hill) at the entrance to the harbor opposite Port Royal, where sentinels on twenty-four-hour guard duty could spot the approach of enemy ships. Once the alarm had been sounded, however, all the inhabitants could realistically do in the event of a real invasion was take to the hills with what little valuables they possessed, and hide.

Spain had declared the New World off limits to the rest of Europe, and for a time it was. During the first half of the sixteenth century the empire was in its glory and the Caribbean was a Spanish lake. Maintaining a strict monopoly on trade with its colonies was essential for keeping the vast Spanish Empire intact, for without the immense treasures she received from the New World, the empire would collapse. By the middle of the sixteenth century Spain was deeply engaged in wars all over Europe, and her inadequate navy was forced to remain in European waters. This gave the other European powers an opportunity to share in the riches of the New World, and the Spaniards were constrained to sit and watch, unable to commit any of their warships, as France, England, and later Holland sent ships to trade with her colonies or, failing that, to take some of the wealth in plunder. Freebooters roamed the Caribbean at will, concealing themselves from pursuers in the myriad deserted bays and coves to be found on many of the islands, and Jamaica, with its hundreds of miles of uninhabited coast, became a favorite hangout. The only defense against them was the determination of the settlers. In 1565, when three French ships sailed into Puerto de Caguaya, the sentry on Henderson Hill spotted them and gave the alarm, and they were put to flight by a small force hastily mustered by the governor. Such resistance was the exception rather than the rule, for the inhabitants there and in other places were so desperate for goods, which could generally be bought at a much lower price than those shipped from Spain, that they would usually trade with the foreigners. The contraband trade eventually became so important that it led to the total disruption of the annual treasure fleets from Spain, as the great wealth of the New World was diverted from the coffers of the King of Spain into the hands of other European rulers and merchants.

During most of the sixteenth century the interlopers were more of a nuisance than a threat, since no nation really dared to fling down the gauntlet to mighty Spain. Then, during the last two decades of the century, Spain suffered a series of disastrous reverses on both land and sea—the worst being the defeat of her Invincible Armada in 1588 by the English, which left her without a navy and with scarcely enough ships to maintain communications with her New World colonies. This gave the other European powers the opportunity to increase their activities in the New World without any danger from Spanish warships. Whereas previously they had been content with making good profits from the contraband trade and the capture of an occasional ship, they now took the initiative and sent large fleets of privateers to attack the major seaports and the treasure fleets. The Dutch were the most successful "in singeing the beard of the Spanish King," and in 1628 they captured a complete treasure fleet of twenty-four ships, which netted them a greater amount of plunder than had been taken from the Spaniards in the New World by all the privateers and pirates of all nations throughout the sixteenth century.

Even more threatening to Spain's power and prestige than the attacks on shipping were the settlements that other European powers were establishing in the New World. The Spanish Crown did not worry much about those founded in North America, but when they began springing up in the West Indies, right on the doorstep of their wealthy colonies, it was a grave matter. Spain had considered most of the smaller West Indian islands to be of little importance and had done nothing to colonize them, but other European powers realized their potential and were quick to lay claim to them. Between 1625 and 1650 the English, the French, and the Dutch established settlements on almost every one of the Leeward and Windward islands. Aware that the presence of foreigners so near the important trade routes could lead only to disaster, Spain made a few attempts to dislodge them, and although Spanish forces were able to drive the settlers from some of the islands, they simply moved to other islands or returned as soon as the Spaniards left. Spain still held all of the Greater Antilles—Cuba, Hispaniola, Puerto Rico, and Jamaica—and it was only a matter of time before the other foreign powers would become greedy and make an attempt to seize them from Spain. Jamaica, being the most poorly defended, was an inevitable target.

Since the reign of Queen Elizabeth, Jamaica had been raided for plunder on three different occasions by English privateers, but no attempt had been made to hold the island. In 1595 Sir Anthony Shirley captured Villa de la Vega with a relatively small force, after the inhabitants made a token show of defense. Finding only a small amount of booty, he held the town for ransom, which the Spaniards were unable to pay, so he burned the town and carried away the only four iron cannon the Spaniards had to defend the place. The Spaniards on the island were so disillusioned by their neglect at the hands of the Spanish Crown that they actually asked the English invaders to hold the island and make them subjects of the English Crown. Even this attack seems not to have opened the eyes of the Spanish Crown to Jamaica's vulnerability, for nothing was done to better fortify the island. Again, in 1603, the island was attacked, by Captain Christopher Newport, who would have captured it if his men had not found a warehouse full of wine and brandy in Puerto de Caguaya and rendered themselves unfit for fighting. In 1643 Captain William Jackson, with only five hundred men, landed at Puerto de Caguaya, where more than two thousand Spaniards were dug in to repel his forces. The ill-trained and badly armed Spaniards lost more than two hundred men before they hastily retreated into the hills, and the English were able to sack the town at their leisure. Before retreating, the English also received a considerable amount of loot in ransom for the town, with the loss of only forty men. None of these raids was an attempt to take permanent possession of the island, for the place had so little value that no one wanted it.

The Lord Protector of England, Oliver Cromwell, was the man responsible for Jamaica becoming an English colony, but he did not particularly want it either; he was after bigger game. In 1654, after defeating the Royalist supporters of Charles I and concluding a brief but intense war with Holland, Cromwell found himself with swarms of unemployed Roundhead troops on his hands and a large fleet of warships in readiness. Although England was then officially at peace with Spain, Cromwell, like most Englishmen, considered Spain England's natural enemy and decided to launch an overseas campaign against one of Spain's American colonies. What better way to consolidate his position with his subjects and make use of his military forces? For the sake of appearances Cromwell first asked Spain for freedom of trade in the New World, well aware that the monopolistic Spanish Crown would never entertain such a petition. When the expected refusal came, it provided Cromwell with an excuse for going ahead with his "Western Design," a plan that called for the capture of either Puerto Rico, Hispaniola, Cuba, or some part of the Spanish Main—but not Jamaica.

Unfortunately for Cromwell, he ended up with the consolation prize—Jamaica—which was the best his forces could accomplish. His grandiose venture was doomed from the start when it left Portsmouth in December of 1654. The leader of the naval forces, William Penn (father of the William Penn after whom Pennsylvania is named), and Robert Venables, who led the land forces, were experienced officers, but both lacked the tactical brilliance and knowledge of the Caribbean that had enabled the Elizabethan sea dog, Sir Francis Drake, to capture a number of strongly fortified Spanish cities there. Contrary to expectations, veteran soldiers had not volunteered for the expedition, and the troops finally raised were far from being a cohesive group of well-trained fighting men. The majority were an undisciplined rabble, recruited for the most part from among vagrants and prison inmates.

The expedition leaders were unable to raise the full quota of eight thousand men deemed necessary for the venture, so they sailed to the English-held island of Barbados, where they enrolled thirty-five hundred men, most of them indentured servants who wished to escape their bondage. While there, the ranks were decimated by illness and death from inadequate rations (the storeships failed to arrive from England) and by tropical fevers, which invariably took their toll of unacclimatized European troops in the West Indies. To replace those lost at Barbados, soldiers had to be obtained from other English islands. When all was ready, the leaders waited an additional two months for the storeships from England, which failed to arrive. With most of the troops on the verge of mutiny, Penn and Venables were compelled to initiate some action against Spain at once or lose all chance of doing so, so Santo Domingo, capital and principal port of Hispaniola, was chosen the target.

There has never been a more inept military campaign in the history of British arms. On March 31 the fleet of thirty-eight ships left Barbados carrying eight thousand unhappy soldiers, several thousand seamen, and a totally inadequate supply of arms, ammunition, and provisions. Rather than make a frontal surprise attack on the well-fortified harbor, a plan that had the best hope of success, the leaders decided to land their forces six miles west of the town and march overland to attack from the rear. The comedy of errors began on April 3, when the ships landed the invading forces more than thirty miles west instead of six. The soldiers had to make an exhausting trek, mostly through swampland, completely losing any element of surprise. Then, to make matters even worse, the leaders decided to camp for a week outside the town, which allowed the Spaniards time to strengthen their defenses and bring in reinforcements from the surrounding countryside. It also gave the dread tropical fevers ample time to weaken the English troops. The assault, when finally attempted, was a total fiasco. For three days the Spaniards defended the city's walls so bravely that the English had to admit defeat and, after burying their many dead, they returned to their ships.

The naval and army leaders blamed each other for the defeat, and although both had been guilty of tactical mistakes, the gravest error of all was to attempt to attack with such badly trained, poorly armed troops racked by disease and starvation. Realizing that they would be in serious trouble with Cromwell if they returned to England empty-handed, the leaders quickly reconciled their differences and a new plan of action was drawn up. Furthermore they knew that if some place was not captured that could supply them with victuals, most of their men would die of starvation before ever reaching England. They needed an easy prize, and Jamaica was selected—for the island's meager defenses were known to the world at large and to the English in particular.

At sunrise on May 10, 1655, the English fleet entered Kingston Harbour, and Admiral Penn, showing one of the few signs of wisdom demonstrated during the entire campaign, anchored his large ships off Port Royal, wisely heeding the warning about the treacherous shallows near Puerto de Caguaya given by those of his men who had participated in Jackson's 1643 raid, while smaller vessels crossed over to land the first wave of troops at Puerto de Caguaya. The handful of Spaniards manning the fort there put up only token resistance and then fled to spread the alarm in Villa de la Vega.

The promising beginning was short-lived, and matters soon settled down to the levels of miscalculation and misfortune that had characterized the expedition all along. Instead of pursuing the fleeing Spaniards and entering the town by surprise, the English set up camp ashore and waited for the rest of the troops to land. This gave the inhabitants of the town all the time they needed, for when the English reached the town late the following afternoon, they found it deserted except for a few Negro slaves. The Spaniards had taken everything of value with them, and still worse, from the point of view of men who had been hungry since leaving England, they had taken all the food and driven their cattle from the surrounding plains to the hills.

At first the Spanish Governor, assuming that the attack was just another raid for plunder, sent emissaries into the town to find out what ransom was being asked this time. He was probably surprised to learn that the English actually wanted to take possession of the island, but he made the best of it. He stalled the invaders for almost a week, pretending to be considering the harsh surrender terms demanded, which was long enough for his people to send their valuables, their women and children, and their aged and infirm north to be evacuated to Cuba, while the able-bodied men and loyal Negro slaves prepared themselves for a long siege of guerrilla warfare.

The English leaders, finally realizing that they had been tricked, sent search parties to ferret out the island's inhabitants, but these were all unsuccessful, and frequently suicidal as well because of ambushes set up by the Spaniards, who were familiar with the terrain. Unable to do anything else, the English stubbornly dug in while events went from bad to worse. In the midst of plenty, the troops continued to starve. The parties that went into the hills to hunt for food met the same fate as those that searched for the Spaniards. Even soldiers sent out to plant crops fared little better, and although they managed to get the job done, they could hardly expect the crops to spring up overnight. The invaders were driven to eating dogs, rats, snakes, and iguana lizards. By January of 1656 this diet, combined with the ravages of dysentery, malaria, yellow fever, and the depredations made by the Spaniards, had reduced the eight thousand invaders to a mere twenty-six hundred. Penn and Venables, finding Jamaica an unhealthful place to be, had deserted their men soon after taking the island and returned to England, where a furious Cromwell had them imprisoned in the Tower of London.

Cromwell was far from happy with his consolation prize, but deciding that it would be held at all costs, sent reinforcements and one of his closest aides, Major General Robert Sedgewick, as military governor. He offered everyone over the age of twelve who was willing to migrate there thirty acres of free land, but there were few takers, for word of the terrible hardships suffered on the island spread quickly. Many of those foolish enough to go to Jamaica returned home after finding that the reports had not been exaggerated.

For several years the English continued to walk a tightrope on the island they now considered theirs; they held only a small area around Villa de la Vega, with scattered outposts on the surrounding plains, all but one within a ten-mile radius of the town. The Spaniards still felt they owned the place and made every effort to prove it. With reinforcements, arms, and supplies sent from many of the other Spanish colonies, they continued to plague the intruders and held almost the entire island.

Port Royal was the one bright spot in the miasma of misery and squalor that surrounded the English during this period. From the moment of their arrival they realized that the cay with its deep water and absence of shoals was the best site for a port, and named it Cagway, a corruption of Caguaya. They also realized that it was the key to the defense of the entire harbor and began fortifying the place soon after arriving. On the seaward side of the cay they constructed a simple fort, consisting of earthen breastworks enclosing a stone Round Tower and armed it with cannon from the fleet's ships. When the fort was completed in 1657, the army moved its headquarters from Villa de la Vega to the cay. It was soon found to be the safest place on the island for the English to be: though Villa de la Vega was attacked on numerous occasions, no guerrilla band was foolish enough to venture near the ships and guns that guarded the cay.

The cay also had a reputation for being more healthful than the mainland, probably because it had little rainfall and consequently fewer fever-carrying mosquitoes. Despite the lack of fresh water, the barren soil, and the need to have all supplies brought in by boat, a busy little civilian community soon grew up there.

However casual the Spanish attitude toward Jamaica had been, the seizure of Jamaica by the English had changed matters, for the Spaniards recognized that the permanent loss of the island would greatly endanger the rest of their American colonies. Spain declared war on England, and plans were formulated to mount an expedition to recover the island, but because the ships were needed at home and the war with England was draining the royal exchequer, the plan had to be delayed. An alternative plan was drawn up, calling for an invasion force to be made up from forces in neighboring Spanish colonies, and the Viceroy of Mexico was placed in command of the undertaking. A base was established at Santiago de Cuba, located only 125 miles from the north coast of Jamaica, but very little was accomplished. Many of the colonies were having problems of their own and could not afford to send many men. Although the Spanish guerrillas on Jamaica numbered well under a thousand, they continued to hold their ground and probably caused the English more problems than an invasion force would have.

The English quickly learned that they were fighting a losing battle against the guerrillas and decided that the best defense is a good offense. To launch it, they used the weapon that was rapidly making them the most feared power in the world—their navy. Admiral Penn had taken most of the large warships with him when he deserted in 1655, leaving behind only twelve frigates and a handful of smaller craft, under the command of Vice-Admiral William Goodson—one of those intrepid, enterprising seamen who fill the annals of British naval history. In August of that year, rather than wait for a Spanish attack he took the initiative by raiding the town of Santa Marta, which was near Cartagena, one of the principal ports of call for the treasure fleets. Although the raid was not profitable—the inhabitants, warned of the attack, carried away most of their valuables, and the only real booty obtained were thirty-two cannon—it shook the complacency of the entire Spanish Main, and the Governor of Cartagena, who had planned to send troops and arms to aid the guerrillas on Jamaica, changed his mind, fearing that his city would soon come under English guns.

During the rest of the year the Spaniards had nothing to worry about, though they had no way of knowing it. Major General Sedgewick, the newly appointed military Governor of Jamaica, opposed the raids and ordered the fleet to stay close to the island. Sedgewick had brought eleven more warships with him, and it must have been frustrating for Goodson to be restricted to home waters when he knew he could do more good by continuing his offensive. To appease him, Governor Sedgewick permitted him to take a squadron of ten ships out again in April of the following year. He first attacked Ríohacha, on the Spanish Main, once more capturing only cannon, and he appeared off Santa Marta and Cartagena, primarily to intimidate the Spaniards. Later in the year, when Sedgewick let him loose again, he inflicted considerable damage: after capturing a number of prize ships off Cuba, he was successful in keeping the Spanish treasure fleets bottled up in Veracruz and Havana for months, thus depriving the near-bankrupt King of Spain of the treasure he so badly needed.

Early in 1657 Goodson was recalled to England, but his successor, Commodore Christopher Myngs, a determined man who had worked his way up through the ranks, proved an even worse scourge, as his nickname El Diablo (the devil) indicates. Cromwell had given him orders to do what Goodson had desired to do, and he harried Spanish shipping throughout the Caribbean and attacked dozens of settlements all along the Spanish Main from Venezuela to Mexico. He terrorized the Spaniards in raids that became more and more profitable, and England's treasury swelled as Spain's grew lean. His biggest success occurred in 1659 at the port of Coro, in Venezuela, when he captured twenty-two chests containing four hundred pounds of silver valued at 1,500,000 Spanish pieces of eight.

Jamaica, on the other hand, had benefited in an even more important way from its fleet's domination of the Caribbean: the

Spanish colonies were too concerned with protecting themselves to send any effective aid to the guerrillas in Jamaica. Nor did the long-waited aid from Spain ever arrive, and for the same reason: English naval supremacy. Ever since the Battle of the Armada in 1588, the Spanish Navy had been weakened by numerous defeats at the hands of the English, the French, and the Dutch. Goodson had been instrumental in dealing Spain a blow almost as serious as the 1588 disaster. In 1656, when the treasure galleons Goodson had bottled up in Havana finally reached home, they ran into an English squadron blocking Cádiz. Six of them were captured or sunk and only two escaped—and two million pieces of eight fell into British hands. A similar fate befell the other treasure fleet that Goodson had bottled up in Veracruz. Admiral Robert Blake destroyed all sixteen ships of this fleet as they lay at anchor off Tenerife, in the Canary Islands. The Spaniards had managed to get all of the treasure ashore and out of reach before the English arrived. However, the Spanish Crown, which needed it desperately, did not get it either. Spain had no ships to carry it back to Spain, nor money to have ships built. Blake's stroke put an end to any hope of a Spanish expedition to Jamaica for years to come. As the war dragged on, Spain's naval power continued to decline, until by 1661 the only warships left were a few squadrons of antiquated galleys in the Mediterranean, which were no match for the powerful English warships and were unfit for the rough waters of the Atlantic.

The English settlers in Jamaica, encouraged by the tidings from Europe and by the performance of the fleet based in Port Royal, felt that the island belonged to them and took a firm hold. More people accepted Cromwell's offer of free land and began to raise crops on the rich plains surrounding Villa de la Vega. A new settlement, numbering sixteen hundred people, all from the English island of Nevis, was established at Port Morant, on the southeast tip of the island. It was isolated from the main English strongholds, so a fort was constructed at the harbor entrance and a large garrison installed there. Before there could be further expansion, however, the guerrillas would have to be subdued or driven out—that much was obvious to everyone.

Under the brave and resolute leadership of Don Cristóbal de Ysassi, who had assumed command on the death of the Spanish Governor, Spanish guerrillas continued to plague the English and still held most of the island. Relying on ambushes and hit-and-run raids, they disappeared into the thick forests and rough mountains, and the English pursuers were never able to find them. The English Navy was more effective by making sea-borne raids against various Spanish settlements still flourishing on the southwestern plains of the island. They burned the dwellings and captured large numbers of horses and cattle and some prisoners, but these raids were only temporarily effective, with the Spaniards quickly moving back into the devastated areas.

Early in 1657 English warships began a constant and very effective patrol of the waters between Cuba and Jamaica's north coast, to cut off the supply of reinforcements and supplies to the guerrillas. A number of Spanish supply ships were captured and large numbers of prisoners taken, and the English succeeded in destroying all the Spanish settlements located along the coast. The culminating blow came in June of 1659, when an English frigate spotted two Spanish troop-transport vessels at anchor off Rio Nuevo. The ships managed to escape but not their hapless cargo, which had already been landed. The Spaniards suffered more than three hundred casualties and the English took over one hundred prisoners, with only a minimal number of casualties on their side. This event marked the end of large-scale resistance by the Spaniards, and the majority of the guerrillas were evacuated to Cuba soon afterward. But Don Cristóbal de Ysassi refused to abandon his homeland and continued fighting with a small band of Spaniards and about two hundred black slaves, still hoping for the long-awaited expedition from Spain. He held out until May of the following year, when he, too, left with his followers for Cuba. Most of the Blacks stayed behind and continued sporadic and ineffective guerrilla activities.

Rio Nuevo marked a beginning as well as an end—the beginning of Jamaica as an English colony rather than a beleaguered military outpost, and the end of Spanish domination of the island. In 1660, when the English monarchy was restored, many feared that King Charles II, known to be sympathetic toward Spain, would return Jamaica to the Spanish Crown. Instead he proclaimed his intention of keeping it and ordered an extensive effort to be made to attract more settlers to the island, and people began to flock there from England and the other English colonies. Now that movement without fear was possible, plantations began to sprout all over the coastal plains and even in the foothills. A settler who arrived about this time, Richard Jourdan, wrote:

In short, this island for the richness and the goodness of the soil, for the pleasantness of its woods, and the abundance of all good things, may well contend with any other American Islands whatever and in this respect excells them, that it hath so convenient and advantageous a situation between the greater islands and the western continent of America. So as if our countrymen would raise up their dull spirits, and seriously set themselves to plant here, they would not only exceedingly advance the public interest and benefit their native country, but very much advantage and enrich themselves, their children and posterity; there being no adventure or merchandize in any part of the world undertaken as yet by the English, that is like to be of less hazard and more certain profit.

Chapter Three

From its early beginnings as a military site, the tiny cay at the end of the Palisadoes quickly developed into a bustling civilian settlement. To celebrate the restoration of the English monarchy, its name was changed from Cagway to Port Royal and the fort christened Fort Charles. Although settlers were spreading all over the island, Port Royal continued to be the most densely populated area, and within a few years the small cay was so jammed with houses and other buildings that it was necessary to fill in the marshy area separating the cay from the Palisadoes to provide more room for expansion. Why people flocked to Port Royal is not hard to explain: they went where the money was. From the beginning, gold, silver, pearls, and emeralds circulated freely in the streets, and much of it came from plunder.

The first civilian government in Jamaica, consisting of a council chosen from among the prominent inhabitants of the island and the army commander appointed interim governor by King Charles II, met there; so did the courts of justice that were now established. Officially Villa de la Vega, which came to be known as Spanish Town, was the island capital under the English as it had been under the Spaniards, but for a number of decades it was little more than a shadow of a town, with a population of only a few hundred. After the 1692 earthquake it grew in importance.

In 1662 the first truly civilian governor, Lord Windsor, arrived, bringing with him many new laws and ordinances for the better governing of the island. Large numbers of merchants also began arriving around this time, opening shops and setting up booths in the streets—trading for the booty taken from the Spaniards by the fleet based there. In return for English products, they obtained plundered Spanish gold and silver. They also obtained Spanish money by a more direct means: contraband trade with the Spanish colonies. Spain claimed, but could not enforce, an exclusive monopoly on trade with its American colonies. Even at the best of times Spain's inadequate merchant fleet was unable to supply its colonies with all the cloth, tools, and other items they required, and after the destruction of their two treasure fleets, in 1656 and 1657, Spain's commerce with her colonies almost came to a halt. No Spanish fleets sailed to the New World for seven years, and when they began coming again, they were much smaller in size and sailed at intervals of three or four years instead of annually. In 1669 Spain was so short of ships and seamen that she had to hire Dutch ships—a humiliating step for a nation that had formerly gone to such lengths to exclude foreigners from any contact with its colonies.

Since Spain was unable to satisfy its colonists' demands for European products, the English at Port Royal were happy to do so—at a handsome profit. Port Royal, protecting one of the finest harbors in the West Indies, was inevitably the center of this contraband trade, which, though less daring and exciting than raids for plunder, brought more wealth to the island and England. Large English merchantmen would arrive laden with cargoes of European goods: textiles, tools, glass, paper, and other items the Spanish colonies did not manufacture themselves and wanted badly. These items were transferred to smaller, swift vessels that could enter small bays and coves and trade for treasure undetected by the Spanish officials who were supposed to prevent illegal trade but often looked the other way.

Thus, through plunder and contraband, many of the riches of Spanish America—silver, gold, pearls, and emeralds—found their way to Port Royal, and what had been a deserted cay only a few years before became the most important trading center in the New World. The port was also a stimulus for the development of Jamaica as a whole: the rapidly increasing population required many kinds of European products, which were paid for by shipping Jamaica's sugar, indigo, cotton, tobacco, mahogany, dyewoods, ginger, and allspice to England via Port Royal.

Not all the ships arriving at the busy port brought cargoes of general merchandise; many brought human cargoes of Negroes from Africa, who were needed in large numbers to work on the island's plantations. Slaves were also in large demand in the Spanish colonies, where they were paid for dearly. On many Jamaican plantations the slaves outnumbered their overseers as much as fifty to one, and because of the inhumane manner in which they were treated, revolts were inevitable and a common occurrence. Rebellious slaves were punished severely, as was described by Alexander Buckland, a visitor to the island:

No country exceeds them in a barbarous treatment of slaves, or in the cruel methods by which they put them to death: A rebellious negro, or he that twice strikes a white man, is condemned to the flames; he is carried to the place of execution, and chained flat on his belly, his hands and legs extended; then fire is set to his feet, and so he is burnt gradually up. Others they starve to death, with a loaf of bread hanging before their mouths. I have seen these unfortunate wretches gnaw the flesh off their own shoulders, and expire in all the frightful agonies of one under the most horrid tortures.

Not surprisingly, a community so committed to worldly gain devoted itself to worldly pleasures, and Port Royal became notorious for its licentiousness. The Reverend John Taylor called it "the most wicked and sinful city in the world," and if the alcohol consumed by the inhabitants was the criterion, wicked and sinful it was. In 1661 the Council issued forty new licenses for taverns, grogshops, and punch houses during the month of July alone; respectable citizens complained that "there is not now resident in this place ten men to every house that selleth liquors." A resident wrote to a friend in England in 1664:

The common drink here is madeira wine, or rum punch; the first, mixed with water, is used by the better sort; the latter, by servants, and the inferior kind of people. The madeira is a wholesome wine and agrees perfectly well with one's constitution in this place. The rum punch is not improperly called Kill-devil; for thousands lose their lives by its means. When newcomers use it to the least excess, they expose themselves to imminent peril, for it heats the blood and brings on fevers, which in a very few hours send them to their graves.

Although the author of this letter may have exaggerated about thousands losing their lives from drinking Kill-devil, it was certainly potent stuff. One of Jamaica's governors, Sir Thomas Modyford, reported that "the Spaniards wondered much at the sickness of our people, until they knew of the strength of their drinks, but then wondered more that they were not all dead."

When King Charles heard of this apparently unquenchable thirst, he promptly proclaimed a royal monopoly on the sale of brandy in Port Royal, and ordered the revenues from it to be used for improving the town's fortifications: by 1668 Fort Charles had been enlarged and two smaller forts, James and Carlisle, constructed.

At first the military stationed there and the sailors of the fleet, behaving like soldiers and sailors on the loose in any town, were the chief contributors to the town's bad reputation. They were joined by women eager to separate them from their money: a common nocturnal sight in any tavern was a sailor with a girl draped on either arm recklessly spending Spanish pieces of eight from a recent raid; toward morning, badly hungover and his pockets empty, he was generally bereft of female companionship.

Very soon the ranks of the revelers were swelled by adventurers, assorted cutthroats, and the men whose exploits were to bring Port Royal its lasting fame: the buccaneers.

United in a desire to get rich at Spain's expense, the buccaneers performed a great service for England and its infant colony during the two decades following the capture of the island from Spain, particularly from 1662 to 1671. In fact, without them the history of Jamaica might well have taken a different turn. Despite rapid advances as a colony, the island's population of a few thousand was negligible compared with that of the Spanish colonies, then numbering hundreds of thousands. Although Spain, its resources depleted by the war with England, could not send an expedition to Jamaica, it never ceased enjoining its colonies to attempt recovery of the island. They were only too eager to do so, for they realized how great a danger to themselves the English stronghold constituted. In turn, the English on Jamaica knew they had much to fear from the Spanish colonies, which lacked a real navy but possessed enough small vessels to transport a large invasion force to the island. To make things worse for the struggling colony, Charles II had recalled most of the fleet stationed at Port Royal as an economy measure; in 1662 he had also ordered Lord Windsor to disband all but a portion of the army, counting on a citizens' militia to defend the island. Unfortunately settlement of Jamaica was not rapid enough to provide a militia capable of withstanding an invasion force of any magnitude. Then, like a gift from the gods, the buccaneers descended on the fleshpots of Port Royal, and the citizenry welcomed them with open arms.

They came from all over the Caribbean, but the majority were from a small island off the north coast of Hispaniola named Tortuga. Early in the seventeenth century, drifters from many nations had gravitated to Tortuga; some were ships' deserters, some political or religious dissenters forced to flee their homelands, still others adventurers seeking a life free from the restrictions of organized society. They were not at first primarily pirates, though occasionally they would attack a Spanish ship passing though the nearby Windward Passage, between Hispaniola and

Cuba. Their principal occupation was hunting cattle and hogs, on the western half of Hispaniola, which had escaped from Spanish farms on the other half of the island. From their occupation came the name they were known by: the meat from the animals was dried over grills of green wood called *boucans* in French; those who dried it became known as *boucaniers,* or, in English, buccaneers. During the dry season they hunted, and when the rains came they returned to Tortuga to sell their animal hides and smoked meats to passing ships. It was a pleasant existence, allowing plenty of leisure for drinking, gambling, and enjoying themselves free of moral restraint.

Unhappy about the colony of foreigners so close to his trade routes, King Philip IV of Spain sent a large force in 1623 to wipe out the settlement on Tortuga. Many of the men were away hunting on Hispaniola when the Spaniards arrived, but the more than four hundred unlucky ones at home were beheaded. All the women and children were sent to the Inquisition's dungeons in Havana and Spain, places from which few ever emerged alive. This barbarous act perpetrated by the Spaniards, followed by a campaign to kill all the wild cattle and hogs on Hispaniola and thus deprive the buccaneers of their livelihood, precipitated the age of piracy in the New World.

The buccaneers who had been away from Tortuga at the time of the attack returned to find their families gone and their homes destroyed. Vowing vengeance on the Spaniards, they quickly erected a large fort and then left some of their number behind to guard the island while the majority put to sea with the aim of scourging Spanish shipping—an objective they more than fulfilled. Their ranks swelled as adventurous men of several nationalities —French, English, Dutch, Portuguese, and even a few renegade Spaniards—decided that the buccaneers' life was for them.

Spain, goaded beyond endurance, took Tortuga again and stationed a garrison there, but it was removed in 1655 during the English attack on Santo Domingo. Since most of the buccaneers were French, they sought protection from the French Crown, which established a civil government on Tortuga in 1657 and made the island off limits to the buccaneers of other nations. Thus when the English authorities in Jamaica encouraged the English buccaneers to bring their prizes into Port Royal, the hospitality was accepted with alacrity. The English buccaneers knew the town well—some had helped capture the island from the Spaniards before going on to more profitable pursuits. Above all, they knew the value of being governed by their own countrymen, who were so ready to countenance depredations against the Spaniards that they granted the newcomers letters of marque, thereby making them lawful privateers (seamen on private vessels commissioned by governments to attack enemy shipping). Although to the Spaniards they remained pirates, to the English the privateers had the standing of an unofficial navy; and the citizens of Port Royal rejoiced in the twofold blessing of plunder and protection.

The importance of the privateers to Jamaica soon became apparent. Commodore Myngs had been recalled to England by Charles II along with most of the fleet, but Lord Windsor insisted that Myngs was needed in Jamaica, and he returned to the island in 1662 with Windsor. The King's instructions to the new Governor were highly ambiguous: at the same time that he was to maintain good relations with the Spanish colonies, he was also to establish free trade with them—if not by consent, then by force. Insisting on Myngs's return to Port Royal left little doubt how Lord Windsor would interpret the royal instructions. The gesture of petitioning the governors of several Spanish colonies for free trade was made, the anticipated refusals received, and then plans for attacking a Spanish settlement were quickly drawn up. The selected target was Santiago de Cuba, which the English had cause to remember as the supply base for the Spanish guerrillas on Jamaica. The attack would serve a dual purpose, revenge and a deterrent to future Spanish schemes for reconquering Jamaica from Cuba.

With more than thirteen hundred men aboard eleven privateering vessels and a 46-gun navy frigate, H.M.S. *Centurion,* Myngs sailed from Port Royal on September 21, 1662, and reached his objective on October 5. Although the harbor of Santiago de Cuba possessed one of the most impregnable forts in the New World,

Myngs and his men took it and the town with little difficulty. After demolishing the fort and leveling the town, they spent a week razing the surrounding countryside before heading back for Port Royal with more than a half million pounds sterling in treasure and other loot.

When they arrived back at a jubilant Port Royal, they discovered that Lord Windsor had returned to England for reasons of health, leaving the government in the hands of Sir Charles Lyttleton, the Lieutenant Governor. The performance of the privateers under his command had shown Myngs how valuable a fighting force they were, and he persuaded Lyttleton that Jamaica would have even better protection if the buccaneers who still remained on Tortuga, most of them French and their Dutch allies, could be enticed to move to Port Royal. An emissary sent to Tortuga with an offer of privateering commissions, in return for using Port Royal as a base, brought back a great many acceptances.

Ever committed to the principal that the way to keep the Spaniards from attacking Jamaica was to attack them, Myngs lost little time in organizing another raid. Word reached Jamaica that the King of Spain had ordered an assault on Port Royal in retaliation for the raid on Santiago de Cuba and had placed the Viceroy of Mexico in charge of it. Myngs convinced Lyttleton and the Council that the best way of dissuading the Viceroy from carrying out his orders was to launch an offense on one of his own ports. Campeche, on the western coast of the Yucatán Peninsula, was selected as the target.

With most of the same men and all of the same vessels used on the previous raid, Myngs and his privateers sailed for Campeche on January 12, 1663. On arrival, Myngs found that the Spaniards had been warned of his approach by some fishing vessels. Formally requesting the Spanish Governor to surrender, he received a refusal, and got down to business. In broad daylight he landed his troops right in front of the town, with a show of flying flags, beating drums, and blaring trumpets to intimidate the defenders. The attackers quickly overran the three batteries leading to the fort and then attempted to storm the fort itself, but the garrison within resisted so stoutly that Myngs decided to bypass it and capture the town first. The inhabitants, reinforced by men from nearby settlements and a great number of Indians, had other ideas. They fought from the rooftops, hurling down not only musket fire but also stones and hot oil and defended each house as though it were a fort. After the better part of a day spent in in fierce hand-to-hand combat, the privateers captured the town, then directed their attention to the fort, which by nightfall was also theirs. They were very disappointed in the plunder, considerably less than what they had obtained in Santiago de Cuba— no doubt the warning of the fishermen had given the inhabitants sufficient time to send most of their valuables into the country for safekeeping. However, they did capture sixteen ships in the harbor (which were added to the fleet of privateer vessels based in Port Royal) and a large number of cannon, small arms, and munitions.

Myngs took his victorious fleet back to Port Royal and found orders awaiting him to return to England with the *Centurion*, the only naval warship stationed in those waters. After reaching London he was knighted by Charles II for his services in protecting Jamaica. Myngs never returned to the scene of his greatest triumphs: his career as a naval officer ended prematurely in 1666, when he was mortally wounded in a battle against the Dutch in the North Sea. This stalwart seaman deserves more credit than anyone else for keeping Jamaica in English hands during the years following the conquest of the island.

The privateers carried on his policy of keeping Spain on the defensive, and the benefits they bestowed were financial as well as military, for there was scarcely anyone on the island who failed to profit from their raids. Merchants bought and sold the luxury goods plundered from the Spaniards; tavern keepers received a good share of the spoils, which the privateers were only too eager to spend on drink; and farmers got their share as well by supplying most of the provisions for the expeditions. Virtually everyone had indirect interests in the privateering ventures, and many had direct investments in them. Wealthy citizens, and on occasion the governors, would lend the privateers money to outfit an expedition, or sometimes even buy their ships, in return for a fixed share of the booty. Rarely did the privateers save enough money from one expedition to finance the next, and in Port Royal they were assured plenty of credit.

Considering how much interest the townspeople had in the success of the expeditions, it is small wonder that there was dancing in the streets whenever privateering vessels returned from a successful voyage (seldom did they return from an unsuccessful one—they owed too much money). As soon as the lookout in Fort Charles sighted a returning privateering vessel, the fort's cannon fired a salute, notifying the townspeople that the fun was about to start. It was a signal to drop everything (merchants and craftsmen closed their shops, and sometimes the courts suspended sessions) and come running. The moment the ship dropped anchor or tied up to the wharf, the King's officials rushed aboard to confiscate a tenth of the booty—the Crown's share in return for granting letters of marque. Next came the creditors, sure to be on hand while the booty was unloaded. The privateer captains generally saw to it that rum flowed freely, to celebrate the occasion and to get the buyers in an expansive frame of mind. Next the plunder —silks, laces, broacades, jewels, intricately worked images, reliquaries, and chalices from the Spanish churches, and any slaves captured on the raid—was auctioned off to the highest bidder. Then the privateers, each with a share of the proceeds of the voyage, managed to quickly spend most of it in the taverns, at the gaming tables, and in the numerous brothels of the town.

Sir Thomas Modyford arrived as Governor in June 1664 with orders from the King to suppress privateering, because more and more of the inhabitants of the island were forsaking their normal occupations in favor of the more lucrative business of privateering, which was detrimental to the growth and development of the island. The new Governor managed to convince a small number of privateers to return to planting, but this accomplished very little, for their places on the privateering vessels were immediately taken up by others. Fearing that if he pressed the matter, the privateers might leave Jamaica for another base or even prey upon English shipping as well as Spanish, he gave up any further attempts to hamper their activities, a move that met with the wholehearted approval of most of the island's inhabitants.

Not all the plunder reaching Port Royal was brought in by lawful privateers, for many, not wishing to give the English Crown a tenth of the profits, refused to accept letters of marque and thus remained true pirates. During the early years of the town the governors and royal officials were powerless to act against them because of their great numbers, and accorded them the same privileges enjoyed by the lawful privateers.

One of the earliest pirates to achieve notoriety was a Portuguese called Bartholomew, a bold and desperate rogue, who scored many successes against the Spaniards and kept Port Royal's merchants and tavern owners happy. On his last voyage he encountered a large galleon of twenty guns bound from Cartagena to Havana with a cargo valued at 250,000 pieces of eight. Though greatly overmatched, for his small sloop carried only thirty men and four cannon, he attacked the galleon. The first attempt to board her failed, but he tried again and succeeded. Heading back to Port Royal, his treasure-laden sloop was captured by three large Spanish warships and taken to Campeche, which was still smarting from Myngs's recent attack. The Spanish Governor, in no mood to be merciful with pirates, ordered them all hanged. Bartholomew managed to escape, after stabbing several of the guards aboard his sloop, and swam ashore using two large ceramic jars for buoyance. After hiding in the woods for days, he put to sea in a small boat and was picked up by a privateer sloop. But luck was not with him on this voyage: the sloop, on its way back to Port Royal loaded with booty, wrecked on a reef off the south coast of Cuba and all aboard were drowned.

Another celebrated pirate was the Dutchman known as Roche Brasilano. A former planter who had been expelled from Brazil by the Portuguese, he made his way to Port Royal and started his pirate career as a common seaman on one of the vessels operating out of there. Fearing nothing, avoiding no dangers, he soon distinguished himself and was elected captain of a band of sea rovers. On his first voyage of command he captured a homeward-bound Spanish galleon carrying a great quantity of silver, right

under the guns of the forts of Havana. The carousing and de-
bauchery that followed his triumphant return to Port Royal set
something of a record even for that degenerate town. Brasilano
probably contributed more heavily than any other pirate or privateer to Port Royal's reputation for lewdness. Claiming he owed
no allegiance to any government, he returned from each successful venture more arrogant and unruly than before. He had a
large band of followers and there was little the Jamaican authorities could do to curb his outrages. These included striking, slash-
ing, or throwing beer at people he encountered in the streets when
he was in a bad mood and, when he was feeling more sociable,
buying a huge barrel of wine, setting it out in the street, and inviting passers-by to drink with him—few refused, since he usually
issued the invitation with pistol in hand. If Brasilano terrified the
English, he terrified the Spaniards even more, for he submitted
all Spaniards he captured to the most cruel and excruciating tortures. Fortunately for everyone, his career lasted only a few years;
he departed on a voyage and was never heard from again.

Roche Brasilano's excesses were unusual. The majority of the
pirates and privateers who used Port Royal as a base took their
pleasure in a less sadistic fashion. Yet it was not uncommon for
a man to find life ashore more perilous than at sea: many a privateer and pirate who had survived Spanish gunfire met his end in
one of the many duels and drunken brawls for which Port Royal
was notorious. Disreputable, dissipated, sometimes dangerous, they
had the run of the town and few attempts were made to control
them, for the inhabitants feared that they might make their base
elsewhere if they found Port Royal uncongenial. Some of the
more righteous citizens complained to the authorities, but to no
avail. What was a little disturbance of the peace measured against
the profits and protection from invasion conferred on the town
by these men?

The exploits of a number of other pirates and privateers made
them legendary in their own time. There was the Englishman
Lewis Scot, who captured and destroyed Campeche a few years
after Myngs's attack. There was John Davis, another Englishman,
who penetrated deep into Guatemala and other Spanish colonies

in Central America, taking a fortune in plunder and leaving a trail of destruction behind him. There was the Dutchman Edward Mansveldt, who marched overland across Central America to attack Spanish possessions in the Pacific. And towering above them, there was the most famous privateer of them all, whose name is as much a part of Jamaican history as that of Columbus —Henry Morgan.

Morgan was born in 1635 in Glamorganshire, Wales, the son of a prosperous yeoman. Concerning his youth, Morgan said: "I left school too young to be a great proficient in either the Admiralty or other laws, and have been much more used to the sword and pike than the book." He left home before his fifteenth year, perhaps bored with the placid country life, and soon afterward was kidnaped at Bristol and sent to Barbados, where he was bound over to a planter as an indentured servant. When Cromwell's fleet stopped there to recruit troops, Morgan, like many others in his position, joined the Army to escape the harsh life of bondage. He participated in the ill-fated assault on Santo Domingo and in the capture of Jamaica. Later, along with other soldiers discharged from the Army, he became a privateer and distinguished himself during Myngs's attacks on Santiago de Cuba and Campeche. His courage and talent set him above the pack, and in 1666 Mansveldt, then the leader of the Port Royal privateers, selected him as his lieutenant.

At that time Mansveldt was facing a bit of dissension in the ranks. Although a Dutchman himself, he made plans to attack the Dutch island of Curaçao. Holland and France had declared war on England the previous year; however, the Dutch and French privateers under his command, somewhat more nationalistic than their leader, balked at a Dutch target. Sir Thomas Lynch, then the Governor of Jamaica, advised Mansveldt to undertake a venture that all the privateers would be willing to take part in. Once the suggestion had been made, it did not take long for Mansveldt to come up with a target everyone could agree on—a Spanish one: Porto Bello, on the Caribbean coast of Panama. This port was one of the most important in Spanish

America; treasure fleets came there each year to pick up the gold and silver from South America and carry it back to Spain.

A fleet of fifteen ships under the command of Mansveldt and Morgan set sail, but en route they captured a Spanish ship just out of Porto Bello and received news that forced a change of plans. Through spies, the Spaniards had learned that an attempt would be made on Porto Bello, and they had fortified and garrisoned it so well that an invasion would be folly. Rather than return home empty-handed, they attacked Santa Catalina (today known as Providencia), a small island off the coast of Nicaragua, on May 25, 1666, and took it with very little resistance from the Spanish garrison stationed there. Very little plunder was taken, a rare occurrence on a privateering venture. Since the place would serve as a good advance base for a future assault on Porto Bello, Mansveldt left a small force behind to hold the island. He took the fleet back to Port Royal and immediately requested that Governor Lynch send settlers to Santa Catalina, but Lynch, who believed that Jamaica could ill afford any loss of population, refused to do so. As far as Mansveldt was concerned, the expedition had been a total failure, for without reinforcements the men left on Santa Catalina could hardly be expected to hold the island. Disappointed, and fearing that the privateers who had sailed under him would blame him for their empty pockets, he left with a few followers to work out of Tortuga, which still harbored a good number of buccaneers, and shortly afterward he died a natural death. As he had foreseen, Santa Catalina was soon retaken by a Spanish force sent by the President of Panama, and all the three hundred privateers there were put to the sword—an event that Morgan vowed to someday avenge.

Morgan succeeded Mansveldt as leader of the Port Royal privateers. For a time, he had to limit his activities to small operations such as capturing Spanish vessels on the high seas: approximately half the privateers in Port Royal were Dutch and French and unwilling to serve under an English leader, so he could not attempt anything on a grand scale. Then, toward the end of 1667, word reached Jamaica that England had concluded peace with Holland and France. The news came as a relief to everyone. Chauvinistic differences were quickly settled, all the privateers were ready for a big expedition, and Morgan was prepared to lead them. As an added boost to a commander going off on his first big mission, Morgan was given the rank of colonel in the British Army by Lynch's successor, Sir Thomas Modyford, who was to prove himself a greater champion of the privateers than any other representative of the English Crown in Jamaica.

Early in 1668 Modyford directed Morgan to organize a force and "find out the truth" about reports of an intended attack by the Spaniards in Cuba against Jamaica. Modyford and Morgan, both ambitious men, hoped to make Spain abandon plans for reconquering Jamaica once and for all and perhaps force a formal recognition of England's claim to the island. The objective selected was Puerto Príncipe (known today as Camagüey), in Cuba. Sailing with five hundred men and ten ships, he anchored his ships in a deserted bay near the port and executed a forced march, planning a surprise attack. However, the inhabitants, warned two days in advance, had ample time to spirit away most of their valuables and to prepare a bellicose welcome for the invaders. Morgan took the town, but only after several days of intensive house-to-house fighting. The booty was disappointing— only fifty thousand pieces of eight and three hundred Negro slaves extorted from the inhabitants through torture and Morgan's threat to burn the town if they refused to pay.

It was hardly an auspicious debut for a commander who was to earn a place beside Sir Francis Drake as one of England's most brilliant tacticians. To make matters worse, the privateers passed the time waiting for the ransom money in a victory celebration with the fine wines of the town. The inevitable brawl ensued, and a French privateer was killed by an Englishman. The French contingent demanded immediate justice, which meant executing the Englishman on the spot, but Morgan ordered him taken back to Port Royal to stand trial. This insistence on legality, interpreted as favoritism, so inflamed the Gallic temper (already irritated by the small pickings) that all the French privateers left in a huff for Tortuga, resolved to make it their base in the future.

Only a few weeks after the diminished band's far from tri-

umphant return to Port Royal, Morgan sailed again, with nine
ships and four hundred sixty privateers, this time after a bigger
prize—the heavily fortified city of Porto Bello, in Panama, Mansveldt's original objective two years before. To make certain that
his hoped-for surprise attack would be effective, he left his ships
well up the coast and piled his men into small boats. Stealing up
on the town at dawn, his men captured a sentry before he could
give the alarm and, after surrounding Santiago de la Gloria,
Porto Bello's main fort, forced him to call upon the defenders to
surrender or meet death without quarter. Being answered by
musket fire, the privateers scaled the walls and, despite great resistance, overwhelmed the garrison. True to their word, they put
all their prisoners into a single room and blew it up with gunpowder. The second of the town's three forts was captured without much difficulty, but the last one, commanded by the Spanish
governor himself, was more of a challenge. Vowing that he and
his men would fight to the death rather than surrender, the governor organized an opposition so staunch that it almost forced
the privateers to retreat.

From dawn to noon the fort withstood all assaults, and Morgan
realized that desperate measures were required and they had to be
quick, for the inhabitants of Porto Bello were fleeing into the
woods with all the valuables they could carry. He ordered his men
to round up the town's friars and nuns and forced them to carry
the scaling ladders to the fort's outer walls in front of his advanc-
ing troops. Morgan was well aware of the great veneration the
Spaniards had for the clergy, and counted on the defenders' laying down their arms. He must have been astonished when the
governor, torn between piety and duty, chose duty and kept his
troops pouring down steady musket fire. Undoubtedly the governor suffered pangs of conscience, but not for long: he and most
of his men died fighting for a losing cause.

The city surrendered as soon as the fort fell, and the privateers
began to sack it and torture their prisoners to reveal hidden
wealth. This time the privateers had no cause to complain about
the plunder, which included more than 250,000 pieces of eight,
a great deal of valuable merchandise from the warehouses, three

hundred Negro slaves, and a large number of cannon from the forts. The President of Panama sent a relief expedition, but it was easily defeated. Morgan sent the president a pistol with a note, claiming that he would be back to fetch it soon. The privateers returned to a rousing welcome in a Port Royal almost delirious with joy. The celebration lasted well over a month, until most of the booty found its way from the pockets of the privateers into those of the citizens. Morgan, more than anyone else, had cause to celebrate: on this expedition he had proved himself a brilliant strategist.

In January of the following year Morgan set sail again and narrowly escaped death at the beginning of the expedition, while anchored near the Isle of Ash, off the south coast of Hispaniola. During a drinking bout, his flagship somehow caught fire and blew up; only he and a few of his officers, in the after part of the ship, escaped. They then raided several small ports along that coast—most likely a bit of practice after a long layoff, for Hispaniola was a relatively poor Spanish colony, and little booty was obtained. Then he headed for his main objective, the Port of Maracaibo, located on a large, almost landlocked extension of the Caribbean known as Lake Maracaibo. The narrow entrance to the lake was protected by a strong fort, and its cannon opened fire as the fleet attempted to sail past, thus forcing a temporary retreat. The following day, when Morgan landed troops to storm the fort, he found the Spaniards had fled. Continuing on to the town, he found that deserted, too. After sending some of his men to scour the countryside, he sailed with the rest to the nearby town of Gibraltar, but found it abandoned also. Morgan was not easily discouraged: he dug in with his men for almost a month, and during that time his search parties managed to round up many of the inhabitants of both towns and extort about 250,000 pieces of eight from them.

Morgan once again proved his audacity and tactical ingenuity. As his fleet was departing for home, they found the entrance to the lake blocked by three huge Spanish warships. Even though his fleet numbered fifteen vessels, it was no match for the enemy, for all his vessels were small, and the total number of cannon among them was less than that carried by any one of the warships. The moment night fell, he filled one of his vessels with inflammable materials and set it afire, sending it against the largest warship. After the collision, the warship caught fire and the stores of gunpowder exploded. The second warship had to cut her anchor cables to escape the flames and in doing so accidentally ran aground, forcing the Spaniards to set her afire to keep her out of privateer hands. The third warship, assaulted on all sides by dozens of ships' boats, was an easy prize.

This exploit so enhanced Morgan's reputation that when he organized another expedition, late in 1670—which turned out to be the most important one of his career—he was able to raise almost forty vessels and more than two thousand men, including many of the same Frenchmen who had deserted him after Puerto Príncipe. He sailed to rendezvous with the Tortuga forces at Cow Island, off the south coast of Hispaniola, after first sending most of his ships to capture victuals from Spanish vessels and ports. While waiting for them to return, ten of the eleven ships with him ran aground during a storm, but all save three were refloated. One of his ships came back with a bigger prize than provisions: a number of important officials captured on a Spanish ship. From them Morgan learned that the President of Panama had recently granted letters of marque empowering Spanish captains to capture all English ships they came across and to put all the prisoners to death. Particular stress was placed on those ships engaged in contraband trade with the Spanish colonies.

Morgan realized that the President of Panama's design, if carried out, could mean the ruin of Port Royal and a serious blow to England's prosperity. The Crown relied heavily on revenue derived from contraband: Much of the currency in England was minted from Spanish coin and bullion obtained via Jamaica. As for Jamaica itself, in 1668 the Council passed a law recognizing Spanish coins as the colony's official currency, since they were virtually the only ones to circulate there. Until then, most Spanish officials had turned a blind eye to the activities of the Jamaican smugglers because their colonies were in such dire need of the goods they supplied. Now that it seemed that this tacit under-

standing was at an end, Morgan decided to shelve his original
plans for the expedition (it is not known what they were) in
favor of striking a blow at the President of Panama that he would
not soon forget: an attack on his capital, Panama City.

The city lay on the Pacific coast, so a large stretch of the
Isthmus of Panama would have to be crossed, making it a difficult
undertaking. Morgan decided to take his men up the Chagres
River as far as possible and then to cover the rest of the journey
by foot. That necessitated the construction of several hundred
piraguas, or dugout canoes, and to get the timber to build them
Morgan attacked and easily took the island of Santa Catalina, the
same island that had been wrested briefly from Spain by Mansveldt. Setting most of his men to work on the piraguas, he sent
three ships and five hundred men led by Captain Joseph Bradly
to capture the fort of San Lorenzo, which guarded the mouth
of the Chagres River. The privateers began the attack on the fort
on January 6, 1671, finding it strongly fortified and well manned.
Three days of fierce fighting availed nothing, and Bradly was on
the point of postponing the attack until Morgan arrived, when a
guardhouse inside the fort caught fire, exploding kegs of gunpowder and breaching one of the fort's outer walls. The privateers stormed through the gap and took the fort, with both sides
suffering heavy losses.

Morgan arrived several days later with his fleet, but while entering the port, five ships, including Morgan's flagship, were
wrecked on a reef. Although no lives were lost, the misfortune
was the first of a series that were to dog the expedition. Leaving
about five hundred men to hold the fort and guard his ships,
Morgan started up the river in the piraguas with fourteen hundred men but without food for them: he expected to pick up provisions from Spanish and Indian settlements along the way. The
advance up the river was slow and difficult and the troops suffered greatly from lack of nourishment, for even in those days a
scorched-earth plan of defense was used and they found little or
no food in the settlements they passed on the river. The seven-day
journey up the river left the privateers weakened by hunger,
dysentery, and fevers—in no condition for a grueling jungle

march. But march they did, their progress impeded by ambushes set by the Spaniards. Their hunger pains increased, and many of the men resorted to eating their shoes, first beating them to soften the leather. After nine days of marching, they finally sighted Panama City from a hilltop and also a galleon leaving the port—which they later learned was carrying nearly five million pieces of eight to safety.

The men, famished and weary, paid little heed to the departing ship. Fortunately there were many cattle near the outskirts of the city, a number of which the privateers promptly slaughtered and roasted to assuage their hunger. The next morning the privateers awoke to drum rolls and trumpet calls within the city and, as they ate the leftovers from the night before, they watched twenty-one hundred Spanish infantrymen and six hundred cavalry draw up in battle formation on the plain in front of the city. Quickly Morgan organized his troops, who numbered considerably fewer than the enemy but had the advantage of not having to face the morning sun, and advanced.

The entire Spanish cavalry charged the privateer vanguard, which held its ground and turned the charge with musket fire of deadly accuracy. Then, as their infantry advanced, the Spaniards had some Indians stampede two thousand head of cattle against the privateer rear guard. It was a cunning maneuver, but it failed: the privateers fired at the charging beasts, dispersing them in all directions. The Spanish infantry, now within range of the privateers' musket fire, faced it with little enthusiasm after seeing the ruin of their cavalry and the failure of the stampede. Most of them fired once, flung their heavy muskets to the ground, and fled back to the city, where fresh troops waited to defend the barricaded streets.

Although a very effective defense could have been put up, the President of Panama decided to destroy his city rather than risk having it fall into Morgan's hands. The most important buildings were set afire and the fort blown up, in such haste that forty of the men inside were blown up with it before they could abandon their posts. The inhabitants fled to the woods with all they could carry, and the invaders encountered little resistance when they entered the gates of the city. The place was like a furnace, for the majority of the city's two thousand buildings were built of wood and the fire spread rapidly. By the time the privateers finally extinguished the holocaust, nearly three quarters of the city had been leveled, including the majority of the more than two hundred richly stocked warehouses and the homes of the wealthiest citizens, leaving little to plunder. Learning that the galleon seen leaving the day before had carried most of the city's treasure, Morgan sent several fast boats from the harbor in pursuit, but it was not to be found.

During the month that the privateers remained in the ruins of the city, raiding parties were sent out to capture the inhabitants, many of whom were harshly treated and tortured to make them divulge where they might have hidden treasure, but the results were disappointing. The privateers overlooked one of the richest treasures of all: the Golden Altar of the cathedral. Before fleeing the city a resourceful monk had coated the altar with white paint, and the raiders, thinking it worthless, passed it by. Most of the 750,000 pieces of eight, which were carried overland in 175 mule loads, were obtained by ransoming the prisoners they had captured. The booty was divided among the privateers before they sailed for Jamaica, and because the loot had to be cut so many ways, shares were disappointingly small. Many of the privateers accused Morgan of cheating them, and the Spaniards claimed to have lost or paid out in ransom far more money than Morgan said they did. Legend has it that he buried a great treasure on the way back to Port Royal, a legend that gained credence from the fact that Morgan's ship left quickly after the division of the booty and returned to Jamaica alone. Today there is scarcely an island in the Caribbean that the inhabitants do not claim as the site of Morgan's buried treasure.

Although Morgan's capture of Panama was an impressive military feat, it almost generated another war between Spain and England. In July of 1670, five months before Morgan left Port Royal for Hispaniola, England and Spain had signed the Treaty of Madrid, which formally recognized England's claims to all territory then in English hands, including Jamaica, and proclaimed a peace. Consequently the attack on Panama was rather embarrassing to the English Crown. Morgan denied any knowledge of the treaty, and so did Governor Modyford, who had as usual countenanced the privateering venture. The Spanish Crown didn't believe them and threatened to declare war on England again unless the culprits were punished for violating the treaty. Charles II, anxious to preserve the peace now that he had title to Jamaica, sent Sir Thomas Lynch back to Jamaica as governor for the second time with orders to ship Modyford back to England under arrest. Still Spain was not satisfied, and a year later, while poor Modyford continued to languish in the Tower of London, Morgan, too, had to be shipped back to London in chains. Fortunately for him, he was regarded as a national hero by the public and neither saw the inside of a prison nor stood trial.

Morgan, with his talent for turning disaster into triumph, cleared himself of the charges and was knighted by Charles II. In 1674, when the tensions with Spain had eased, Modyford was finally released from the Tower, and Morgan returned to Jamaica as lieutenant governor under a new governor, Lord Vaughn, replacing Lynch, who was extremely unpopular with the people because of the measures he had been ordered to take to suppress privateering. Contrary to what many believed, the appointment of Morgan was not an encouragement of privateering. King Charles wanted to maintain peaceful relations with Spain, and his new officials were given strict orders to issue no further letters of marque, to cancel all those extant, and to do everything possible to suppress piracy and privateering in the West Indies. Very likely the choice of Morgan for the job was dictated by the adage "Set a thief to catch a thief."

When Morgan returned to Port Royal, it was estimated that still about a fifth of Jamaica's population of twenty thousand were engaged in privateering, and these men could hardly have been eager to abandon an adventurous life on the high seas for farming or something equally mundane. Nevertheless Morgan persuaded many of his former companions-at-arms to give up what had now become illegal piracy. When persuasion failed, he resorted to sterner measures, sometimes ordering the hanging of old cronies. Morgan was merely doing his duty, which he performed with zeal, but not even his efforts could stamp out piracy entirely. In 1677, six heavily armed pirate ships entered Port Royal to dispose of plunder acquired at Santa Marta, on the Spanish Main, and Morgan, without the forces to stop them, had to sit back helplessly as they went about their business. In 1681, he proved his loyalty to king and country beyond a shadow of a doubt. Learning that a Dutch pirate named Everson and his force of a hundred men had two vessels anchored in Cow Bay, he sent a ship after them. One of the vessels escaped, but the other was captured and brought into Port Royal. Morgan sent the pirates, most of whom were English, to the governor of Cartagena to stand trial, and they were all hanged. Gradually Port Royal became less and less popular as a haunt for pirates, especially after 1685, when the English Crown sent a warship there expressly to combat them. A few continued to risk it, because the merchants were always willing to buy Spanish goods and were not particular about where they came from; the majority, however, simply returned to Tortuga and worked out of there.

At first glance, Morgan's severity seems like a complete about-face, and there is no doubt that it cost him many friends, who regarded him as a turncoat. It must be remembered that Morgan had been a privateer, not a pirate, and as such had served his country all along. Privateering commissions do not, of course, excuse the many cruelties attributed to Morgan and other privateers, but it must be taken into account that they lived in an age of cruelty, when the authorities of many countries inflicted indescribable tortures on their own countrymen in the name of religious orthodoxy and sentenced men to be hanged for stealing a loaf of bread.

In 1682 Morgan retired as lieutenant governor and spent more and more time in taverns, to the detriment of his health. A few months before his death, the personal physician of the governor, the Duke of Albemarle, described him as "lean, sallow-colored, his eyes a little yellowish, and a belly a little jutting out. . . . much given to drinking and sitting up late." Finally the tavern dissipations took their toll and Morgan died on August 28, 1688, leaving most of his property to his wife, and some to close friends. The greatest privateer of them all was buried in Port Royal's cemetery, which sank into the sea four years later.

Even with most of the privateers and pirates gone, Port Royal continued to prosper. Contraband trade with the Spanish colonies, which all along had accounted for most of the island's wealth, was the leading industry. Spain, with virtually no navy at all, could no longer make much of a stand against the English upstarts, and decided that if it couldn't beat them, it would join them: In 1689 an agent of the Spanish Crown arrived in Port Royal to sell licenses permitting the merchants to sell Negro slaves to the Spanish colonies, which needed them badly to work in the gold and silver mines. Aside from enjoying considerable profits from the slave trade, the merchants found the authorization to enter the Spanish ports a great boon to illegal trade, for the ships carrying the slaves were always laden with a good supply of contraband goods. Others also managed to get rich through (wonder of wonders for that town) legal trade. A flourishing commerce had sprung up between the New England colonies and Jamaica: Flour, dried and pickled meats, shingles, tar, and the like were exchanged for sugar, molasses, rum, and various spices. There was also a thriving trade with England, which provided most of the basic commodities ranging from ale and cheese to linen fabrics in return for the island's products and Spanish money. As a commercial center, Port Royal had no peer in the Western Hemisphere.

It was also the center of a new and thriving industry in the Caribbean—treasure hunting, or "the wracking trade," as it was then called. The treasure sought lay at the bottom of the sea on countless sunken vessels, and the majority of the divers used in this pursuit were escaped Negro slaves who had worked in the Spanish pearl fisheries on the Spanish Main. In 1682 William Phips, an American from Boston, and later governor of Massachusetts, hired several dozen divers in Port Royal and then sailed on an expedition that culminated in the recovery of treasure worth over three million dollars from a Spanish galleon sunk on a reef off the north coast of Hispaniola. It was the greatest sum recovered from a single wreck until the present century. One of Phips's principal backers, the Duke of Albemarle, was so persuaded by the return on his investment that there was a fortune to be made from this new industry that he prevailed upon the King of England to appoint him governor of Jamaica, thus making sure to be on hand when further treasure hunts were undertaken. Unfortunately, Albemarle was also addicted to excessive drinking, like his friend Henry Morgan, and followed him to the grave two months later, having governed the island for only a year.

The absence of the pirates and privateers did little to change the town from its notorious ways, and the scandal became so great that in 1682, at the orders of the English Crown, a law was passed providing

> that whatsoever person so licensed as alehouses, taverns, and victualling houses shall entertain or receive anyone to tipple or drink in the time of divine worship or service shall forfeit twenty shillings for every such offense; that anyone caught gambling in any public place shall pay a fine of ten pounds sterling; and anyone blaspheming the name of God shall pay a fine of twenty pounds sterling and also face corporal punishment as the Supreme Court of Judication shall see fit, loss of life and limb only excepted.

So strong was the opposition of the citizens that the law was either weakly enforced or ignored. In a place where there were so few forms of recreation, it is not surprising that people resented any curtailment of their freedom to tipple, gamble, and carouse—for what else was there to do? Only when disaster struck, on June 7, 1692, did many of Port Royal's residents decide to atone for their sins and amend their ways, and for many this was only a temporary measure, for they were soon back to their old pleasures once their fears subsided.

Chapter Four

Few of Port Royal's survivors slept the night of June 7, for earth tremors were felt hourly and it was believed that an even greater earthquake was imminent. Crowded together aboard ships in the harbor, the decent survivors were at the mercy of unscrupulous shipowners who demanded exorbitant prices for the food they consumed. During the night more than fifty of them died from injuries sustained in the quake: there were few doctors and very few medical supplies left. Conditions worsened in the days that followed. The weather, ever more oppressive and sultry, hastened the decomposition of the hundreds of corpses floating in the harbor. Eyewitness accounts describe the unbearable stench floating over the area and tell of large numbers of sharks which feasted on the floating bodies for days after the disaster.

On the third day following the earthquake the rector of St. Paul's, Dr. Heath, took a small band of followers ashore on what remained of Port Royal to bury the dead, but not before obtaining a safe-conduct pass from the men who were still pillaging the town. They were appalled to discover that many of the corpses had fingers missing: in their eagerness to remove the gold rings worn by the dead, the looters had wielded their knives freely.

The period of lawless plundering lasted about two weeks, until there was little left to take. Then most of the looters, not caring to linger and face inevitable punishment, left Jamaica and dispersed throughout the Caribbean. To those who remained, John White issued a proclamation stating that they might keep a third of the booty taken if they returned the balance to the rightful owners. A few accepted the offer; most preferred to clear out with their ill-gotten gains. If disaster can be said to have a bright side, it was that it drove many of the lawless elements from Port Royal and left the place to the law-abiding citizens, most of whom, however, no longer wanted it.

On June 20, White wrote to the Lords of Trade and Plantations in London, relating details of the catastrophe and begging their assistance in trying to get the colony on its feet again. He was particularly concerned about the island's defenses, knowing full well that if France, which he still believed had a stronghold on the north coast, or any other nation chose to attack Jamaica, she could offer little resistance. A few days intervened before the ship sailed for England with over two hundred of the survivors from Port Royal aboard, and White was able to add a postscript containing the reassuring tidings that the danger was not immediate. H.M.S. *Guernsey,* out on patrol when the earthquake occurred, had returned after having defeated the French intruders in St. Ann's Bay and driven them from the island.

The letter reached England in late September. But it reached an England that had just suffered its own cataclysm, for on September 8 an earthquake had struck, causing damage as far away as Germany and devastating England even more than had the Great Fire of London in 1666. Beset with the need to tend to domestic matters, King William and Queen Mary could send little assistance to their Caribbean colony. They did, however, appoint a new governor, Colonel William Beeston, an army officer with a distinguished record of service characterized by initiative and efficiency.

Meanwhile back in Jamaica earth tremors continued for two months after the disaster, and what was left of Port Royal seemed to be sinking a little more each day. Many believed that it was only a matter of weeks before the ten-acre cay would totally disappear. A few stubborn souls thought otherwise, and on June 28 they received permission from White to return to Port Royal to reconstruct their homes and shops. Little by little, as fear subsided that the cay would sink entirely, others also returned to rebuild on Port Royal.

Members of the Council and the majority of the surviving townspeople decided to found a new town across the harbor from Port Royal. What was to become Kingston began as a collection of wretched huts providing little protection from the elements. The people crowded into them and, already weakened by hardship, without proper food or medical supplies, succumbed to disease. Within a span of two months there were more than three thousand deaths in the new town, including that of John White, who was replaced as acting governor by John Bourden.

Those who had chosen to return to Port Royal fared no better. By the end of September, all the government offices had moved back to Port Royal, because it was considered a more healthful environment than Kingston. With the exception of property deeds, which had been kept in Spanish Town, all government records had been lost in the earthquake. The treasury was empty, and royal officials could do little to begin rebuilding until aid arrived from England—which was not until the following spring.

One of the first laws passed by the Council after moving back to Port Royal was to declare every June 7 a day of mourning. The Act read:

For as much as it hath pleased Almighty God, the Great Creator and Judge of Heaven and Earth, on the seventh day of June, one thousand six hundred ninety two, justly to punish the inhabitants of this island, for their manifold sins and wickednesses committed against his Divine Majesty, by a most terrible and dreadful earthquake, which not only laid waste our estates and places of habitations in general, but also destroyed many hundreds of people; which tremendous

Judgement was succeeded by a raging sickness and mortality, that few or no families escaped. Now, that so single a Visitation may be had in Perpetual Remembrance, and we and our posterity may be humbling ourselves, endeavour to appease God's imminent Wrath, and prevent heavier Judgements; be it hereby enacted and ordained that every seventh of June, shall be for ever hereafter set apart, to be kept and observed by all the inhabitants of this Island, as an anniversary day of fasting and humiliation; and that all and every inhabitant aforesaid, shall upon the said day, resort to some usual place where prayers and preaching are used to be ministered.

Colonel William Beeston, now Sir William by virtue of the knighthood conferred upon him before leaving London, arrived to take up his post in March of 1693. At once he made energetic efforts to revive the colony. He had engineers map out Kingston, and the new town began to grow. As for Port Royal, he regarded it as the key to defense of the harbor; he saw to it that Fort Charles was repaired and other fortifications erected. Determined to have a town re-established on the cay, he ordered that all standing buildings be used again by their owners or sold to others, and that much of the land lost to the sea be reclaimed by driving piles into the water and filling in the sunken areas with stones and sand from the Palisadoes. Beeston was determined that every Jamaican, rich and poor, contribute to restoring prosperity to the island, and to see that this was accomplished, one of his first acts in office was passing a law "For punishing idle persons and vagabonds." Any fit and able person found not to be engaged in some lawful occupation was ordered apprehended by the constables and given up to thirty-nine lashes on his naked back.

The new governor also ordered that every able-bodied man on the island be properly trained in the use of arms and formed in companies of militia—a wise move, which probably saved the island from falling into French hands the following year. Their slowness in acting after the earthquake no doubt cost the French the opportunity of capturing the island. On June 17, 1694, a French fleet of three warships and twenty-three transports, carrying over fifteen hundred troops, reached Jamaica and began to systematically destroy and sack settlements and plantations both east and west of Port Royal on the south coast of the island. Jean du Casse, the leader of the expedition, boasted that after having control of the surrounding countryside, he would force the inhabitants of Port Royal and Kingston to surrender by depriving them of food supplies from the rest of the island. Before he could make good his boast, Beeston acted. He led a surprise attack with more than three thousand militiamen and soundly defeated the French on July 23 in Carlisle Bay.

After the battle, things returned to normal, and for several years it appeared that Port Royal might once again achieve the importance it had had before the 1692 disaster. The island in general began to prosper and Jamaica soon became England's most important colony in the West Indies. By 1698 the population had increased to about fifty thousand whites and forty thousand blacks—with more settlers arriving daily.

Nor did it take long for Port Royal to regain its notoriety as a wicked seaport, as attested by many contemporary visitors—few, if any, of whom had much good to say about the place. From one who visited in 1700 we have the following description of the town and its inhabitants:

> From a spacious fine built town it is now reduced, by the encroachments of the sea, to a little above a quarter mile in length, and about half so much the breadth, having so few remains left of its former splendour. The houses are low, little, and irregular; and if I compare the best of their streets in Port Royal, to Kent Street in London, where the broommen live, I do them more than justice. They have a church, 'tis true, but built rather like a markethouse; and when the flock were in their pens and the pastor exalted to overlook his sheep, I took survey round me, and saw more variety of scare-crows than ever seen at the Feast of Ugly-Faces in Eng-

land. The generality of the men look as if they had just knocked off their fetters, and by an unexpected providence escaped the danger of a near misfortune; the dread of which hath imprinted that in their looks, which they can no more alter than an Ethiopian can his colour. Everything is very dear and an ingenious or an honest man may meet with this encouragement, to spend a hundred pounds before he shall get a penny. They regard nothing but money, and value not how they get it; there being no other felicity to be enjoyed but purely riches. They are very civil to strangers who bring over considerable effects; and will try a great many ways to kill him fairly, for the lucre of his cargo: And many have been made rich by such windfalls. A broken apothecary will make there a topping physician; a barbers apprentice, a good surgeon; a bailiffs follower, a passable lawyer; and an English knave, a very honest fellow. A little reputation among the women goes a great way; and if their actions be answerable to their looks, they may vie wickedness with the devil. An impudent air, being the only charms of their countenance, and a lewd carriage, the studied grace of their deportment. They are much who have been scandalous in England to the utmost degree, either transported by the State, or led there by their own vicious inclinations; where they may be wicked without shame, and whore on without punishment. In short, virtue is so despised, and all sorts of vice encouraged by both sexes, that the town of Port Royal is the very Sodom of the Universe.

Another visitor to the town only two years later described it in even stronger terms:

It is the dunghill of the universe, the refuse of the whole creation, the clipping of the elements, a shapeless pile of rubbish confusedly jumbled into an emblem of chaos, neglected by the Omnipotence when he formed the world into its admirable order. It is the nursery of Heavens Judgement, where the malignant seeds of all pestilence were first gathered and scattered to punish mankind for their offenses. The town is the receptacle of vagabonds, the sanctuary of bankrupts, and a close-stool for the purges of our prisons. As sickly as a hospital, as dangerous as the plague, as hot as hell, and as wicked as the devil.

Not surprisingly, many predictions were made that divine wrath would once again strike the New World Babylon, and the prophets of doom didn't have long to wait. In the three decades following the 1692 upheaval Port Royal was destined to face three more disasters, spaced at ten-year intervals. The first, in 1702, when the town had grown to almost five hundred buildings, was described by an eyewitness:

On saturday the 9th January, about 11 a clock in the forenoon, it being a very windy day, we was suddenly surprised with the lamentable cry of FIRE, FIRE, upon which I ran out into the street without either hat, coat, or waistcoat and saw the devouring flames coming with such terrible fury along as hardly ever was known; for the wind was so violent and strong that in three hours time most of the houses, being of timber building, were all in flames, and by ten at night all burnt to the ground—even the church and chapel—nothing remaining but the two forts [Fort Charles and a newly built fort named Williams]. The beginning or occasion of this amazing conflagration is variously discoursed of some imputing it to the carelessness of a storehouse keeper, in the house of Captain Hudsdon, who accidentally leaving a candle burning among some loose tarry rope and other combustible matter, in an instant communicated the raging flames all over the town which stood upon fourteen acres of the richest ground perhaps that ever belonged to the Crown of England. But some others are of opinion that it was set on fire by lightning, it being seen to lighten very much that morning, and there being much loose powder in the said house, that was preparing to be ship'd off, 'tis not improbable but such an accident might be occasioned thereby.

But to return to the particulars; most part of provisions, silks, linens, cloaths, spices and indeed most sorts of merchandizes to an incredible value, besides what is above expressed, were totally burnt and consumed by the devouring flames; nay it was so violent sudden swift and amazing that few could have time to carry off their cash, much less any goods or household stuff; for those which were hurried into the streets had the same dismal fate, having no opportunity to carry them farther being surrounded by the sea. The terror and confusion we were in is scarcely expressible not knowing which way to go with our families to escape with our lives; having lost all our substance, nay many hundreds of people who the day before were worth some thousands of pounds, are reduced by this dismal calamity to such extreme necessity as to want bread for themselves and families. Tis strange to relate, but true matter of fact, that the wind turned six times during the fury of the fire, which hastened the total destruction of the place.

The Governor ordered us to settle ourselves as well as our miserable conditions will admit, at Kingston, where we now are, Port Royal being no more, nor do we know if it will ever be rebuilt again. Kingston, may be a very fine place in a few years if God please to preserve it, of which at present we are much afraid: For last night [a week after the fire] about midnight an earthquake happened here, which tho' it lasted not a minute, yet shook me more in my bed, than a coach has done when I have rode in it through Fleet Street, London. Today, being sunday about ten in the morning another shock of an earthquake happened while we were at church at our devotion insomuch that the timbers of the said church began to crack, which put the people in a dreadful consternation and amazement that we ran out in such confusion and disorder that we ran over one anothers bodies, great numbers of them being thrown down by the frightful throngs of people that endeavoured to get out first. For we had not forgot the dismal judgement which befell this island in 1692 and it appeared that God was punishing us again with two tremendous judgements at once.

The Governor of Jamaica forbade further resettlement in Port Royal, but at the insistence of the merchants, King William III rescinded the order. The number of lives lost in this disaster was not recorded, but it is known that about half of the survivors chose to remain in Kingston when the others returned to Port Royal. The town, rebuilt slowly, was beginning to achieve a permanent air once again when it was leveled in 1712 by a hurricane that also caused considerable damage to Kingston. The few resolute souls who elected to remain and rebuild saw the place collapse in ruins around them as a result of an even more devastating hurricane in 1722.

During the next 250 years the town was destroyed on at least two dozen different occasions: twice by earthquakes in 1766 and 1907, twice by fires in 1750 and 1815, and all of the other times ravaged by hurricanes—the last of which struck in 1951. Understandably, Port Royal never regained any degree of its former glory, but not even recurring disasters could finish it off completely. It sprang up again and again for the same reasons that had caused the English to first settle there: its location and natural advantages as a port.

Port Royal's role throughout the eighteenth and nineteenth centuries was as a base for the British Navy. Occasionally during periods of war, the privateers appeared again like ghosts from the past. However, times were no longer conducive to the emergence of a Henry Morgan. The privateers were generally limited to capturing enemy merchant ships on the high seas and any neutrals who traded with the enemy. As soon as the need for them ended, their services were dispensed with. The English Navy, firmly in control of the waters around Jamaica, had no desire to encourage a spirit of free enterprise in the Caribbean.

Indeed a primary task performed by the Navy was to suppress

piracy, which continued to plague the area until early in the nineteenth century. Extreme measures were taken—many pirates met
their end at a place on the Palisadoes known as Gallows Point—
but it was a time when extreme measures were needed, for many
of the eighteenth-century pirates were true desperadoes.

Policing the waters of the Caribbean was only a part of the
function of the English naval forces based at Port Royal. The
mother country was often at war—with Spain, with France, or
with the rebelling American colonies—and there was no dearth
of activity. Many renowned British admirals were based and flew
their flags at Port Royal. Early in the eighteenth century Admiral
Benbow commanded the West Indian squadron based there;
wounded in a fight with the French, he returned there to die.
During a war with Spain that started in 1739, called the War of
Jenkins's Ear, Admiral Vernon was in charge of the fleet. This
venerable salt, called Old Grog because of the grogram cloak he
wore, bragged that he could capture Porto Bello with only five
ships, and he actually did. During the years of the American
Revolutionary War, when France, aided by Spain, attempted to
seize British possessions in the West Indies, it was Admiral Rodney who led the resistance from Port Royal. By 1782 Tobago, St.
Kitts, and Nevis were in French hands, and the combined fleets
of France and Spain seemed poised to capture Jamaica. It was
then that Rodney defeated the French fleet in the famous
"Battle of the Saints," off Dominica, and Jamaica remained in
British hands. Twice, the most famous British naval hero of them
all—Horatio Nelson—was stationed at Port Royal. There was
scarcely a British naval leader of any note who did not turn up in
Port Royal at one time or another.

The Caribbean became less and less a theater of warfare as ter-
ritorial squabbles among nations were resolved, and Port Royal's
significance as a naval station steadily declined. During the nineteenth century the port was mainly used by the British Navy for
repairing ships and as a hospital center for the men who served
on them. During the first half of the twentieth century only a
small garrison remained to man several coast-artillery guns and
to attend the occasional naval vessel visiting the island.

Even though the cay became connected to Palisadoes again during the eighteenth century, Port Royal failed to attract a civilian population of any magnitude: a visitor to Jamaica reported in 1774 that the town had only a hundred houses, while Kingston had 1,165. In 1804 the number had doubled, but no one could have mistaken the place for a metropolis. By 1900 the number had decreased to less than fifty. Like Pompeii, Port Royal's days of glory are a thing of the past.

Chapter Five

Port Royal today is a small village of pastel bungalows basking quietly in the tropic sun and attracting a few underwater treasure hunters and tourists lured there by tales of a city standing intact under the sea with the streets strewn with gold, silver, and precious jewels waiting to be recovered by any adventurous soul brave enough to go down and pick it all up.

In 1953 a Hollywood movie inspired by such tales was made. Called *City Beneath the Sea* and starring Anthony Quinn and Robert Ryan, it fired the imagination of thousands. A plastic mock-up of the city was built in a tank, and in the film it appears that the divers stumble over hundreds of chests of treasure lying everywhere on the bottom. Over the years, countless books and magazine articles have added to the Port Royal myth with stories of fabulous treasure recoveries from the sunken city—tales painting a very romantic but regrettably false picture of the actual state of Port Royal.

Prior to my excavation, the only retrieval of artifacts off Port Royal that is a matter of historical record was fortuitous, when some fishermen in 1788 caught a fifteen-foot tiger shark, ripped open its belly, and discovered three leopards' teeth covered with gold leaf (probably brought from Africa on a slave ship), a number of glass beads, and a few half-digested bones. Several years later another large shark was caught in the same area and a Bible and a man's belt were found in its stomach. Sharks had been numerous off Port Royal since the town was first settled. In addition to feeding on the refuse from the town's markets and the ships, they devoured the corpses of those hapless slaves who had not survived the voyage from Africa and were thrown into the harbor. Some dauntless Port Royalists hunted shark purely for sport and attempted to kill them with knives; no doubt, some of them, too, fell prey to the sharks. Before the eyes of many townsfolk, only several years before the disastrous earthquake, four fishermen had been eaten by sharks when their canoe overturned near Fort James.

The reason no treasure had been recovered during the previous 250 years was that there were very few attempts after the initial salvaging had been carried out following the quake, and in all likelihood very little remains to be found. Contemporary accounts tell us that on the very day of the disaster people were already salvaging everything of value from those buildings still above the water. Most of the city sank gradually, and the upper parts of many buildings remained above water for years. In July of 1693 a visitor wrote:

> The principal parts of Port Royal now lie four, six or eight fathoms underwater.
> Indeed, 'tis enough to raise melancholy thoughts in a man now to see chimneys and the tops of some houses, and the masts of ships and sloops, which partaked of the same fate, appear above the water, now habitations for fish.

Since most of Port Royal's roofs were constructed of wood and shingles, which could have been torn off without difficulty, access to the standing buildings must have been very easy not only for divers but for other salvors, who did not descend into the water. They used two different methods: dredging and fishing. To dredge, they lowered heavily weighted fishing nets and dragged them over the bottom, snagging loose items. To fish, they first spread oil on the surface of the water to calm it so they could see clearly to the bottom, then used long poles or ropes, with grappling hooks attached, to catch hold of what they wanted.

As for the sunken buildings, Port Royal was the center of the "wracking" profession, and there were many divers on the scene at the time of the quake. The deepest part of the city lay under less than sixty feet of water, and a great part of it under less than twenty feet; consequently salvage would have been quite simple for them, especially since the underwater visibility in those days was excellent. Some of the salvors used diving bells, allowing them to remain submerged for an hour or more. The rest, who used no diving aids and were known as free divers, were capable of reaching depths of well over a hundred feet and remaining submerged as long as five minutes on their own breath.

Little of Port Royal's treasure would have been overlooked by the divers, dredgers, and fishers immediately on the scene, and it is a matter of record that salvaging continued on a large scale for several decades after the earthquake—but they did miss some treasure, which was discovered during our excavation of the site.

Another Port Royal legend as romantic as the one of untold riches to be found on the sea floor concerns St. Paul's Church, which is supposed to lie about three hundred yards from the present shoreline: a permanent navigation marker, known as the Church Beacon, stands over the site. The legend began midway through the nineteenth century, when a large Spanish church bell made of bronze was dredged up there. Even at that time, a great number of standing walls of a large building could still be seen on calm days in the area where the bell was found, and the people assumed that they belonged to the town's largest church. There was no real basis for any such assumption, for there is no proof that the bell came from St. Paul's. It could have been part of the Catholic chapel or one of the bells used in the town's three markets, or even part of the cargo from a ship lost during the 1692 earthquake or during one of Port Royal's other disasters. On the other hand, there is no proof that it did not come from

St. Paul's: being of Spanish origin does not rule out the possibility, since we know from a document dating a few years before the 1692 disaster that the inhabitants thought the church needed a new bell, and they might well have obtained one the way they obtained so many other things—plunder from some place sacked by the privateers. The steeple of St. Paul's was one of the first things to topple during the quake, and the subsequent tidal wave could have carried it anywhere.

The identity of the bell remains a mystery, but we do know that the building below Church Beacon is not St. Paul's. About a decade after the bell had been found and the legend born, the building's true identity was discovered in 1859 by Jeremiah D. Murphy, a helmet diver stationed at the English naval base whose normal employment was inspecting and repairing naval vessels.

After repairing H.M. Ship Valorous, I went down on the 9th of September at what is called at Port Royal the "Church Buoy," but what ought to be called the "Fort Buoy," it being placed on the remains of old Fort James. But the day was unfavorable, the water being muddy, so that I could not see much; and being impressed with the idea that it must have been the remains of the church on which I was, my explorations that day were not satisfactory. About twelve o'clock (being then down four hours) the water cleared a little, and getting a much better view I concluded that the ruins which I was on must have been those of a fort. But soon after I found a large granite stone somewhat the shape and size of a tombstone, which was covered with a coral formation, so that I could not tell whether it had an inscription or not. Fancying this stone to be a tombstone, thereby indicating the vicinity of a church yard, I was not satisfied what the character of the building could have been. I came to the surface about one o'clock determined to wait a more favorable day. In the meantime Mr. de Pass was so good as to obtain for me, from the collection of Henry Hutchins, Esq., a map of the old town as it stood before the earthquake, by which I learned that the ruins, of the nature of which I had all along my doubts, were in fact the ruins of Fort James, and that the church stood about the east end of the present dockyard.

Monday, the 19th instant, being a very clear day, I went down about two o'clock, and had a very good view of the fort. At times I could see objects one hundred feet away from me. The fort forms an obtuse angle to the west. . . . The walls are built of brick, and are as solid as so much rock. . . . After being down about two hours, I found an iron gun in one of the embrasures almost covered in the ruins, with a heavy copper chain to the breech. After sending up the gun the next day, I found the end of another chain not far from where the gun lay. On heaving it out of the sand and mud, I found it attached to a granite stone similar to the one I had seen before. I have no doubts these stones were part of the embrasures and that the copper chains were used for slinging the guns.

Murphy's description of what he had seen, published in a Jamaican newspaper, the Falmouth *Post,* should have squelched the legend, but it persisted.

In 1967, while working on the sunken city, I received a letter from a high-ranking retired British naval officer, who wrote:

My mother who died in 1941 used to tell me about the sunken city of Port Royal. Prior to the 1907 earthquake, people used to go out in a boat when the tide was flowing in a certain direction, and some sort of pipe was lowered to a depth of about eighty feet and one could hear the muffled clang of the cathedral's bell or bells. In 1910 or thereabouts some Americans tried to get into the cathedral which had collapsed, hoping to get an immense treasure which is reported buried under the High Altar, but sharks stopped their efforts. When I was a young boy of about ten, I dove on several walls of the sunken city, without the use of diving equipment and located a large ceramic jar and several broken bottles. When you get around to excavating the cathedral, please be careful because there is a belief that a giant octopus is guarding the treasure under the altar.

About thirty years ago the church legend was given a new lease on life through a magazine article, which has since been reprinted at least two hundred times in magazines around the world, written by a helmet diver who claimed to have found the church standing intact at the site of the Church Beacon. The article was accompanied by a painting of a massive cathedral, and the author alleged that he had found it in thirty fathoms, or 180 feet, of water. However, the water around the Church Beacon is less than forty feet deep: in fact, nowhere in the harbor is the water deeper than sixty feet. The diver claimed to have walked right into the cathedral and to have discovered a room full of church treasure, but most unfortunately a twelve-foot crab attacked him at that climactic moment and he had to fight his way out of the building and to the surface. The diver's story, full of excitement and derring-do, is pure romance, and romance dies hard. Even today there are people living at Port Royal who will swear that when the weather is rough, fishermen passing by the Church Beacon can hear bells ringing.

It is said that Debussy's *La Cathédrale engloutie,* with its rich musical evocation of a bell tolling mournfully for its dead, far beneath the sea, was inspired by the story of St. Paul's.

Truth should have supplanted the legend a century ago, for Murphy was right: the building under the Church Beacon is Fort James. From maps of Port Royal predating the disaster, it has been established that St. Paul's lies nearly a quarter of a mile east of Fort James. It did indeed sink into the sea during the earthquake, but its remains are now covered by land. This happened through a natural process that began shortly after the city sank, when mud and sand piled up around the foundations of the buildings. The currents that deposited enough sediment from nearby rivers to once again connect Port Royal to the Palisadoes, during the eighteenth century, also built up a land mass that eventually entombed more than half of the submerged city. The rest, still under water, is for the most part covered by sediment. Although as late as 1880 a scientific observer using a glass-bottomed bucket stated that on clear days many of the sunken buildings could still be seen, during the next few decades the majority of the buildings were silted over by harbor sediment. Around the beginning of this century extensive dredging was done in the harbor, particularly around Port Royal, for the construction of a naval coaling station. Since the sunken city is located on one side of the narrow entrance to the huge harbor, the outgoing tides caused a great deal of the sediment dredged up to be deposited over the site. To further complicate matters, the earthquake of 1907, Jamaica's worst since 1692, caused the majority of the buildings still standing underwater to topple over, and they, too, were soon buried under sediment: my own excavations have turned up items from the first decade of this century under fallen walls of buildings dating from the 1692 upheaval. The task of excavating Port Royal becomes increasingly difficult as the years pass, because more and more sediment is accumulating on the site each year.

During the first two decades of the nineteenth century a considerable amount of salvaging took place on the site—but not for treasure. Thousands upon thousands of bricks were recovered from sunken buildings and used in the construction of the massive, two-story Port Royal naval hospital. There are also accounts during this same century of many bricks being removed for use in construction elsewhere on the island.

Murphy's account of his dive on Fort James precipitated a flurry of interest when it appeared in print, and he was eventually to regret ever having explored the site. He was accused of having found several chests full of treasure and of shipping them back to England. For several years following this publicity, a bad case of "treasure fever" raged on the island. In 1861 a bill was introduced by a member of the Jamaica House of Assembly "for the recovery of the treasure which was submerged in the earthquake of 1692," but nothing came of it. The following year a famous paleontologist, Lucas Barrett, explored the drowned ruins in the course of making a geological survey of the harbor and accidentally discovered a fair number of artifacts, which he placed on exhibition. Confident that he could get into those buildings which were standing, even though they were full of sediment and debris, he resumed his explorations and was drowned on one of his dives.

Perhaps his death impressed people with the dangers of diving or led to a feeling that some vigilant demons protected Port Royal's sunken treasures. In any case, nothing more, with the exception of a brief American expedition in 1910, appears to have been done to work the site for the better part of a century, during which the only known recoveries were the result of the dredging operations for the coaling station. Recently, with the growth of skin diving as a sport and the resultant increase in the number of qualified divers, interest in Port Royal has revived. Some would-be treasure hunters still dream of discovering gold, silver, and jewels; others, more realistic, dream of the genuine treasure to be found there: historical artifacts, valuable clues for the reconstruction of the past.

The first skin divers to make any known recoveries from Port Royal were Mr. Cornel Lumière, a well-known producer of underwater films, and Mr. and Mrs. Alexis DuPont of Wilmington, Delaware. During the summer of 1954 they spent a week exploring the site, most of the time without success: they could locate no trace of the sunken city, for nothing was to be seen protruding above the muddy sea floor except coral heads and thousands of spiny sea urchins. Then, on the last day of diving, near Fort James, they discovered an arched brick doorway with ten steps leading up to the entrance. Digging in the surrounding mud with their hands, they retrieved the upper portion of an earthenware jug, some loose bricks and roof tiles, and a few bottles that once contained liquor (called onion bottles because of their shape), all dating from the time of the earthquake. The local press played up their find, declaring that they had discovered "a tavern from the days of the buccaneers."

Two years later, another group of underwater explorers led

by the noted inventor and treasure hunter Edwin Link arrived at
Port Royal at the invitation of the wife of the American Consul
General in Jamaica, who was an amateur archaeologist. Before arriving, they had spent several weeks fruitlessly searching for a
Spanish galleon reportedly sunk on a reef off the south coast of
Jamaica. As chief diver with Link was a professional diver named
Art McKee, who in the course of twenty years had found considerable sunken treasure at various places in the Caribbean. They
began their explorations near Fort James and, like the first group,
did not find any traces of the sunken city at the start. Using an
underwater metal detector, they located several areas with heavy
metallic concentrations, and employing a small suction pump began digging into the sediment. They soon discovered that from
four to six feet of sediment had to be removed before there was
any sign of the old buildings, which were covered with a thick
growth of coral. Deciding that the pump was inadequate for the
job, they left after raising a cannon from Fort James, with the intention of returning at a later date with better equipment.

In June of 1959 Link came back under the sponsorship of the
National Geographic Society, the Smithsonian Institution, and the
Institute of Jamaica, with an enthusiastic group of divers. To give
the expedition the stamp of an underwater archaeological project,
and not just a treasure hunt, Mendel Peterson, Curator of Armed
Forces History at the Smithsonian Institution, was invited to
participate.

After his 1956 visit to Port Royal, Link had set about building
a new vessel, suitable for excavating the sunken city. As inventor
of the Link Trainer and many other aeronautical and electrical
devices, he was able to draw on a fund of experience in designing special tools for unusual jobs. His new vessel—*Sea Diver*—
was a 91-foot-long, steel-hull ship powered by twin diesel engines,
with accommodations aboard for twelve persons. The principal
excavation tool he brought with him was an air lift consisting of
a tube ten inches in diameter connected at the bottom to a hose
through which a great volume of compressed air could be
pumped down from the *Sea Diver*. The air rising up the tube
created suction that drew up great quantities of bottom sediment,

as well as any artifacts that the divers, holding the tube on the bottom, failed to grab from the mouth of the tube, and deposited everything onto a barge on the surface. Another efficient tool on the *Sea Diver* was a water jet, similar in operation to a fire hose: the powerful jet of water blew bottom sediment away, especially from around the walls of buildings.

While the *Sea Diver* was under construction, Link spent some time in London doing historical research on the site and located a number of documents and old charts pertaining to the sunken city that were of great help during his expedition. The same thing was done in the Jamaican Archives by a research assistant, who managed to uncover hundreds of pages of property records of old Port Royal. Guided by charts of the city before and after it sank, the Link group under the supervision of a navigational expert, Captain P. V. H. Weems, a retired U.S. naval officer, began to map those sections of the site they planned to excavate. To locate the sunken buildings they tried using echo-sounding equipment, which proved impractical (most of the walls lay under sediment, but so did large masses of coral and modern debris, and the echo sounder could not distinguish one from another), and after a week they abandoned it. However, with it they did locate many of the walls of Fort James, some of them thickly encrusted with coral, standing as high as fifteen feet above the sea floor.

The first area in which Link decided to excavate was where he estimated the King's Warehouse, or Custom House, to be, since he considered it the most likely to contain treasure. It turned out to be an unfortunate choice. Although at the time of the disaster it may have held treasure along with the usual stock of export items such as cotton, sugar, tobacco, and molasses awaiting shipment to England or elsewhere, in all probability the treasure would have been salvaged soon after, since the building lay in very shallow water. Moreover it was a large building, 234 feet long by 65 feet wide, and searching amid the remains for a treasure chest was like looking for a needle in a haystack. After a week in which nothing but a few broken bottles and some pieces of pottery came to light, they moved to an area near the walls of Fort James. Here they had better luck, finding artifacts of historical importance. The first recovery was a long-handled brass ladle, and this was soon followed by several pewter spoons, a badly corroded pewter plate, about two dozen onion bottles, and a great quantity of animal bones. From the nature of the objects brought up, Peterson and Link deduced that they had been working in the ruins of a private dwelling or a tavern.

During the first four weeks of the ten the expedition spent on the site, most of the diving was done by amateur divers, including several from a local skin-diving club. Then Link got the loan of six U. S. Navy frogmen, who took over most of the diving. Diving on the site was far from safe or easy—particularly since underwater visibility was sometimes only a few inches. An account written by Mrs. Marion Link states:

> There was constant danger of cave-ins, as the dredge sucked at the base of old brick walls. The air lift itself, with its heavy weight and powerful suction, was an ally to be respected. Many times the divers' gloves were seized in its greedy maw and deposited on the barge above. We almost expected someday to see the elongated form of a diver himself erupt from the upper end of the pipe. Sea urchins, sting rays, moray eels, and scorpion fish lurked, mostly unseen, on the muddy bottom. Sharks and barracuda were often glimpsed near the surface, and although for the most part invisible to the diver in the murky depths, they were no less dangerous. In spite of all these hazards, when the summer's activities came to an end, no more serious damage could be chalked up than an injured toe and a few squeezed eardrums resulting from their owners' changing depths too quickly.

In other areas they recovered a large pewter platter, some clay smoking pipes, a linen smoother made of glass, several copper cooking pots, a brass candlestick, and many other artifacts. One very exciting find, spotted by the alert Navy frogman who was on the barge to catch any objects coming up through the air lift, was a brass pocket watch. Opening the case, Link was disappointed to find that the minute and hour hands had long since disintegrated,

The tip of Port Royal, where the sunken
[cit]y lies. The barge and skiff working on the
[sit]e. *Photo by Marx.*

2. Chart showing the area of Port Royal
before and after the quake and the outline
today of the coastline. Lower area is what
land remained after the quake. Upper area
is portion now sunk. *Photo by Marx.*

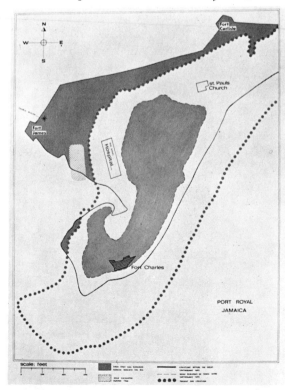

3. Painting of H.M.S. *Swan*, which sank during the quake. *Photo by Marx.*

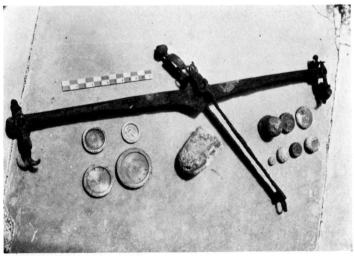

4. Steel scale balance and brass and lead weights found in the meat-market site. *Photo by Marx.*

5. Part of the brick walls at Fort Rupert, on the edge of the lagoon. *Photo by Marx.*

6. Three silver pieces of eight (Spanish coins) found on the site. *Photo by Marx.*

7. Chinese porcelain plate. *Photo by Marx.*

8. Dutch bellarmine jug, found in many pieces but restored. *Photo by Marx.*

9. Brass oil lamp found on the site of the Jewish synagogue. *Photo by Marx.*

10. Brass slave collar before cleaning. *Photo by Marx.*

11. Ornate head of a man on clay smoking pipe. *Photo by Marx.*

12. Clay smoking pipes. *Photo by Marx.*

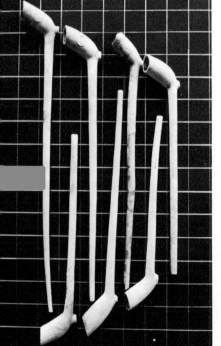

13. Pipes with makers' marks on them. *Photo by Marx.*

14. Men on the barge with air lift in action.
Photo by Marx.

15. Author removing coral encrustation from large iron cannon ball. *Photo by Marx.*

16. Ruins of old Port Royal excavated on land in 1970. Note the well in the center. *Photo by Marx.*

7. Marx coming ashore with large, coral-crusted musket. *Photo by Marx.*

18. View of our camp site at St. Ann's Bay. Bob Judd and two others are searching through the material brought up in a core. *Photo by Marx.*

19. Ship's calking tools found on land in Port Royal in 1960. *Photo courtesy of Jamaica Tourist Board.*

20. Kenute Kelly with some of the tho sands of bricks brought up off the si *Photo courtesy of Jamaica Tourist Board.*

21. Author's wife, Nancy, with human jaw
and leg bone. *Photo by Marx.*

. Nancy finding a complete ceramic plate
the mud. *Photo by Marx.*

23. Small medicine bottles, found in a me
icine chest. *Photo by Marx.*

but by X-raying the face of the watch he was able to establish that it had stopped at 11:43—the time corresponding to the upheaval as revealed in the contemporary accounts. Investigations in England after the watch had been cleaned disclosed that it had been made by one Paul Blondel, a Frenchman living in the Netherlands, around 1686.

Another interesting artifact was a wrought-iron breech-loading swivel gun, or small cannon. It was first identified as dating from the fifteenth century by an expert at the Smithsonian Institution, and caused a great deal of excitement: since Columbus had lost two ships on the north coast of Jamaica on his last voyage to the new world, it is perfectly conceivable that the gun was salvaged from one of them and found its way to a resident of Port Royal. However, further research indicates that the date cannot be pinpointed so precisely, for guns of the same type were still in use at the time of the earthquake. A more likely possibility is that it came from one of the trading or privateer sloops lost during the disaster.

Link was forced to conclude his excavation because of business commitments and departed for the United States in the *Sea Diver* with every expectation of returning again. Although his expedition was considered an outstanding success by the press, it was not considered such by many serious underwater archaeologists. The use of such a large air lift caused a great number of artifacts to be damaged and destroyed, which could have been avoided with the use of one or more smaller air lifts. And on the barge some sort of screen should have been used to catch small objects spewed out of the air-lift tube—it was a near miracle that the pocket watch was caught before it was washed back into the water. Link did do two important things that helped me a great deal when I began working on the site: he had all the property-record documents published and also, with the assistance of Captain Weems, produced a good chart, which he compiled from old charts of the sunken city and his own explorations on the site.

Only a few months after the Link expedition left, another American, named Norman Scott, requested permission from the Jamaican Government to work on the sunken city. When Link heard of Scott's intended plans, he contacted the government, stating that Scott had no previous archaeological experience and that if he were given a permit to work on the site, he would have to be closely supervised. Despite Link's interference and the fact that there were no qualified persons available to supervise Scott's expedition, he was granted a permit to work on the site for six weeks, providing that everything recovered be turned over to the Jamaican Government. The area selected for excavation was around Fort Carlisle, located on the easternmost edge of the sunken city—which proved to be a poor choice.

Bad luck plagued them from the start. Before leaving Miami they discovered that their diving vessel needed extensive repairs and were forced to go without it and without most of the diving and excavation equipment they had planned to utilize. On their arrival in Port Royal, the Jamaican Government provided them with a barge and some other equipment. Scott and his six divers set out with great enthusiasm, but on the very first day of their dig the air lift was damaged beyond repair, delaying work for several days while another was obtained. Two weeks of excavation produced very little—a wooden wheel (probably from a gun carriage), several clay pipes, and two onion bottles—and the Scott group returned to the United States very disheartened by the outcome of the expedition. Certainly, if they had been permitted to work in another area of the site, they would have had much better results. It appeared to many persons, not just Scott and his men, that he had been forced to excavate an area where there was little likelihood of making any significant discoveries.

Late in 1960 a very exciting discovery was made, on land rather than in the sea. Workmen digging foundations for a new hotel, on land reclaimed from the sea, unearthed a cache of ships' calking tools—axes, hammers, scrapers—and other tools, numbering almost two hundred in all. An expert identified them as dating from the time of the earthquake and belonging to a pitch-boiling house (there was still pitch clinging to many of them). They were used for careening and repairing ships, and the location of the cache indicates that these same tools may well have been the ones used on H.M.S. *Swan.*

Since most of the land on which the present town of Port Royal is built was the original site of the old town, artifacts and sometimes even coins are very often found by accident. During the period I spent working at Port Royal, three different holes were dug for septic tanks and dozens of interesting artifacts were uncovered—most of which were sold to tourists by the Port Royalists.

Chapter Six

The first people to show an interest in marine archaeology were a group of English archaeologists and antiquarians who, in 1775, sponsored an expedition to recover historical artifacts from the Tiber Riber, near Rome—Greek divers using a bell worked for three years with very little success, for they had no means of removing the accumulation of river mud that covered the Greek and Roman artifacts they were hoping to salvage. After that, there was very little interest in recovering relics until early in the twentieth century, when objects brought up from the Mediterranean by Greek and Turkish sponge divers aroused the interest of archaeologists working on land sites nearby. The archaeologists hired and supervised divers to recover more artifacts and obtain archaeological data for them.

Today virtually all marine archaeological work is confined to the Mediterranean. In the late 1930s, even before scuba equipment was available, the noted underwater explorer Dimitri Rebikoff began exploring, surveying, and excavating dozens of ancient shipwrecks and sunken cities off the coasts of France, Italy, and Greece. He was followed by Jacques Cousteau and others, who worked on several ancient shipwreck sites off France and Tunisia.

In recent years a great amount of marine archaeological work has been undertaken in Greek and Turkish waters, largely because of the enthusiasm of an American, Peter Throckmorton, who in 1959 discovered thirty-five ancient shipwrecks. His most important find is a shipwreck dating from 1200 B.C. called the "Bronze Age Wreck," which lies in 120 feet of water off Cape Gelidonya, Turkey. Soon after making this discovery Throckmorton became associated with the Department of Archaeology of the University of Pennsylvania, under whose auspices and under the direction of Dr. George Bass major excavations have taken place on several shipwreck sites during the past decade. During the past few years no less than twenty marine archaeological expeditions took place all over the Mediterranean: in Spain, France, Italy, Greece, Yugoslavia, Turkey, Israel, Tunisia, Malta, and Crete—almost all carried out by Americans. The sad fact is that most of those few Americans who are qualified to conduct a proper marine archaeological excavation prefer working on the more ancient sites in the Mediterranean, which results in a scarcity of archaeologists to work sites on this side of the Atlantic.

The Caribbean is the most promising area for marine archaeology in the Western Hemisphere. Though hardly comparable in antiquity to the Mediterranean, the Caribbean was the focus of the richest maritime trade in the world. All but a small portion of the legendary wealth that flowed from the Spanish colonies in both North and South America, plus the great variety of goods the colonies imported from Europe in return, funneled through the waters of the Caribbean. The wealth of the Spanish colonies soon attracted the Portuguese, the French, the Dutch, and the English, who came to the Caribbean to gain a share of the wealth either through plunder or through contraband trade. Later, when these other nations, with the exception of Portugal, founded settlements in the Caribbean, the volume of shipping greatly increased because of the trade between these nations and their colonies.

Over the centuries thousands of ships were lost in the waters of the Caribbean, but shipwrecks are not the only source of data for the marine archaeologist: the fact that the Caribbean is ringed by an earthquake belt has provided another type of underwater site—sunken cities. Early in the sixteenth century the town of Nueva Cádiz, on Margarita Island, off the coast of Venezuela, sank into the sea; during another earthquake, in 1687, the towns of Jamestown, on the island of Nevis, and Orangetown, on St. Eustatius, toppled into the sea; and then we have Port Royal—the most famous of them all.

Despite all the opportunities and advantages the Caribbean offers in the field of marine archaeology, very little work has been done to date. During the past decade a number of underwater projects have been carried out that mark an advance from salvage operations toward marine archaeology—in Mexico, Haiti, Jamaica, and the Virgin Islands. However, prior to my own work at Port Royal, all these projects fell short of acceptable archaeological standards on three counts: failure to map the site adequately, to plot the positions of the finds, and to publish any scholarly work on the over-all operation.

Since the popularization of skin diving in the early 1950s, the Caribbean has lured ever-increasing numbers of professional and amateur divers in search of the ubiquitous sunken galleons loaded with treasure, creating serious problems for the future of marine archaeology. The amateur who simply picks up a cannon ball or other artifact lying on the sea floor to decorate his living room undoubtedly does not realize he could be removing a valuable clue to the location and identity of the site. But professional treasure hunters have often caused irreparable damage of much greater magnitude. By removing the best signposts of many old wreck sites—anchors and cannon—they have unwittingly made it difficult, if not impossible, for marine archaeologists to locate these sites in the future. Dynamite and huge dredging devices are common tools employed in their "excavations," which can ravage an entire site, destroying most of the less intrinsically valuable artifacts such as glassware, ceramic ware, etc., and leaving only the gold and silver that are being sought.

A large share of the blame for this damage lies with the governments of the various Caribbean countries, for until recently there was little official interest and no laws protecting underwater sites. Mexico was the first country to prohibit the exploration and excavation of underwater sites except under official auspices. Some of the other countries have taken confusing measures, inconsistently enforced, to protect their underwater sites, which serve only to discourage the well-intentioned while permitting the unscrupulous to carry on as before.

The Link expedition, which received international newspaper and magazine coverage, made the world aware that the sunken city of Port Royal is the most important marine archaeological site in the Western Hemisphere. The artifacts recovered aroused the interest of scholars everywhere, and they began to press for a thorough excavation of the site. The Jamaican Government hoped that Link would return to continue his work, but business commitments prevented his doing so, and for six years no work was done on the site except for the ill-fated Scott expedition. Then, in response to the increasing public interest in Port Royal, the Honorable Edward Seaga, then Minister of Development and Welfare in Jamaica and the man in charge of all cultural projects on the island, decided that a marine archaeological excavation on the site should be undertaken as soon as possible. Actually, as I later learned, other matters also swayed his interest in having the sunken city excavated.

The job of directing the project was offered to me in November 1965, and I accepted without a moment's hesitation. The prospect of excavating the sunken city would excite anyone, but I have for years had an interest in Port Royal that amounts almost to an obsession. It dates back to when I was ten and happened to read a book written by a treasure hunter who claimed to have dived on the sunken city. At that time I could barely swim, and the thought of becoming a professional diver and marine archaeologist had never entered my head, but the book changed all that. The author spun a good yarn about what he had seen under the sea: the standing cathedral under the Church Beacon, taverns in which skeletons sat at a table with tankards in their bony hands, chests of treasure ready for the taking everywhere. I don't think I swallowed it all, even at ten, but

the parts about the sunken cathedral and the treasure I never
doubted for a minute. Only when I visited Port Royal did I
discover that the book catalogued under non-fiction in the library
should have been catalogued under fantasy. I hold no grudge
against the author, even though he was an out-and-out liar.
Far from it. I'll always be grateful to him for awakening my
interest in the incredible world under the sea and marine archaeology.

After learning how to skin dive in murky lakes and rivers
around Pittsburgh, where I spent most of my youth, I made
several unsuccessful attempts before I was fifteen to reach Port
Royal by running away from home; the farthest I ever got was
Miami. Finally, in the spring of 1954, while serving in the U. S.
Marine Corps as a diving instructor, I got to Port Royal. My
heart was beating like a triphammer as the plane began its
descent to Palisadoes Airport. Over the intercom the pilot was
intoning a speech he had probably given hundreds of times:
"Off to the right is Port Royal, and directly in front of it in
the sea is its famous sunken city, which contains millions in
treasure. The sea is rough today, but when it is clear you can
see the buildings still standing on the bottom. Under the navigation beacon is the sunken cathedral, and fishermen say they
can actually hear the bells tolling as they pass by." I had my
face pressed so hard against the window that I almost stopped
breathing, trying to see some signs of the sunken city, but all
I could see was turbid water below.

After checking into a hotel I was on my way to Port Royal
in a matter of minutes, where I found a strong north wind
blowing, driving large waves against the sea wall. Undaunted,
I plunged into the water wearing fins and mask and headed out
for the Church Beacon. Jellyfish were as numerous as snowflakes
in a blizzard, and the water visibility was a mere one to two feet,
but nothing was going to stop me from seeing the sunken
cathedral. I knew that I could at least feel the walls of the
cathedral even if I couldn't see them. Reaching the Beacon,
I gulped air into my lungs and jack-knifed down. I felt something
all right: the sea floor. My head and arms were imbedded in the

soft silt before I saw it coming. Extracting myself, I found I could see nothing except my own face: the combination of muddy water on the bottom and the glass of my own face mask acted like a mirror. Still determined to find the cathedral, I groped in the darkness for a wall, any wall. Suddenly it felt as though a thousand needles were being driven into my right hand: I had caught hold of a large, black, spiny sea urchin.

The pain was excruciating enough to force me out of the water. Eager to get back in, I welcomed medical assistance offered by some fishermen ashore, who claimed they knew a foolproof method of extracting sea-urchin spines. It consisted of digging into my hand with a knife. Many of the spines came out, but so did a lot of surrounding flesh, and my hand became infected, swelling to twice its size by the next morning. For a few days I was as restless as a caged animal because I had to stay out of the water. In order to be doing something, I took a boat out to the Church Beacon, hoping I might hear the bells tolling. I didn't, nor could I see anything; the water was too black.

When I was finally able to dive again, conditions were more to my liking, with the sea flat and calm and visibility more than ten feet. Unable to find any scuba equipment on the island, I almost killed myself by free diving for eight straight hours before I had to give up from sheer exhaustion. I saw no signs of the cathedral or of any other buildings—only a number of coral-encrusted projections on the sea floor; walls, which in my great inexperience I overlooked. The only artifact I discovered turned out to be a whiskey bottle dating from the late nineteenth century. The next few days were virtual repetitions of that one, and I became more and more depressed, beginning to doubt that Port Royal had ever sunk into the sea at all. Convinced that I was wasting my time, I left to join some friends who were salvaging a Spanish shipwreck in the Florida Keys.

My interest in Port Royal revived the following year when I heard about the success of the Lumière-DuPont group. I was still in the Marines and had already used up most of my leave for the year, but I managed to get back to Port Royal for several days.

This time I brought several diving tanks with me. Hiring a fisherman to take me to the exact location of the brick archway and steps, I almost overturned the skiff in my haste to get down. Visibility was good, and I spotted the ruins at once. During the first hour of diving I located several clay smoking pipes, two onion bottles, a cannon ball, and countless pottery shards. I could hardly believe it, for I had been all over the same area the year before and had found nothing. I climbed aboard the skiff like a man in a daze, almost overturning it again. The fisherman didn't share my bewilderment; he explained that the building had probably been exposed by a recent storm or current and suggested that I search the area for other buildings that might have been uncovered as well. I took him up on it, and before I exhausted my tanks, discovered many other walls.

The next day, while my tanks were being refilled at the local oxygen-supply house in Kingston, I paid a visit to the Institute of Jamaica, where I met the director, an American named Bernard Lewis, who was profoundly interested in Port Royal. He turned over files full of documentation on the sunken city, and by the end of the day I was aware of the importance of doing historical research on all underwater sites before doing any exploratory work on them. Little did I realize at that time that eventually I would spend almost four full years doing original research in dozens of archives, libraries, and museums all over Europe and North and South America.

One of the first documents I came across was Murphy's 1859 account of discovering Fort James under the Church Beacon. Any last bit of faith I had in the author I had read as a boy vanished. Murphy's story had the ring of authenticity, and other documents and charts I consulted backed it up. Before leaving I thanked Lewis and vowed that someday I would be back to excavate the sunken city.

The following day I was back at the Church Beacon, and this time I did not dismiss the projections on the sea floor as coral reefs. For hours I chipped away with a crowbar through almost a foot of coral until I reached a brick wall—Fort James. I could not have been more jubilant about the discovery if I had been the first to make it instead of being beaten to it by almost a hundred years. I spent the rest of the day digging in the bottom sediment near the wall, locating a large cannon, cannon balls, onion bottles, etc.; the deeper I dug, the more artifacts I uncovered. Then, after reburying everything I had recovered (I had turned over the other artifacts I had recovered two days before to Bernard Lewis, but he asked me not to bring any more to him, because they had no means of preserving them), I surfaced with the feeling that I had done a good day's work. A year later Link and his team raised the cannon I had discovered.

My leave was up and I returned to my base, having seen for myself that the sunken city really existed and was a bonanza of priceless historical relics. The childhood dream of finding treasure was soon replaced with a new one—the dream of excavating Port Royal and learning about her famous past. I wasn't ready for it then, and I knew it. I was a good diver, but I had no knowledge of how to excavate an underwater site properly. Not that very many others had either: no underwater excavations had then been attempted in the Western Hemisphere, and of the few carried out in the Mediterranean, details had not yet been published.

During the ten years that intervened before I finally started serious work on the sunken city, I devoted my life to learning all I could about archaeology and maritime history. I acquired some of my knowledge from college and reading everything I could find relating to the field, but most of it came from actual experience. In those years I searched for and located the USS *Monitor* off Cape Hatteras, excavated sunken wrecks all over the Caribbean, dived in Mayan sinkholes in the Yucatán Peninsula, surveyed and excavated ancient shipwrecks and sunken cities in the Mediterranean, and spent several years reading musty old documents in archives. It was an exciting though grueling apprenticeship, but it prepared me well for the immense undertaking at Port Royal.

In July of 1964 I felt that I was finally ready to tackle Port Royal, so I went to Jamaica and met with Bernard Lewis, and he seemed anxious to help. Since he claimed that there were no funds to get the project started just then, I offered to work without any pay and to raise the necessary working capital from outside sources. While browsing around the basement of the Institute of Jamaica during this visit, I accidentally stumbled across a large number of the artifacts that had been recovered by the Link group in 1959, and I was astonished at what I saw: Dozens of perishable artifacts made of iron, glass, and wood—which should have been given preservation treatment, or at least placed in water-filled storage tanks—had been piled in heaps and left to disintegrate. I began having second thoughts about the sincerity of Lewis's interest in archaeology and history. I brought the matter to his attention—even offering to purchase storage tanks for the objects myself—but he said he would see that they were properly taken care of himself. When I returned a year and a half later I found the artifacts just as I had last seen them: still lying in the same piles, but in even worse condition.

I spent several months trying to raise funds from various foundations for the Port Royal project, but met with no success. Through a close friend I was put in contact with several of the officers of the Reynolds Aluminum Company, and they offered to finance the project for several years: Reynolds mines and exports vast amounts of bauxite from Jamaica and is the leading American firm engaged in business on the island. The Reynolds people felt that the publicity they would derive from financing the project would be well worth the expense, especially since Jamaica had recently become an independent country and they had been receiving bad publicity in the island's newspaper as the "foreign capitalistic exploiters of the people."

I had planned to arrive in Jamaica during the first week in April of 1965 to start the project, but Lewis informed me that for reasons beyond his control, the project would have to be delayed for a few months. Then in July I phoned Lewis, anxious to get started, and was told that he had heard that Link was coming back to work at Port Royal again and that I had to delay my arrival even longer, until he could straighten out everything. He also informed me that because of the strong nationalistic feelings on the island, the government did not want my project financed by an American company and that I should notify the Reynolds people of this decision. Several days later Lewis phoned, saying that the rumor about Link returning was false and that I was still in the running to direct the Port Royal project.

Unknown to me at the time, in December 1964 proposals had been submitted to the Jamaican Government for the development of Port Royal into a major tourist center—similar in many ways to Williamsburg, Virginia—by a group of Jamaican and international business interests known as the Port Royal Company of Merchants. The chairman of the group was a Major E. H. Marley, a London banker, and among the founders of the company was Commander Edward Whitehead, of Schweppes fame, and Edwin Link. These proposals included construction of two large hotels, several condominium complexes, a yacht marina, and other tourist facilities. The company's plans provided for the use of the old Royal Naval Hospital as a terminal building for a cruise-ship pier and for the dredging necessary to create a deepwater port off the western tip of Port Royal. To undertake such a monumental project, the company planned to raise around twenty million dollars by selling shares of stock to the public. In return they demanded the exclusive rights to excavate the sunken city and to retain everything recovered from the site, which they offered to display in a museum they would construct. Naturally they wanted Link, one of the founders of the company, to excavate the sunken city.

Early in October of 1965 the Port Royal area suffered a series of minor earth tremors, which actually helped me a great deal in finally getting to start my project. The local diving enthusiasts who rushed to the sunken city immediately afterward discovered that the sea floor had been affected by the tremors, exposing dozens of walls. Also, innumerable lightweight artifacts had been forced to the surface of the sea floor and were lying there uncovered. This resulted in a mad stampede by the divers—something on the order of the California gold rush—to pick up the artifacts. One diver, in only six hours, recovered about fifty onion bottles (more than had been recovered on Link's 1959 expedition), numerous roof and floor tiles, clay smoking pipes, and ceramic shards—all dating from the time of the earthquake. By the time Bernard Lewis learned of the matter, the bottom had already been picked cleaned, and the majority of the artifacts had been sold to tourists.

As a result of this event Lewis finally convinced the government that the best way to protect the site from future unauthorized diving and looting was for them to undertake their own excavation of the site. Soon after, I was contacted by Lewis and asked to direct the excavation of Port Royal as an employee of the Institute of Jamaica. I quickly abandoned my excavation of several Spanish galleons in Colombian waters and lost no time in going to Jamaica, where I arrived during the third week of November. More than a year passed after my arrival before I actually received the employment contract, which I had been told would be waiting for me when I arrived; in fact, it was five months before I was even put on full salary.

Bernard Lewis was waiting at the airport when I arrived and rushed me off to the office of Edward Seaga, the Minister of Development and Welfare, under which the Institute of Jamaica operates. I was pleased to find that Seaga had a degree in anthropology from Harvard University and was very interested in history and archaeology. Seaga pointed out that there was a great urgency for me to get started on the project—not just as a means of stopping the looting on the site by the amateur divers but because the site was in a greater danger. The construction of a large drainage system, called the "Sandy Gully Project," to control floods in the Kingston area had just been completed. He had received a report several days before from several geologists stating that when the heavy winter rains began, they expected vast amounts of silt would be carried into the harbor, a great deal of which would be carried by currents and deposited over the sunken city.

I told the minister I was ready to begin work the following day and presented him with an outline of my plan of operation and a list of equipment and personnel I would need. My plan entailed a preliminary survey and mapping operation of the whole site, which I estimated would take from six to eight weeks. The major items of equipment on the list were a helicopter for making

an aerial photographic survey, a small vessel, a rubidium magnetometer (for locating all large metallic concentrations), and a subbottom-penetrating sonar unit (for locating the walls of all the
buildings, both those buried beneath the sediment and those protruding through the sea floor)—all essential items for establishing
the over-all extent of the whole site and selecting the best areas
to excavate first. In addition I requested two full-time assistants.
Seaga promised that I would have everything I needed in a matter of days, and I foolishly believed him.

The following day I made the first of hundreds of exploratory
dives on the site. Visibility was down to three or four feet, and the
water so abounded in jellyfish that soon all the exposed parts of
my body was covered with welts. Nevertheless I accomplished
quite a bit. The arched doorway and steps and many of the walls
I had seen years before were again covered with sediment, but
I located more than twenty other walls, the remains of two shipwrecks, about a dozen large anchors, and a great many artifacts
dating from the time of the earthquake—all of which had probably been uncovered during the recent earth tremors. My big find
was a complete Arawak Indian clay cooking pot, the first evidence
of a possible Arawak settlement at Port Royal, which caused a
stir among the Arawak specialists on the island. The day's diving
ended with a bang. As I ascended from my last dive with my
aqualung tank nearly empty, I spotted three large hammerhead
sharks cruising on the surface overhead. Not being one to engage
in combat with the numerical odds so clearly against me, I waited
for them to go away, but they seemed content to hover there, no
doubt discussing their next meal: me. At last, completely out of
air, I had to ascend in a hurry, and broke surface right in the
middle of the huddle. Before they had a chance to attack, I
struck the water with the flats of both hands. The noise was as
loud as a thunderclap, and they took off as though the avenging
furies were after them.

Ashore I found a British gentleman, Sir Anthony Jenkinson,
the owner of Morgan's Harbour, the local hotel and yacht club,
waiting for me with a rather sour look on his face. He got to the
point quickly: he announced that he was one of the founders

and the local representative of the Port Royal Company of Merchants (which I had not even heard of until then) and told me briefly of their plans for the development of Port Royal and about their negotiations with the government. Naturally I was a bit surprised that neither Lewis nor Seaga had even told me about this matter, but my surprise quickly turned to anger when Jenkinson announced that he and other members of his group would make every attempt possible to stop us from ever excavating the site, which he stated had been promised to his group. I soon found that he was more than serious in making that threat.

Several days later, after Edward Seaga had publicly announced in the press my appointment and the government's plan to excavate Port Royal, Jenkinson and several other members of his group went to Seaga threatening to break off all further negotiations with the government and cancel their plans for the development of Port Royal unless the planned excavation was called off. I was never informed of what really transpired at this meeting, but later that day I ran into Jenkinson, who announced: "You better join our group and work with us, or you'll never excavate the sunken city." I told him to "go to hell."

Meanwhile, while waiting for the equipment and personnel I needed to undertake my preliminary survey of the site, I continued diving on the site daily. After spending the first week exploring the whole site, I decided that my next move would be to remove all the modern debris: automobile chassis, stoves, sinks, and incredible amounts of other junk which had been thrown into the sea by the inhabitants of modern Port Royal. Fortunately I had brought some diving equipment with me; otherwise I wouldn't have been able to do even this. For almost a month, working alone except on weekends when I had a few volunteer assistants, I brought tons of modern trash to the surface, placed it in a small skiff I borrowed from a friend, and then threw it all back into the water in areas off the site. This was probably the hardest work I have ever done in my life, but it had to be done.

During the first weekend of what I called "Operation Junk Removal" I invited the local chapter of the British Sub-Aqua Club to assist me, and on the first day more than thirty of them arrived, but I soon learned that I had made a drastic mistake. Some of the club members used this opportunity to search for and pick up artifacts instead of trash. After discovering this fact, I chastised them, and when the same thing occurred on two other occasions I was forced to work without their aid.

Two of the members of the club, Stan Judge, the assistant chief engineer for the Jamaican Omnibus Service, and his teenage daughter Louise, were a cut above the others—in fact they resigned from it and worked with me as volunteers throughout the project, and I owe them a great debt of gratitude. Along with my wife, Nancy, who soon became a history professor at the University of the West Indies, Stan and Louise contributed every free moment they had to the project.

Several cocky American divers, whose yacht, the *Lone Star*, had been anchored at the Port Royal marina for almost a year, soon came under suspicion, but though they were watched closely by the local police, no one could figure out how they were getting artifacts from the sunken city, which they were known to be selling to tourists. Then one day I accidentally bumped into one of them while I was on a routine dive. We both had a shock: neither of us had expected to meet anyone under water. I was ascending with an armful of trash when I spotted a diver swimming with a bulging gunny sack. I pretended that I hadn't seen him and gave him a head start, following him back to his yacht. Then I saw him enter a hatch in the bottom of the hull of the yacht and disappear from sight. I had to admire the James Bond ingenuity of the maneuver: with the hidden hatch, the comings and goings of those aboard were unknown to the people ashore or on the surface. Ingenious or not, what they were doing was criminal. I reported my discovery to Seaga and they were ordered to leave the country. But this wasn't the last we heard of them.

Their exposure discouraged others from making illegal dives and I had no further need to play detective. Edward Seaga had a large sign erected along the roadside on the outskirts of Port Royal notifying divers of prosecution for picking anything up off the sea floor or in any way interfering with my project.

This brought vehement protests from the members of the British Sub-Aqua Club, who claimed that since there was no law then in effect in Jamaica, Seaga had no right to prevent them from picking up artifacts on the sunken city. They should have left well enough alone; Seaga had a law passed to this effect, which also even prohibited all diving at Port Royal. Then Jenkinson, with the aid of several members of the island's opposition party, jumped on the bandwagon, claiming that the law was detrimental to the tourist business because many persons came down to the island to dive at Port Royal. Seaga at this time was one of the most powerful men in the government, not one safe to cross swords with, and the law went into effect.

During the third week of Operation Junk Removal I began having problems from another quarter—fast boats and water skiers trying to run me down in the water. After about twenty near misses during a period of a few days, the final one was the last straw as far as I was concerned. As I surfaced from a dive about two hundred feet from shore, a speedboat passed about ten feet off and as I turned to shout at the driver, who turned out to be Jenkinson's teen-age son, the skier came right at me, straddling my head with his two skis. I rushed to the Morgan's Harbour Hotel in a fury. Jenkinson was sitting at a table near the bar grinning in contentment, with a police officer as his guest, who I later learned was a close friend of his. After I announced in no uncertain terms that I would shoot him or his son if my life was further endangered, the police officer jumped up and said that if I didn't leave the premises immediately, he would have me arrested "for threatening a person with bodily harm." Seaga came to my rescue again. A notice appeared in the *Daily Gleaner,* the island's main newspaper, prohibiting all boating and water skiing in the areas I was working.

My problems with Jenkinson made me sort of a hero with the people of Port Royal, who hated Jenkinson for a number of reasons. When Jamaica received her independence from Great Britain in 1962, the British Government retained a large section of Port Royal on a ninety-nine-year lease, to be used as a military base in the event of a major war, and somehow Jenkinson had managed to sublease this property from the British Government—which consisted of one quarter of the land area of the township of Port Royal—and had built the Morgan's Harbour Hotel and Marina. Tourists had freedom of the facilities, but it was restricted for Jamaicans, who had to pay a large initiation fee and become club members. Naturally this excluded the poor inhabitants of Port Royal, who couldn't possibly meet the requirements. Although I was solvent enough to pay the fee, my application for membership was refused on the grounds that I was "an undesirable applicant."

In the center of the town was a bar named the Buccaneers Roost, where most of the men hung out, and I soon made it my temporary headquarters. It was the only place to get a hot meal other than at Morgan's Harbour, but the selection wasn't too large: one ate either fried fish or conch chowder—the latter so richly spiced with hot peppers that few of my visiting friends could stomach it. Actually it was far from what one could call a tourist facility, for brawls were a daily occurrence and there were even occasional knife fights—mostly precipitated by Kingston fishermen, who were not especially welcome at Port Royal. However, I was quickly accepted by the locals and rarely had any problems with them. In fact, on a number of occasions when bad elements from Kingston came over to Port Royal and began giving me trouble, they were quickly driven off by the Port Royal people.

I finished Operation Junk Removal a few days before Christmas and was ready to go on to the next stage of the preliminary survey of the site, but even though a month had passed since Seaga had promised to supply everything I needed, "in a few days," I hadn't received a single item, nor did I get authorization to hire two assistants. At a Christmas party I finally confronted Seaga, who had been difficult to reach for days, and soon learned why. He announced that no funds for my project would be available until the next fiscal year, which started April 1 of the coming year. I could hardly believe what I had heard. What was I to do for three months—wait and be patient?

I knew that somehow Jenkinson and his Port Royal Company of Merchants were responsible for the delay of my project—which proved correct—and I wasn't going to sit around and let them get the better of me. I decided that I would continue the project on my own initiative, as I had been doing for the past month. But before I could get started, I needed the necessary equipment, so I headed for the United States a few days after Christmas with the hope of somehow obtaining it all.

The two main things I was after were the magnetometer and the subbottom sonar unit—which, combined, cost over twenty-five thousand dollars—but I was unable to convince any of the companies that manufacture these items to loan them to me for the project. I had better luck with diving-equipment firms, who contributed several thousand dollars' worth of equipment; with the Nikon Camera Company, who gave me two cameras; and with several chemical firms, who offered to supply all the chemicals I would eventually need for preserving the artifacts I knew we would recover. I later learned that a special license was required to import chemicals into Jamaica—one I was never able to obtain.

I knew that we would need a good person to work on the project as a preservation specialist, and I convinced Alan Albright, who was then employed by the Smithsonian Institution in this capacity and was recognized as an expert in this field, to come down and work with me. Unfortunately funds were never made available to hire him, but he did come down on several occasions and spent weeks helping on the preservation aspects of the project.

Each year, Mendel Peterson holds a party for his treasure-hunting and underwater-explorer friends. That year it happened to coincide with the time I was in Washington, D.C., visiting Alan Albright, so I attended. Link was also at the party, and I cornered him about my problems with Jenkinson and demanded to know if he were actually trying to come back and excavate Port Royal. He stated that he had considered it over the years, but just didn't have the time, and was happy that I would be directing the project, since it would take him off the hook of his obligation to return to Port Royal. He appeared sincere and I believed him.

A week later, the Port Royal Company of Merchants held a board of directors' meeting in New York attended by both Jenkinson and Link. When Jenkinson returned to Jamaica, he presented Seaga with a new proposal concerning Link's returning to excavate the sunken city—this one much more favorable for the government. They offered to spend two full years excavating the site, using a minimum of ten divers at all times, and they would foot the whole bill, including the cost of building a museum at Port Royal. Instead of demanding 100 per cent of what was recovered, they now offered to split it down the middle with the government. Seaga notified Jenkinson that the new proposal was under consideration and asked him to invite Link to come down for a conference.

When I discovered that these negotiations were going on behind my back, I had one of the many stormy sessions I was to have during the next three years with Seaga. He claimed that he had been pressured into considering the proposal by other members of the government, who were fearful that if it wasn't accepted, the company would probably call off all their plans of developing Port Royal, thus depriving the island of a sizable income. Seaga said that he would accept the proposal if the Link group would accept me as the marine archaeologist codirector of the project with Link. I knew that these terms would not be acceptable to the company, so I began gathering ammunition for the battle I knew was imminent.

Bernard Lewis was completely on my side and was aghast when I told him what I had heard from the Hon. Seaga. He quickly sent him a memorandum:

Mr. Marx came to me yesterday morning in a most upset state of mind as he has found himself in an impossible position in view of recent developments and statements which have been made to him at Port Royal. Provision has been made for salary for Marx in our proposed budget for 1966/1967 and, with our verbal commitment that he would be undertaking the excavation work at Port Royal, he went to the U.S. at his own expense to get additional equipment and to re-establish contacts for assistance with the Port Royal project. Since his return he has encountered great embarrassment because of rumors which are circulating about himself and statements which have been made that he is not going to be able to carry out our programme because firm contracts are being made with others to do the work. Most of these rumors appear to have originated from Sir Anthony Jenkinson or those associated with him.

When Marx first met Sir Anthony, about the time of the press release, he was told that Government had acted unethically in bringing him to Port Royal when negotiations were in progress with his Company. He tried then and there to induce Marx into his employ. Marx, of course, did not entertain such a possibility. He has subsequently encountered a most disconcerting atmosphere of suspicion and I, myself, have heard from different quarters that he is here under false pretences, that he is unqualified, that he has a bad record, etc.

I do not know what took place at the discussion at your Ministry on Monday last but it appears that many rumors are now circulating that Government has capitulated and that the Port Royal Merchants will be in full charge of the programme. Marx believes that he has been used as a "pawn" in the negotiations with the Port Royal Merchants and I can quite understand how upset he must be especially since he has thrown himself into this project most completely and is heavily involved financially. He is characteristically a man of action and undoubtedly the unfavorable tales have magnified in his eyes. Personally I am convinced that Marx is sincere and suitably qualified, and that if he is fairly treated, he can and will exercise loyalty and integrity and do an excellent job for us.

Mr. Minister, it is essential that we see you as quickly as possible because we are in a most difficult situation. If Marx is to do anything at all a release from the Ministry will have to be made providing him with appropriate credentials and authority.

Several weeks later Link appeared, and Seaga held a meeting in which about twenty persons attended from both sides: Government and the Port Royal Company of Merchants. I was not invited, nor did I know about it until it was underway and I received an anonymous phone call informing me. Link was talking as I entered and didn't notice me, stating that although he and I were friends, he felt that I was unqualified to codirect the project. Upon which I jumped up and took the floor and presented the ammunition I had been gathering. From more than twenty archaeologists, historians, and other types of scholars, I had solicited and received letters stating that I was the best-qualified person to direct the Port Royal project, and most of them stated that the Jamaican Government ought to undertake the project on their own, without any outside help. After only a few of these letters had been read by a secretary, Link and all his associates stormed out without as much as a good-bye. Seaga had been a bit upset by my intrusion, but after the competition had left, he said: "Marx, you must be a descendant of some buccaneer, because I've never seen such a bullheaded man like you."

That evening I had an even greater surprise: The acting Prime Minister, the Honourable Donald Sangster, phoned me at home. He told me that shortly after the meeting at Seaga's home several of the members of the company had come to his residence (it was on a Sunday) and presented him with an ultimatum, demanding that I be fired from the government service immediately and that it be announced publicly in the press that Link would be given the concession to excavate Port Royal, or they would call off their plans to develop Port Royal. This was a bad move on their part and it angered Sangster. He told them they could do as they wished, but the Government would not be coerced into anything.

The following day, Sangster announced in the press, radio, and on television that my appointment as marine archaeologist and director of the Port Royal excavation, which would be a Jamaican Government project entirely, without any outside help, had been approved and would be funded by the Government. My problems with the Port Royal Company of Merchants were over—or at least it seemed so at the time.

Meanwhile I hadn't been idle all this time. My first task after returning from the States was to take aerial photographs of the site and adjacent coastline; aerial photographs had helped me locate a number of shipwrecks in the past, but in clearer waters. With the use of a helicopter from the Jamaican Defense Force, I spent several days photographing, using different kinds of film including infrared and with different filters including a Polaroid filter. But the waters at Port Royal were so dirty that the photographs failed to reveal any details of the sea floor. They did come in handy soon after, when I had the Survey Department make a more up-to-date chart of the Port Royal coastline. Those then available weren't up to date: during a minor earthquake in 1957 a six-hundred-foot-long and eighty-foot-wide section of the southern shore had sunk into the sea along with other, smaller portions of the coast.

During the helicopter rides, I discovered that the illegal divers were not the only intruders on the sunken city: during one two-hour ride I counted more than thirty sharks on or near the surface. Most of them arrive in Port Royal in the wakes of ships, feeding on the garbage thrown overboard. When the ships stop, they stop too, and many choose to remain, for Port Royal is a fishing base, and fishermen cleaning their catches throw the guts and other waste into the sea, where the sharks pounce on them much as their ancestors undoubtedly pounced on the discarded scraps from the fish market that existed before the 1692 earthquake. Although the children at Port Royal spend a great deal of time swimming in the same water, the last known shark attack off Port Royal occurred more than twenty years ago.

The Survey Department helped me considerably by erecting permanent markers ashore—spaced every one hundred feet— along the three quarters of a mile of the shoreline that borders the sunken city. They also produced a set of charts with grids; these were invaluable for the preliminary mapping survey and later for plotting the major finds.

Working alone most of the time, I knew the mapping procedure was likely to take a long time, and because I knew that there was a good chance that earth tremors or even an earthquake might occur and render a map of the sunken city inaccurate overnight, I decided to map only part of the site before beginning the actual excavation. The first area I chose was the north side of the old Port Royal about midway between Fort James and Fort Charles—the section of town where the residences and wharves of the wealthy merchants had stood. Since the buildings in this section had been thrown into the sea within minutes after the quake and lay in much deeper water than the rest of the sunken city, there was a good chance that the early salvors, primarily interested in treasure, had over-looked many interesting artifacts.

Without the use of the rubidium magnetometer and the sonar unit, I had to rely on more primitive equipment in making my survey. A friend of mine, John Bender of Houston, Texas, generously donated an underwater metal detector to locate the large metallic concentrations on the site. To locate the walls of buildings and other non-metallic objects, I elected to use an eight-foot metal rod (it should have been at least twice that length, I later learned, because many objects were buried still deeper in the sediment) as a probe; upon striking anything solid beneath the sediment, I would dig down with my hands to identify it. Whenever I located anything interesting to plot on the chart, I had to attach a buoy to it, surface, take bearings from the markers ashore, and plot the location and identification of the object on a plastic slate—then start all over again.

After a full week of mapping, my fingers and hands were covered with cuts from sharp objects in the sediment such as glass, metal, and coral, and gloves were no help at all, for often I could not see the objects because of the muddy water and had to rely on touch for identification. By this time I had covered only a small area, approximately sixty by forty feet, and I was pretty discouraged; at that rate it would take me years to map the whole site. The greatest loss of time resulted from the necessity of digging into the sediment with my hands to identify every solid object encountered by the metal rod, and more often than not it turned out to be a rock or a large piece of coral. Then Stan Judge, who was to come to my rescue many times throughout the project, devised a simple suction pump with its engine mounted in a large inner tube on the surface, to dig into the sediment, and with it I was able to accomplish in minutes what before had taken hours.

Although my wife and Stan and his daughter assisted me in their spare time, the majority of the time I was forced to work alone. To speed up the operation, I invited three diving friends to spend several weeks working with me as volunteers, but only a few days after their arrival I had troubles again. Some members of the British Sub-Aqua Club had learned of their presence and protested to the government, claiming that since they were no longer able to dive at Port Royal, they considered it an injustice to have foreign divers doing so. I was ordered not to use my volunteers any more—to my great regret.

I kept pestering Seaga and Lewis about their providing funds so I could hire several assistants, and about all I could get out of them was "Soon come," Jamaica's most frequently used expression. It could mean anything from a matter of minutes to a matter of months. Funds for the project were not forthcoming until the middle of April, and even then in only a limited amount.

Around the end of February I lost several days because of the yacht *Lone Star*, which had been ordered to leave the island two months before. Jenkinson had a lien placed on the vessel, claiming that the owner owed him over one thousand dollars for repair work. They had abandoned the boat and left the island a few days after being ordered to leave, but they returned and finally paid the debt to Jenkinson. One of them came to me and announced that they were going down to Pedro Shoals, a reef about 130 miles south of Port Royal, to salvage a Spanish wreck. I told him that they couldn't do it without a permit, but he only laughed and told me that Jamaica didn't have the means to stop them. In fact, the Jamaican Defense Force did have a navy, consisting of two old World War II torpedo boats, but neither was working at the time. Two days after they left, Seaga sent a plane out to check on them—and true to their word, they were anchored illegally on Pedro Shoals, after clearing Jamaica for Miami.

Seaga ordered me to find a boat and go after them, taking three armed policemen with me. Realizing that they had a much faster vessel than the one I was able to get, we slipped up on them during the night, without any lights showing, and at sunrise the following morning boarded them. On the way to their boat, one of the policemen in the skiff with me became seasick, and while vomiting, lost his false teeth. It took me several months and reams of letters to have him reimbursed by the government to get a new set of teeth.

The pirates were anchored right over the wreck, and their vessel was covered with salvage equipment, but apparently they had heard us approaching during the night, for we were unable to find any treasure or artifacts aboard their vessel. While the search was underway, one of the pirates began emptying buckets of chopped-up fish overboard, which made me suspicious, and he said: "This is to make sure you have plenty of sharks for company if you decide to dive." In a matter of minutes there were over a dozen sharks in a feeding frenzy, which prevented me from diving, so I began using a glass-bottomed bucket to search the bottom for signs of anything they might have flung overboard, but with negative results. Several years later I ran into one of the pirates, who confirmed my suspicions: they had buried three sacks of artifacts in a cave in the reef during the night, after hearing us approach. Americans around the world seem to get away with murder, and these pirates were no exception. We radioed back to Seaga what had occurred and he ordered us not to arrest them, since we hadn't found proof that they were illegally working on the wreck. We ordered them to leave, which they did, but a month later they were back again—this time only too happy for someone to find them.

Their vessel had hit a reef and sunk, and they were rescued after several days of floating around on a small life raft.

After spending two months on the mapping operation, during which I spent seven or eight hours a day diving without even the use of a boat, I had mapped a large enough section so that I was ready to get the excavation underway. I had also made a complete survey of the area between Forts James and Carlisle, which covered over two thirds of the over-all site. In the eastern section of this area I analyzed the composition of the sediment: the first three feet was very soft silt and small amounts of loose gravel; then came four to five feet of hard-packed mud, and below that a mixture of about 70 per cent sand and 30 per cent gravel. In the western section of this area, east of Fort James, the top two feet was composed of soft silt in which long-bladed eel grass grew; the next four to five feet consisted of about 20 per cent hard-packed mud with a mixture of around 80 per cent small fragments of dead coral; below this level the sediment was the same as in the other area. The bottom surface in the whole area was covered with black, spiny sea urchins, and about 10 per cent of it had live coral growing—some of it on sections of walls sticking up through the bottom.

Just when I thought that my mapping operation had been successfully completed, I had to start all over. The Port Royal Company of Merchants was back in the picture again. They announced that in a matter of months they would begin their development of Port Royal by dredging their deepwater port off the western edge of Port Royal—in the area of the sunken city I had not mapped or considered for initial excavation. Armed with a lengthy report from an engineering firm, which allegedly made hundreds of core samples in the area of the proposed deepwater port sometime before I arrived on the island, the company requested permission from the government to dredge there. I was ordered to confirm their report, which stated that no traces of the sunken city were found in that area. Even without diving I knew that the report had to be incorrect, because the old charts showed that about one third of the sunken city—between Fort James and Chocolata Hole (the area where small vessels had anchored prior to the 1692 quake)—was lying there. Using the small dredge, I dug over fifty holes in the area, and in every one of them I found traces of the old buildings or artifacts. As a result of my discovery, the government refused to issue them permission to dredge this area until I had completely excavated it.

Once again I began having problems with Jenkinson, who was furious, especially when I announced that it might take as long as two to four years to thoroughly excavate that area, which consisted of over five hundred thousand square feet. His announcement in the press that "the insufferable delay" caused by my excavation of the area would undoubtedly terminate any future plans for the development of Port Royal by his company, got him nowhere with the government. Trying to be reasonable and seeing it as a means of getting more funds and assistance for my project, I wrote to Major Marley, the chairman of their company, suggesting that if his firm made a sizable donation to my project, I could employ a greater number of divers and assistants and could conceivably completely excavate that area in a year. Marley refused my offer and once again they began demanding that Link be permitted to come back to excavate the site—this time working side by side with me. Seaga refused to even consider the matter.

Another campaign was launched to stop me. Rumors were started that I had been kicked out of several countries for illegal diving and stealing artifacts, and the government was forced to investigate these rumors. After being questioned by several government officials, Jenkinson changed his story and claimed that I had been kicked out of only one country: Mexico. Three days later the rumor was squelched by the arrival of Pablo Bush Romero, whom I had asked to come to my defense. Don Pablo, as he is called by friends, was the president of CEDAM, the official marine archaeological society of Mexico, with whom I had worked a number of times over the years. He praised me and my past work so highly that I didn't hear another peep out of Jenkinson or his associates for months.

According to the old charts and documents, the new area I had to map and then excavate was one of the poorer sections of the old town, where the less prosperous citizens had had their homes and where the fish and meat markets, as well as both prisons, had been. I realized that it would yield fewer interesting artifacts than the area I had first selected for excavation, especially since it was the area where the town had sunk gradually, with the tops of many buildings remaining above water for years. It was also the area off the old Royal Naval Hospital, where extensive salvaging of bricks had taken place early in the past century. Nevertheless it was imperative that whatever was there be recovered before the dredging began. Although the government had stated that no dredging would take place until I had completely excavated the whole area, I knew that governments have the habit of reversing decisions, so the project took on great urgency.

Before I could even start the mapping operation, I had a major obstacle to overcome. There were at least ten times as many sea urchins on the bottom in this area compared with the other I had mapped—in fact, there wasn't a square foot of the bottom that didn't have at least one sea urchin. Before I could use my metal detector or probe, they had to be eliminated. At first I tried picking them up with a metal hook, throwing them in baskets, and depositing them farther out in the harbor, but this method was too time consuming. Heedless of my past problems with the divers of the British Sub-Aqua Club, I decided to ask for their assistance once again. I went to their clubhouse one evening when I knew they were having their weekly meeting, and at first it was like walking into a den of lions. On one of the walls I noticed a recent newspaper photograph of myself, which was full of holes. I was informed that it was used as a dart-board target. In any event, after we all had consumed a few beers, the ice melted and I convinced them to help me eliminate the sea urchins. Fortunately there was a three-day holiday weekend coming up, and an average of about thirty of them appeared each day, armed with hammers and other tools, with which they smashed thousands of sea urchins.

After an area of three hundred by two hundred feet had been cleared I began my mapping survey, which took almost a month. This was by no means the end of the sea-urchin menace: throughout the course of the excavation my team and volunteers spent hundreds of hours eliminating more of them. They are able to walk on the sea floor, and I soon found that in only a matter of days they could fill in a cleared area.

Fortunately most of the land of the shoreline of the new area was taken up by the naval hospital and surrounding grounds, and not by houses, which meant there was considerably less modern debris to be removed. But there were a large number of enormous coral heads—some weighing over a ton—and many of them had to be removed before the excavation could start. The composition of the bottom sediment was uniform in most of the area: the first two feet were soft silt, with small amounts of dead coral fragments; the next two to three feet were very hard-packed mud, also with a small amount of dead coral; and below this to an average depth of twelve more feet, there was a mixture of 70 per cent sand and 30 per cent gravel.

As a result of the complete over-all mapping operation, I discovered that in most areas the site extended around one hundred feet farther out from shore into the harbor than had been thought or had been indicated on the Link-Weems Chart of Port Royal. The over-all extent of the site covered approximately 1,500,000 square feet, and since this covered about 40 per cent of the original town, it is safe to assume that somewhere between seven hundred and eight hundred buildings, or at least the sites on which they stood, were lying in the water off Port Royal.

Around the middle of March of 1966 Lewis notified me that although the funds for the project were not yet available, I should start hiring personnel and buying equipment on credit; this proved easier said than done, for I found that most businessmen in Kingston are reluctant to sell to the government on credit. I almost had a seizure when he announced that my budget for each month was a little less than one thousand dollars. In my original outline for the excavation of the project I had indicated that I would need a minimum staff of fifteen persons:

an assistant director, six divers, a preservation expert, a photographer, an artist, a watchman, and four laborers. There was just no way that I could obtain such a team with the amount of money I had to operate with—which also had to cover buying equipment, chemicals for preservation, fuel for the compressors, and other things. I had to be content with just two divers and four laborers and rely on volunteer help to cover the other work that must be done on the project.

April 1 was designated as the day we would begin the excavation, and there was a lot that had to be done in the meantime. I was extremely fortunate in finding two good Jamaican divers who were willing to work for about one tenth of what I would have had to pay a diver in the States. The first, Kenute Kelly, was a professional diver and champion swimmer who had won a number of international competitions. When I first met him he was working as a salvage diver, but he became so fascinated by the project that he quit his job to join my team, even though it meant a drastic cut in salary. I had good reason to be glad he made that decision, for Kelly is one of those rare people who seem to have been born for work under the sea: fearless at all times and capable of getting the job done under the most adverse conditions. Moreover, I sometimes thought he had extrasensory perception, judging from the way he knew what I wanted him to do before I would tell him, and from the number of times he assisted me in emergencies. My second diver, Wayne Roosevelt, lacked Kelly's diving experience, but showed himself quick to learn. His real love was judo, a sport in which he holds a black belt, and with his earnings from the project he hoped to open a judo school. I had planned to use grown men as laborers, but because of the low salary I was able to pay them, most of the laborers I used throughout the project were teen-age boys.

The natural choice for a shore base of operations was in the partially ruined old naval hospital, which was owned by the government but had six large families of squatters living in it. Although the building was more than one hundred fifty years old, it was still in fairly good condition: it is reported to be

the first building in the Western Hemisphere built out of struc-
tural steel and concrete. To my surprise I found that the room
in the best condition, although it lacked doors and windows,
was the only one vacant, and couldn't understand why it wasn't
being used by the squatters. I soon found out: Several months
earlier a derelict Dutch seaman had died in the room from an
overdose of strong Jamaica rum. Jamaicans are very superstitious
and believed the man's ghost, which they call a "duppy," haunted
the room. Stan Judge, late of the British Sub-Aqua Club,
came to my rescue, and his company donated cement, paint,
lumber, and just about everything else we needed to fix the
room up—which was to serve as a combination storage room for
equipment and a laboratory for storing and preserving artifacts.
The location was ideal, as the area we would be working in
for the next two years was only several hundred feet away.
Although the room appeared large at first—one hundred by thirty-
five feet—once we began bringing up large amounts of artifacts
we quickly ran out of space and had to clear out squatters
and take over more rooms.

During the preliminary survey of the site I had been using
aqualung diving tanks, but I decided against using them for
excavating: not only are they too cumbersome while working
on the bottom, but the divers would have to surface every hour
to get new tanks, and there was also the time-consuming task
of having to refill them every day. Instead, I decided to use a
newly invented breathing apparatus called an Aquanaut, which
consisted of a small compressor set inside a tube that floats
on the surface. Hoses connected to it carry air to a full face
mask worn by the diver, and they were a great deal more com-
fortable to use, since they eliminated the diver's having to bite
on the mouthpiece of a regulator. With a surface attendant
filling the fuel tank of the unit every hour, the diver could
stay down indefinitely. In the area we were planning to work,
the average depth of water was around twenty feet, a depth
that permitted a diver to remain down for any length of time
without having to worry about decompressing before coming to
the surface.

The problem of selecting the correct excavation equipment was not so easy to solve. From the start, I was determined to recover artifacts with as little damage to them as possible. Some divers working off the coast of Florida had developed a new type of excavation tool, called a propwash, which though more than satisfactory on some sites, was too powerful and dangerous to use on my site. I had the choice between using an air lift, as Link and Scott had done, or digging by hand—a procedure so slow it was out of the question. Realizing that too large and powerful an air lift could suck up fragile objects such as bottles, pottery, and glassware and smash them to bits before the diver holding the tube could rescue them, I experimented with smaller air-lift tubes and finally settled on a tube four inches in diameter with a screen on the bottom to prevent any object larger than a half-dollar piece from going up the tube. This reduced danger to the artifacts to a minimum but greatly increased the amount of work to be done by the divers, and also the time it would take to excavate the area threatened by the proposed dredging operation.

Three divers would be needed on the bottom at all times: one holding and directing the tube around and grabbing artifacts as they were caught on the screen, another placing the artifacts as they were uncovered in buckets and moving large objects such as coral heads and sections of walls out of the way, and the third carrying the artifacts to the surface and keeping a careful watch on the wall of the hole, warning the other two if any large objects were ready to fall out of the sediment on top of them.

The decision to use an air lift solved one problem but created another: what to do with the sediment and debris that was sucked up. During most of the underwater excavations involving air lifts, the top end of the tube is pointed in a direction away from the area being worked, so that the sediment and debris coming up will be carried away from the area by currents. This may work well on shipwreck sites, most of which are confined in a small area, but I knew that on our site it wouldn't do: much of the sediment removed from one area was bound to settle in another, making more work for us later. To prevent that, I decided to use a barge as a receptacle for everything coming up the air lift; whenever the barge was filled, it could be emptied off the site or in an area already excavated. Using a barge had a further advantage, since it could hold a large screen of finer mesh than the one on the bottom of the air-lift tube, to catch smaller objects such as pins, beads, or coins sucked up the tube. Later I found that I needed four laborers on the barge to watch the screen for small objects, to maintain the balance of the barge by keeping the sediment equally distributed, and to unload the barge every hour or so.

Still another problem created by the air lift was where to put the large compressor that provided the air for the lift, which I had obtained on an indefinite loan from the Public Works Department. Lack of funds prevented me from obtaining a vessel large enough to hold it, so I decided to keep it ashore and run the air hoses from it to the bottom of the air-lift tube. This worked well except for a few occasions when passing boats ran over and cut the hose with their propellers. With this method we were able to make do with a small skiff as the base of operations in the water and as a container for the artifacts we recovered.

All these problems concerned mechanics; some were difficult to solve, but none were insurmountable. Now I faced the big one: drawing up a plan for the actual excavation that would adhere as faithfully as possible to established archaeological principals. The sudden cataclysm that caused Port Royal to sink into the sea has frequently been likened to the volcanic eruption that destroyed the Roman city of Pompeii, A.D. 79. When archaeologists began excavating Pompeii more than fifty years ago, they discovered a fantastic time capsule, since the site had been covered quickly by volcanic ash and remained virtually untouched for almost two thousand years. Everything was as it had been at the moment the disaster occurred: buildings stood with their furnishings in place, and exact impressions of the inhabitants in their death agonies were preserved in the volcanic ash that first covered them and then solidified around their bodies. After a long, arduous excavation and close study of the findings, archaeologists were able to determine a great deal about what life was like in Pompeii at the time of the disaster.

Because of the similarity in the ways the two cities met their end, many scholars believed that an excavation of Port Royal would show results as dramatic and spectacular as those of Pompeii. Unfortunately, this was not so for many reasons. Marine archaeology, a science still in its infancy, poses problems that do not arise in the excavation of a land site, and salt water does not have the same preservative qualities as volcanic ash. Ideally, archaeological excavation should be undertaken stratigraphically, layer by layer, with the exact depth and location of each find recorded. Stratigraphical digging on land often leads to very precise determination of the age of the object uncovered and the reconstruction of the society it was part of. On most sunken cities, because the sea floor is constantly subjected to disturbances caused by currents, storms, and the like, to say nothing of the disturbances caused by man, such precise data are the exception rather than the rule.

One case in which land archaeological methods were applied under water with outstanding results occurred on the Bronze Age shipwreck discovered by Peter Throckmorton off Turkey. Dr. George Bass, who directed the expedition and was determined that it could be done by using land archaeological methods, had everything in his favor. The wreck lay in crystal-clear water at a depth of one hundred fifty feet, too deep for the salvors of the past to reach. No storms had broken it to pieces over the centuries, currents had not disturbed the artifacts aboard, and it was apparently covered over by sand quickly, before shipworms had eaten all of the wooden hull. The team consisted of excavators, draftsmen, artists, a photographer, a historian, a classicist, and several preservation experts. With their help Bass was able to map the site properly on a grid chart, dig stratigraphically, and record the position and depth of the wood remaining on the ship and of every artifact recovered. Later with the data collected he and his assistants were able to reconstruct the ship on paper, ascertaining how it had been built and what it looked like, what it carried, where each item aboard was stored, and practically everything else that scholars might want to know about the ship.

This shipwreck was an archaeologist's dream, but the world may not see its counterpart for many years. Certainly the chances of obtaining such sensational results in the Western Hemisphere are slim, where almost every marine archaeological site is located in shallow waters and has been subjected to countless disturbances from nature and man. The exception would be the discovery of an old shipwreck that sank in at least a hundred feet of water. But unfortunately only a small number of old wrecks are known to have sunk in such depths. More than 99 per cent of all old shipwreck losses in the Western Hemisphere occurred in depths between ten and forty feet of water, and because of the destructive effects of nature and man, only a limited amount of archaeological information can be obtained from them. Although very little of the original ship's hull remains on these shallow-water sites, thus making it impossible for the archaeologist to determine how the ship was constructed or what it looked like, other data can be obtained: what kind of armament, anchors, equipment, and cargo it carried. However, due to the movement of these objects on the sea floor in storms and currents, it is impossible to determine where and how they were stored aboard the ships.

During my preliminary explorations of the sunken city, I discovered that the condition of the site was neither as ideal as that of the Turkish Bronze Age wreck nor as disturbed and destroyed as the average shallow-water shipwreck—mainly because brick buildings survive much better in the sea than the hulls of wooden ships. The numerous natural disasters afflicting Port Royal through the years have caused buildings to collapse and have altered the sea floor throughout much of the site; in these areas the chances of finding a time capsule of history were slender. How much so, I found out early, during my first week of mapping: Probing the sediment for walls, I heard a loud noise overhead. I surfaced to see a large freighter stopping to take on immigration and customs officials and dropping anchor only a hundred yards from where I was diving. I descended again, curious to know whether the anchor had touched any part of the sunken city, and as soon as the freighter departed, I swam over and got quite a shock. Not only had the two-ton, sixteen-foot anchor landed on the site, but the day's gusty weather had caused it to drag, making a trench four feet wide and five feet deep that extended over more than two hundred feet of the site. Scattered over the sea floor for some distance around lay hundreds of artifacts dating from the time of the earthquake, which had been plowed up, while in the trench lay bottles, tin cans, automobile tires, and other modern debris that had fallen into it. It was obvious that disturbance and contamination of the site like this was no unique occurrence, for thousands of ships had anchored on the sunken city over the centuries; and I realized that stratigraphical excavation of the site was not going to be a foolproof method of determining the age or the original locations of objects discovered. However, I was hoping that there might be some sections of the site that had not been disturbed by nature or men. Even though I did not anticipate a success like Pompeii, I knew that there was a great deal to be learned about old Port Royal, and I resolved at the start that my excavation of the site would be done by the best archaeological standards possible.

I never even got into the water during the last week of March, as there was so much that had to be done before we could start the excavation on April 1. After discovering that I was not able to obtain many of the items I needed on credit, I resorted to getting them as donations. Fourteen different firms donated almost two thousand dollars' worth of equipment—everything from the fuel to run our air compressors to the aluminum tubing for the air lifts. Several weeks before, I had made arrangements to rent a large steel barge, but when I went to pick it up and tow it back to Port Royal, the owner announced that he had rented it to someone else for a better price than I had been able to offer to pay. Stan Judge came to my rescue again: he took two days off from his normal job and built me a barge out of wood—measuring twenty by twenty feet—which was kept afloat by attaching sixteen empty 55-gallon fuel drums. I had obtained around a hundred of these drums as donations from the three major petroleum companies on the island—Texaco, Gulf, and Esso—to be used as storage tanks for keeping the artifacts we recovered immersed in fresh water while awaiting preservation. At times during the next two years, when the project was low on funds and I needed diesel fuel for the large air-lift compressor and gasoline for the Aquanaut diving units, these same companies donated the necessary fuel.

Then, the day before the excavation was to begin, new problems developed and I spent a very frustrating and agonizing month before they could all be resolved. Lewis notified me that we could not start the project until my two divers had their contracts approved by the Crown Solicitor, which seemed to me a simple matter that could be done in a day, but which actually took three weeks. During this period I was told that they were not permitted to dive because of legal problems that could arise if they were injured while not under an official employment contract. The irony of the matter was too much: I had been diving daily for four months without a contract—in fact I didn't receive one until I had been working for over a year.

On April 14 I was asked to attend a meeting at the Beach Control Authority office, where I was informed that they would not permit any excavation to take place at Port Royal. A professor in the Zoology Department of the University of the West Indies was opposed to the excavation on the grounds that the sediment we would stir up with our air lift would clog the salt-water intake system of his marine laboratory, which was located next to the old naval hospital. The harbor master had also objected, claiming that the same mud would fill up the nearby shipping channel. After hours of arguing, it was finally agreed that I should spend a week of trial pumping with the air lift to ascertain where the mud and silt went.

Forced to dive alone, I spent a week pumping with the air lift in different areas on the site, with observers present at all times to witness, watching where the light sediment was carried. Fortunately the prevailing southeast trade winds blew every day and the sediment was carried into the middle of the harbor, away from the shipping channel and the marine laboratory. All the observers agreed that the pumping would have no adverse effects on the shipping channel or the marine laboratory, provided that no pumping was done when the winds were anywhere from the west to northeast.

During the last week of the month, when Kelly and Wayne were finally able to dive with me, we had the arduous task of lifting and removing the massive coral heads that dotted the surface of the sea floor in the area we planned to excavate. Fortunately I was able to borrow a barge with a powerful lifting crane from a diving company that was then engaged in laying a pipe line in the harbor. Without the use of that barge, I doubt if we would have been able to complete this job.

I received another shock while this operation was underway. The commandant of the Police Training School, which is located on the western tip of Port Royal, paid me a visit and said that I might be interested in using the lifting barge to pick up six large iron cannon that were in several feet of water off the parade ground of his school. Four years before, while digging the foundation of a building near the parade ground—which now covers the area of Chocolata Hole, the old anchorage for small vessels before the earthquake—the cannon and a large number of artifacts had been found. The cannon, which were in an excellent state of preservation, had been thrown into the sea at the orders of "someone" in the Institute of Jamaica—as the best means to preserve them. This was almost too much to believe: salt water destroys rather than preserves iron objects. Then, to add insult to injury, I was refused permission to raise them by Bernard Lewis, who claimed that they didn't want them raised because they didn't have any room to display them in the Institute. I still had plenty to learn about the Jamaican attitude toward historical artifacts.

Finally the excavation got underway.

Chapter Seven

On May 1, 1966, at seven o'clock in the morning, the dig began. It was one of the most thrilling moments of my life, and the team shared my excitement. The four normally noisy young boys who were to man the barge were as quiet as they would have been in church. Wayne, too, was solemn. Kelly, on the other hand, was exuberant. Seeing that they were all keyed up for the occasion, I warned them not to expect too much, for there was a good chance the area had been completely salvaged. To that, Kelly said he had bet one of his swimming trophies that we would find more artifacts in a month than the Link expedition had found during its entire stay. It was my private opinion that he stood to lose, but I kept it to myself. A good thing I did, too: Kelly collected on that bet before two weeks were up. When we got started, there were only a few curious spectators around offering us words of advice and encouragement, but by the middle of the day a crowd of over two hundred had gathered.

The spot I selected to launch the dig lay under fifteen feet of water about one hundred twenty feet from shore on the southern extremity of the area threatened by the prospective dredging. During the week I spent digging test holes, I had found six complete onion bottles and some other artifacts in this spot, only two feet below the surface of the sea floor, and figured that it was a good spot to begin in. Anticipating poor visibility, I had contrived a device to enable me to plot the locations of any finds in the gloom. It was a 20-by-20-foot frame of aluminum tubing with holes punched in it every foot: working inside the tube and excavating down a foot at a time, I could take bearings by feeling for the holes like a blind man using the Braille system. To ascertain at what depth below the bottom sediment the finds lay, I had a length of aluminum tubing, also with holes, to use as a ruler. The data obtained would be noted on an underwater writing slate and later transferred to a grid chart ashore. With great pride in my powers of invention—the combination of frame and ruler struck me as a brain storm worthy of a Benjamin Franklin at the very least—I turned on the air lift.

In a matter of minutes, after removing only a foot of sediment, we began turning up one artifact after another. I quickly discarded my gloves in order to distinguish what the objects were I was uncovering. Visibility, almost three feet when we started, had dropped to near zero because of the mud and silt washing off the barge into the water. By the end of the first hour we had filled three buckets with clay smoking pipes, ceramic shards, several onion bottles, and various coral-encrusted iron objects. Also, though the three of us below didn't know it yet, we had recovered our first piece of treasure: a small opal gem stone, probably from a ring, that had gone up the air lift and been caught by the screen on the barge. I doubt if the knowledge could have made us any happier. Kelly was doing a sort of war dance, Wayne was all smiles, and as for me, it was all I could do to refrain from turning somersaults.

If the first hour of the dig was profitable, it also had its negative side, exposing a few real problems. The first was the air-lift tube, which jerked and jumped so that holding it was like trying to control a bucking bronco. This didn't worry me unduly, for I knew that attaching lead weights to the bottom of the tube would make it easier to handle (the next day and thereafter I used the weights and had no further trouble). The second was far more serious. I discovered that my carefully contrived system for plotting the major finds was not going to work. As we excavated deeper and deeper into the sediment, the sides of the hole we were making kept collapsing, carrying the artifacts they contained into the deepest part of the hole. With the bottom constantly shifting under us, the ruler was of no use in measuring the depths of the finds, because most of the artifacts had fallen from a higher stratigraphic level. Moreover, the square frame proved something less than infallible; it couldn't be held stationary, because of the nature of the soft sediment, and kept moving about and falling into the hole. After two hours, when we had reached a depth of four feet, I sent it up to the surface.

There was a delay while the surface crew emptied the barge. Shutting off the air lift, I took stock of the situation. Employing my system for stratigraphical digging was clearly out of the question, and some other method had to be developed to plot the location of the important finds, for it was my hope that through consulting the old property deeds of the town I would be able to determine what artifacts came out of what houses. I seriously considered quitting for the day in order to form new strategy before going on. The hole we were digging was now twelve feet in diameter, and further excavation was bound to increase the problem.

Then, all of a sudden, I made a discovery on the edge of the hole that drove all thoughts of stopping work out of my mind: part of a wall. Since I had every expectation of finding a standing house in this area of the site, I could barely control my impatience until the barge was back in position. During the mapping operation of the area I had struck a solid object with my probe rod in this spot but didn't attempt to identify it because I had located several large coral heads in the surrounding area and had assumed that it was just another one. Only minutes after turning on the air lift, I realized that this was no standing building but a fallen wall. A disappointment, but I didn't let it discourage me. If the wall had fallen during the disaster, there was a good chance of finding some valuables under it: the early salvors might not have been inclined to lift a wall when there were so many other things to be found in standing homes or strewn about on the sea floor.

An hour of excavating revealed that the wall consisted of a single layer of bricks, measuring eleven and a half feet long and eight feet wide, lying level only six inches below the surface of the sediment. Eager to see whether my hope of finding artifacts underneath the wall would be fulfilled, I didn't take the time to disassemble the wall, but began excavating along the sides of it. Sediment and various objects lying under the wall began dropping into the hole I was making. Almost at once I found a pewter spoon; minutes later, another. I moved farther along the wall, and out from under it came a pewter charger (a large, round platter for serving food) with four pewter plates stacked on it so neatly that the pile might just have come out of a good housewife's cupboard. I had called the turn accurately; the fallen wall was a good source of artifacts. How accurately, I had yet to learn, for as it turned out, almost every valuable artifact we recovered was located under a wall.

When I had excavated a trench along most of one side, I discovered by touch that the wall was tilting down over the hollow, and realized that there was great danger of the wall's falling on us at any moment. Turning off the air lift, I took Kelly and Wayne up to the surface for a consultation and to have a better look at our finds. The sensible thing to do, of course, was to take the wall apart before excavating any further, but we were all too eager for further discoveries to accept this solution. Instead, I set up emergency procedures. I instructed Wayne to remain on the surface: in the event that the wall fell and trapped Kelly and me, there had to be a diver available to extricate us. As another precaution, I arranged a series of signals to cover any contingency that I could send by turning the air lift off and on. In this underwater Morse code system, turning the air lift off and on quickly three times meant we needed help; turning it off and on, waiting fifteen seconds, and turning it off and on again alerted the boys on the barge that something good had slipped through the screen on the bottom of the tube and they should grab it.

Descending again, I moved the air lift to the opposite side of the wall that I had been working and began pumping away sediment so that the wall would lie flat again. While I was at it, Kelly, anxious to make a find of his own, crawled under the tilted side of the wall to see if anything else was there. After a while I missed his presence at my side and began to wonder where he was—visibility was then only a few inches. Shutting off the air lift, I circled the wall and located a pair of legs sticking out from under the wall. I was furious but calmed down considerably upon seeing what he brought out: a pewter tankard and a pewter porringer. By pressing our face masks together we could talk underwater to one another, and I made him promise not to take such a risk again. We were both admiring his finds when we felt a tug on our air hoses, the signal to come up. Wayne, relegated to the surface and away from where the action was, had become conscious of his stomach. Small wonder, for we had been down on the bottom for nine hours, and in the excitement no one had noticed how much time had passed. Once out of the water, Kelly and I both felt cold from our long submersion, despite the protection of our rubber diving suits. I decided to end operations, satisfied that we had done a good day's work.

The boys on the barge were even colder than we were, for they had spent the day under a constant shower of the muddy water flying out of the air-lift tube and a brisk wind kept them chilled to the bone. Worse still, they all complained of headaches resulting from the gravel and other objects raining down on their heads while they grabbed objects off the screen. Both problems were easily resolved the next day by supplying them with seamen's rain gear and aluminum construction helmets. The last item became a status symbol for them and they wore their helmets even when not at work on the barge. We divers also had a complaint: when the boys refilled the Aquanaut breathing units' fuel tanks each hour, they accidentally spilled some gasoline each time and the fumes from it were sucked into the air intake of the unit and pumped down into our masks. It gave us a nauseous feeling for a few minutes and one time caused both Kelly and me to vomit—when a wave rocked the skiff, causing the boy to spill a larger amount of gasoline. This problem was also easy to overcome. After determining the exact amount of fuel the unit used each hour, we used rum bottles filled with just the right amount, which were easier to handle than a large fuel can.

I still had to figure out a new way to plot the position and depth below the sea floor of the major artifacts found. To plot the position, I decided to place buoys in a square around the area of each day's dig, recording their location on a sectional chart by taking compass bearings from my shore markers. That left the problem of determining the stratigraphical depth, and I was going around in circles over it when my wife came up with the solution. She suggested painting a scale of feet and inches on the top of the air-lift tube, which protruded above the surface of the water and was attached to the barge. Since we knew the depth of water we were working in and the length of the tube, which was always kept vertical when in use, the surface team could easily determine the depth below the sea floor we were excavating. Then and there I made myself a solemn promise never to underestimate the ingenuity of women. The complete procedure I worked out was that each time we recovered an important artifact or noted a high concentration of common ones (we made no effort to record the precise position of every single pipestem and ceramic shard) we would signal the surface team through my Morse code method to note the depth and position in relation to the four buoys; then one of us would take the item up to the skiff attendant to be tagged and recorded, and with this information I would later plot the find on a sectional chart. The same method was used for plotting walls after they had been measured on the bottom. This new system was much sounder than my original one, and indeed it worked very well in practice. There remained one major problem: when the sides of the hole we were excavating collapsed, which couldn't be avoided because of the nature of the sediment, artifacts fell out of the sediment and slid into the bottom of the hole, so it was impossible to determine their original position or depth. There was no real solution for this except to keep our eyes open for falling sediment and note its landing place—provided, of course, that we could see anything, which wasn't too often.

Before excavating any further, I decided that our first task on the second day was to disassemble the wall. I planned to finish pumping enough sediment to get the wall flat again, a job I had left half done when we quit the day before. Then, while Wayne and Kelly broke the wall apart and raised the bricks, I intended to excavate in another area. The plan pleased Wayne, who preferred any underwater activity to sitting on the barge, but Kelly was a little disappointed, having envisioned a more adventurous morning. I assured him that there would be plenty of excitement later. Although I knew his promise to avoid taking risks with the wall was sincere, I was afraid his enthusiasm would get the better of his good intentions and thought it wiser to eliminate the temptation.

As it turned out, it wasn't Kelly whose enthusiasm led him to take a risk that proved almost fatal; it was my own. Pumping away the sediment to level the wall, I very soon came upon a cluster of four pewter spoons, and it was enough to make me throw caution to the winds. I began pumping deeper than I should have in one spot. Before I knew what hit me, the wall slid over on top of me, pinning my head and torso to the bottom. Luckily for me, it didn't break my air hose. Instead it broke the air-lift tube in two, and the boys on the surface immediately realized that something had happened. One of them pulled Kelly's air hose to bring him to the surface, and told him to check on me. Although he and Wayne had been only a few feet away from me, digging in the sediment with their hands, they had seen nothing of what happened. By groping around the edges of the wall, Kelly located my legs just as I had located his the day before and tugged at my left ankle to let me know he was there. Then he disconnected the air hose from the broken air-lift tube and, using it as an air jet, began blowing away the sediment under my body. It was a risky maneuver: there was every chance in the world that the wall would slide even farther, trapping him as well as me, and in the ten minutes or so I lay there I was torn between admiring his courage and condemning his foolhardiness. Admiration won out when I felt myself being pulled out from under the wall.

I surfaced to catch my breath and think things over, while the boys attached another air-lift tube to the air hose. I had really learned a lesson and made up my mind that it would be sheer folly to try excavating around a wall before it had been disassembled. Entering the water again, I set Kelly and Wayne to breaking the wall apart with crowbars, removing the bricks from the highest side first so there would be no danger of the wall sliding over them. Meanwhile I began excavating a new hole about twenty feet away and soon uncovered a seventeen-foot wooden beam. It proved to be a roof beam with rectangular squares cut in it to support crossbeams. Nearby were two similar beams and hundreds of black slate roof tiles scattered over the area. My first thought was that the remains of the house they belonged to would be found below, but strenuous work with the air lift failed to turn anything up. I concluded that the wall and the roof beams were probably parts of the same house.

While I was excavating this area, the second accident of the day occurred. The four boys on the barge had thus far had no trouble keeping it level, for the first few feet of bottom sediment going up the air-lift tube consisted mainly of mud, which was washed over the sides of the barge and carried away by currents. Now that I was penetrating deeper, what went up the tube at a rapid pace was heavy black sand and gravel. Unknown to me as I happily ran the air lift for all it was worth, two of the boys had swum ashore for lunch, and the remaining two couldn't cope with the large quantity of sand pouring onto the barge. Rather than alerting me to the situation so I could cut down the pressure in the air lift, they chose to be heroes, working like demons to distribute the sand evenly, but without success. The barge overturned, deluging us with sand and gravel, but fortunately both boys managed to jump clear in time and weren't hurt. All artifacts on the barge had been transferred to the skiff only a few minutes earlier, so the only consequence of the mishap was the time lost in pumping the sand back onto the barge. To prevent this happening again, I hired another boy the following day and made a rule that only one could go to lunch at a time, always leaving four on the barge.

The day ended on a happy note: Shortly before we had to call it quits for the day, a circular object got caught on the screen at the bottom of the air lift, so I cut off the air lift and the object dropped into my hand. It was a silver Spanish piece of eight—treasure, by anybody's definition. I grinned from ear to ear. Kelly, eager to see what had caused such jubilation, snatched the coin from my hand, then gave me a handshake that almost paralyzed my arm.

I had determined from the start that, because of the danger the site was in from the planned dredging operation, we would work a seven-day week. On weekends my wife, Nancy, and Stan and Louise Judge did a lot of diving when they weren't busy in the laboratory piecing pottery together, making drawings, etc.

After the first few days a daily routine was established, which I tried to keep to throughout the excavation. I would wake up at five-thirty and pick up Kelly and Wayne, who also lived in Kingston, at six and drive to Port Royal, which took about half an hour. While either Kelly or Wayne rounded up the boys who worked on the barge and skiff—not always an easy task and sometimes they had to yank them out of bed—I would place the four buoys in a square around the area we would excavate that day and plot their positions on a chart while the other diver refueled and started our air-lift compressor. Then followed a daily event that I was against but powerless to do anything about: everyone on my team with the exception of Kelly and myself would smoke one or two marijuana cigarettes, claiming it gave them the needed strength and energy to carry out the day's work. The use of marijuana, or "ganja," as it is called on Jamaica, was and still is quite common, and although there are laws against its use, I never heard of anyone being arrested for smoking it. In fact, when a police instructor at the training academy heard that I had a bad cold, he sent me a small bag of ganja with a note instructing me to boil it in water and drink the tea—which actually cured my cold.

Usually between seven and seven-thirty we were underway each morning and continued working, without stopping for a lunch break, until four or five in the afternoon. Sometimes when we were in a good area and making many interesting finds, we would work as late as seven in the evening. Sometimes we would take a brief rest during the periods when the boys were emptying the barge, but generally we used this time to scour the area for any artifacts that might have been overlooked during the air lifting, to move large coral heads out of the way, and to measure and disassemble any brick walls we had uncovered. Since I generally ran the air lift I had to wear more weights than the other divers—forty or fifty pounds, which helped hold me stationary on the bottom and enabled me to better control the bucking air lift—and the only way I could get to the surface was by crawling up the air-lift tube. In an emergency I could quickly drop the weights, which were on belts around my waist, and ascend rapidly. We found that after spending long hours on the bottom in almost total darkness, the sunlight on the surface hurt our eyes, so we rarely went to the surface unless it was absolutely necessary. As soon as we did surface, one of the boys on the barge would give us a pair of dark sunglasses to wear until our eyes got acclimatized to the bright light. Wayne, who usually had the task of taking artifacts and bricks to the surface, wore a face mask with tinted glass on it.

Though we worked long hours on the bottom, the time sped by, because there was always something happening down there. Poor visibility was by far our most serious handicap, and we soon developed the sensitive touch of the partially blind and did almost everything by feel. Before long I was able to identify everything we uncovered by touch alone—even to the point of distinguishing an old piece of glass or pottery from modern ones. To ascertain that the boys on the barge weren't sleeping on the job and overlooking small artifacts landing on the screen, sometimes I would carry small replica coins hidden in my rubber suit and send them up the air lift—checking at the end of the day to see if they had found them.

At the end of each day's excavation there was still plenty of work to be done ashore. All the diving equipment and the day's find had to be hosed down in fresh water and necessary repairs made to anything that might have been damaged. Then everyone usually helped me separate the finds: clay pipes placed in one pile, iron artifacts in another, ceramic shards in another, and so on. After a photographic record was made of the finds, they were then catalogued and stored in fresh water until they could be given preservation treatment—some of which I did in the laboratory, but a great deal of which I did at home in the evenings with the help of Stan Judge.

Generally I didn't get home until seven or eight in the evenings and was so tired that I seldom participated in the social life on the island—for I still had notes to write up each evening on the day's dig. My eating habits, like those of Kelly and Wayne, were also strange. We felt that eating breakfast or even lunch made our stomachs upset while diving, so we generally ate only one huge meal after returning hime in the evening. And I do mean a huge meal: sometimes I would knock off a three-pound steak at a sitting.

The rest of the month went much as the first and second days had gone, except that our workdays were free from accidents. By the end of May our hole measured thirty by forty feet. To be thorough, we excavated to a depth of fifteen feet, even though we never uncovered any artifacts below nine feet and most were found higher. Of the thousands of artifacts recovered, the most valuable were those made of pewter. The month's total of pewter ware amounted to three chargers, twelve plates, six spoons, one fork, one tankard, one porringer, and two shoe buckles. Of special interest to me were items I had not expected to find after the passage of almost three centuries, among them many leather objects, a few swatches of cloth, and several pieces of rope. The most remarkable find of all was a complete tobacco leaf, in a remarkable state of preservation because the wall it lay under had pressed it deeply into the mud, which had protected it.

As our excavation progressed, I became convinced that we were working on the site of a private home. During the month, we located six walls of similar construction, along with seven roof beams and about four thousand loose bricks. What I was curious to know was whose house we were excavating in, and for a while the identity of the owner remained a mystery. During the first week of excavation I had several clues to his identity. One was Kelly's pewter tankard, which had a French word, "L'Lavoscat," engraved on the handle. However, the documents I consulted did not reveal ownership of property in Port Royal by anyone of that name. The owner of the tankard might have been a visitor, or the person who possessed it at the time of the earthquake might not have been the original owner —a good possibility, considering how property was obtained and how quickly it changed hands in old Port Royal. Or the word might have been an archaic spelling of the French word l'avocat and thus have denoted the owner's profession, that of lawyer or advocate.

A better clue was provided by other pewter ware found under the same wall: two plates, one fork, and two spoons bearing the letter C and underneath it the letters I and R. From the position of the letters, I deduced that C was the initial of the owner's surname, and the other letters the initials of the given names of husband and wife. Consulting the property records of old Port Royal, I found that many landowners had surnames beginning with C, but only a few had first names beginning with R. The one who owned property closest to the area we were working in was a Richard Collins; his house originally stood only two hundred feet east of the spot where we discovered the pewter ware. Further excavation, which turned up known landmarks and enabled me to pinpoint the part of the sunken city we were working on, left little doubt in my mind that we were on the site of Richard Collins' house. To establish the point beyond dispute, thereby providing a tidy solution to the mystery, it would be gratifying to be able to report that Richard Collins had a wife named Isabelle or Irene. Unfortunately, nothing is known about his wife, or for that matter, about the man himself, other than that he owned property. However, I believe I have made an interesting discovery about him: that he either owned a tavern or rented part of his land to someone who did. In the area around the house we found great quantities of broken wineglasses, slip-ware and stone-ware tavern mugs, two hundred onion bottles, and more than five hundred clay smoking pipes. The glasses and mugs might have belonged to a private dwelling, and it is not beyond the realm of possibility that one house might have contained so many onion bottles, though they are far more likely to have been in a store or tavern. The clay pipes are a different matter entirely. At first I thought they might have come from a store, but more than a hundred of them bore makers' marks, and these were of sixty-six different makers. It is unlikely that any store of the period would have been selling so many different kinds of pipe. Moreover, most of them showed signs of having been smoked. Knowing from contemporary accounts that it was customary for men to own several pipes (they had to be allowed to cool after each smoking, otherwise they cracked) and to leave pipes at their favorite places of diversion, I formed the tavern theory. The location of Richard Collins' property bore it out: his land lay very near the anchorage of the trading sloops, and men with throats parched from a sea voyage would undoubtedly have made a beeline for any tavern that stood nearby.

JUNE

To get the month off to a good start and to make sure that none of us collapsed from fatigue, I drew up a new work schedule, limiting diving to six hours a day, six days a week. During May all of us had been under water an average of seven and a half hours a day, seven days a week. It was an insane pace, dictated by our enthusiasm, and I knew it was only a matter of time before it caught up with us: we had already lost about ten pounds each. Although I managed to keep Kelly and Wayne on the six-day-a-week schedule, only a few weeks went by before I found it necessary to spend my Sundays diving again; there were always huge piles of bricks that had to be raised, large coral heads to move, and thousands of sea urchins to crush.

Despite the soundness of my strategy, June did not get off to a good start, for nature did not go out of its way to co-operate with us. Time and time again our work was slowed down by exceptionally heavy rains, which made it impossible for the boys on the barge to work. Down below we had problems as well: the swollen rivers deposited great quantities of mud into our hole, so that we had to spend an hour each morning removing the overnight accumulation before we could resume our dig. By the third week of the month things were even worse. During May we had lost only a small amount of working time because of contrary winds that would cause our sediment to be washed toward the marine laboratory and shipping channel. Now the winds were blowing from the north when we arrived each morning and continued in that direction until around noon each day, when the southeast trades would start blowing. Consequently, during the mornings we were unable to use the air lift and had to excavate by hand, which isn't one twentieth as productive as using the air lift. Before the heavy rains, about one to two feet of sediment collected in our hole overnight; but with the north wind, as much as four to five feet accumulated —all of which had to be removed before we started digging in a new area. During the month, of the 215 hours I spent under water, only ninety-six of them were utilized in excavating new terrain.

Around the middle of the month, nature provided us with an unexpected phenomenon—a minor seismic upheaval. I was down on the bottom and Kelly was nearby loading bricks into the buckets when I felt the bottom move under me. Thinking at first it was simply the vibrations of the air lift, I paid no attention. Then I felt a stronger movement and headed for the surface, where I found Kelly already up, gazing toward the west. We climbed aboard the skiff just in time to observe a tidal wave two feet high, extending over the water as far as our lateral vision could see, coming toward us at a rate of about twenty knots. It was too small to do any damage to our skiff and barge, and the two others that followed were only about six inches high. A few days later there was another minor upheaval, virtually the twin of its predecessor. Even though they disrupted our routine, they fascinated me; I felt I had passed the tremor test to become a true denizen of Port Royal.

During the month, we also had problems with sharks. Both before and after June we seldom saw them; perhaps the noise of the air lift kept them away or perhaps they were always around and the dirty water prevented us from seeing them. Actually we couldn't really see them this month either, but we knew they were around by the presence of many remora fish in the vicinity, which kept attaching themselves to us. The remora, or suckerfish, attach themselves to sharks or other large creatures by means of suction discs on their heads, getting free rides, and dining on the scraps dropped by their hosts. The boys on the barge, watching for fins cutting the surface of the water, would tap a signal on the air-lift tube to alert us when sharks were near. This warning system proved far from foolproof, for visibility was so poor that we never knew sharks were upon us until they were breathing down our necks. Once Kelly bumped into one as he was surfacing with a bucket of artifacts. Another time I felt something nudging my back, and thinking it was Kelly bracing himself against what he took to be the side of the hole, I reached out a hand to push him away, only to touch something that had the texture of sandpaper. I turned to find myself looking doom in the eye: the shark was only a foot away. Possibly I scared it more than it scared me, or perhaps my rubber suit and glass face mask didn't make me a very appetizing morsel. In any case, the shark quickly disappeared. At least twenty times while swimming above us, sharks snared our air hoses with their fins and tails and we were either jerked off the bottom until they broke free, or our air hoses were ripped off our face masks, leaving us without air.

A day on which I could see a shark a foot away was a day of good underwater visibility. Most of the time we worked in total darkness, which led to a number of accidents. Frequently our hands suffered lacerations from sharp objects caught in the air-lift screen, or from sea urchins. Kelly and I each touched a poisonous scorpion fish, and for a few days were barely able to move our arms because of pain. More serious were the frequent cave-ins while on the bottom of the hole. Each morning before starting to excavate we made an inspection tour of the hole for any large objects that might fall out of the sides during the day's work and tied them to plastic lifting bags—parachutes in reverse—filled with air, which carried them to the surface, where they were then dropped in safer areas. Because of the poor visibility and because many large items were hidden in the sediment, we occasionally missed a few. The first time, a coral head six feet in diameter fell across Kelly's knees, but he was able to roll it off, suffering only a few bruises. The second encounter was with a coral head twice the size of the first; it missed striking me but landed on my air hose, cutting off my air supply. Quickly ripping off my face mask and discarding my weight belt, I surfaced with nothing worse than a momentary scare.

The most serious accident of all, with consequences felt on the project for months, had nothing to do with underwater visibility but stemmed solely from Wayne's determination not to miss out on anything. From the start, he had minor sinus-congestion problems; then, early in the month, came down with the flu but refused to admit he was sick. On one dive he found his eustachian tubes were so congested that he was unable to clear his ears, but he went down anyway and within minutes his face mask was full of blood. He had ruptured both eardrums, and it was months before he could dive again. During the month I hired six different men to replace him as a diver, but none of them lasted a full day before quitting, claiming that the work was either too dangerous or too rugged—or both.

At times I began to wonder if the old inhabitants hadn't placed a curse on Port Royal, for it seemed that there was no end to the problems that kept cropping up almost daily. Early in the month the harbor master tried to force me to move from the area we were excavating, claiming that it interfered with the movements of the Port Royal ferryboat, which loaded and unloaded passengers at the sea wall near where we were working, but I refused to do so and the matter was dropped. Although we flew the "divers' flag" to warn that divers were below and everyone should stay at least one hundred feet away, small boats were constantly passing overhead, and on two occasions our air hoses were cut. Finally the Beach Control Authority passed a law forbidding boats from coming closer than four hundred feet from the shore—well out of the area we were working.

Ever since our project began, it had received a great deal of publicity, and the people of Port Royal felt that their town was being reborn again. The publicity also brought many spectators to witness the operation, and not all of them were good people. One morning we discovered that someone had drained all the oil from our large compressor, and several hours were lost before we could replace it. Fearing that thefts of artifacts or our diving equipment might take place, I decided to hire a full-time watchman who could live right in the old hospital. After inquiring around as to who was the meanest and toughest man in Port Royal, I ended up employing a large fisherman who was known as Ivan the Terrible, so feared that only a few words from him would send any unwanted visitors scurrying off the premises.

Despite the weather, the sharks, the accidents, and the various problems, we accomplished a great deal in June. We found numerous fallen walls and brought them to the surface brick by brick, in the hope that eventually they would be used to build a museum to house the artifacts we were bringing up. Seaga had been really impressed by our work and was trying to raise funds to build a museum, which would be constructed to resemble one of the buildings of old Port Royal. I attempted several times to bring up large sections of walls intact in order to study the masonry methods of the period. However, I was never able to recover a section of any appreciable size: the mortar—a mixture of lime, molasses, water, and horsehair—kept crumbling.

The walls continued to be a valuable source of artifacts, and after removing them we found a large number of pieces of pewter ware, as well as two silver spoon handles engraved with the Tudor rose. Kelly soon became wall-happy and repeatedly urged me to abandon my systematic excavation and concentrate on hunting for walls. No amount of explaining that we had to enlarge the hole inch by inch could shake his new obsession. Luckily we recovered enough artifacts from areas that had no walls to keep him quiet most of the time. We found, among other things, ceramic plates, bowls, and cups; copper and brass candlesticks, buttons, buckles from shoes, belts, hats, nails, spikes, ships' fittings, and a food strainer; lead bottle stoppers and two official seals made of lead; iron hammers, saw blades, axes, adzes, padlocks, keys, knives, swords, pike points, cooking caldrons, and a frying pan; and various artifacts of glass, bone, horn, wood, and leather. Most fascinating to me were some items recovered from a particularly barren area: two small glass marbles, a piece of white chalk, a piece of graphite shaped like a flat, wide pencil (it wrote on paper when I tested it), and a fragment of black slate with the numbers 6, 8, 10, and 12 marked on it. Did some schoolboy, terrified when he saw the earth open up, drop them as he raced to take cover?

The vast quantity of artifacts we were recovering soon threatened to crowd us out of our room in the naval hospital. This was resolved by the simple expedient of taking over three more rooms. The real problem was preserving all the artifacts. Those of ceramic, bone, and glass (except for the onion bottles) gave us no trouble; the only treatment they required was a prolonged bath in fresh water to free them of sea salts. Copper, brass, and lead received the same treatment, then were rubbed with very fine steel wool to remove the green patina that covered them.

The major problems were created by the pewter, the silver,

the thousands of iron objects, the wood, and the onion bottles. Wood, which would normally shrink to less than a quarter of its original size if exposed to air, had to be impregnated with a special wax to preserve it and to prevent shrinkage, but a large oven and other sophisticated equipment were required, and the best we could do was to keep the wood immersed in water for the time being. The iron objects and onion bottles met the same fate for the time being as the wood objects, for we didn't have the necessary elaborate equipment required for their preservation.

The most valuable artifacts we recovered during the first two months were those of pewter and silver; items of historical importance, for many of them bore marks that helped identify the owners of the buildings in which we were excavating. At this time very little was known about cleaning and preserving either of these two metals. Fortunately an authority on pewter then resided in Jamaica—Mr. Lewis Purnell, Deputy Chief of Mission at the American Embassy. Excited as a boy over his first bicycle when he saw our collection of pewter and silver artifacts, he quickly offered his services. Together we spent evening after evening in the makeshift laboratory in the hospital, experimenting with small fragments of both metals until he was satisfied he had found the best way to treat them. Later he set up a small laboratory at home so he could spend every free minute on this project. For the pewter, he devised a method whereby the artifacts were placed in a mild acid bath to remove the coral growth. Next, to remove traces of corrosion they were placed for a few minutes in either a bath of boiling water and caustic soda or an electrolytic bath. Sometimes the pewter had to be subjected to alternate baths of acid and caustic soda to achieve the desired results. Then came the most time-consuming part of the operation, which consisted of rubbing the artifacts with fine steel wool and jewelers' rouge—a spoon sometimes requiring six hours of rubbing, a large charger as many as thirty. The silver items were treated in the same way, except that only electrolytic baths could be used and not caustic soda. The outcome was that most of the pewter and silver artifacts emerged looking as good as on the day they left the hands of their craftsmen.

JULY

The third month started off with a great deal of excitement that had nothing to do with our work. On July 2 the Kingston *Daily Gleaner* ran an article entitled "Ganja Threat to Old Port Royal":

Ganja smoking is the new fever which has hit Port Royal. The weed is on sale more or less openly in the old Naval Hospital and the heavy flow of ganja has been introduced into the town by fishermen from Kingston who now occupy the old Naval Hospital premises. Many a night ganja smoking sessions have ended in fights and sometimes knives are brought into action. There is fear among the citizens that something serious will happen if this state of affairs is allowed to continue. Visitors and citizens alike have to pass through the old Naval Hospital premises because the Port Royal-Kingston ferry docks there, but now many persons fear to do so. Everyone is hoping that the authorities concerned will take steps to get the herbalists out of the premises.

The following morning, while we were preparing for the day's work, a contingent of nearly fifty soldiers and policemen suddenly appeared and began ordering all the squatters to take their possessions and vacate the premises. Most of the squatters had become my friends and I hated seeing them kicked out of the only homes they had, so I tried to intervene in their behalf with the officers in charge, but they had their orders and they carried them out. One old woman, who claimed to be over one hundred years old, had lived in the operating room of the hospital for more than fifty years, and I did convince the authorities to let her remain until I could find her a place to live. A few days later the matter was forgotten and almost every one of the squatters moved back on the premises. Ganja continued to be smoked and sold openly.

A week later I had still another surprise. While on the bottom one morning, a strange diver appeared and tapped me on the shoulder. I surfaced to find a group of about forty American divers from the Chicago area either in the water or preparing to enter, and the leader of the group showed me a letter he had received from the Jamaican Tourist Board inviting the club to dive at Port Royal. Naturally I was upset, but so were the divers, who had spent money to come down to dive on the sunken city. Things worked out for the best on their own. While I was phoning the Tourist Board director for an explanation, all the visiting divers went into the water, but after only a few minutes of seeing how dirty it was, they were back ashore and griping about the poor visibility. Within an hour they were gone and I never saw them again: apparently Port Royal diving didn't appeal to them.

Rain and dirty water continued to plague us for the first half of the month. Wayne, unable to dive, was limited to supervising operations on the surface, and Kelly and I bore the full load of the underwater work. Luckily we stayed healthy except for the usual cuts and bruises. For three days I had to stay out of the water with an ear infection, but losing three days was getting off lightly, considering that the harbor water is foul enough to keep anybody's ears constantly infected. Our large air-lift compressor broke down and was out of action for eight days, and we were still losing a few hours each morning because of north winds. In the past we had excavated by hand when we were unable to air lift, but I came up with a better solution to the problem. We used the air hose from the air-lift compressor as an air jet to excavate, just as a water jet operates. Although it was not as effective an excavation tool as the air lift, it was much more effective than working by hand, and very little sediment was carried into the prohibited areas. We actually found more artifacts this month than during both of the two previous months.

July was also notable for presenting us with a mystery, which I eventually solved. During the first three weeks we excavated an area roughly fifty by fifty feet in which we failed to come upon a single wall (needless to say, Kelly's disappointment was acute) and found neither pewter nor silver. What we did find were thousands of artifacts that had come from a ship. The majority were of iron—nails, spikes, tacks, cannon balls, calking tools, and a large variety of ships' fittings. We also found brass calking tools, ships' fittings, nails, and spikes; copper wire and copper sheathing; pieces of pitch, wax, rope, and canvas; more than thirty lignum-vitae sheaves (parts of the blocks used for hauling in lines); and a lead sounding weight and two lead draught markers (Roman numerals placed on the bows and sterns of ships to show how deep they were in the water). The draught markers, Roman numerals VII and IX (or XI), indicated that the ship they belonged to had to be a large vessel, for a sloop would draw no more than four or five feet.

I was greatly puzzled. All the evidence pointed to a shipwreck, but where was it? As a rule, no matter what the age or origin of an old shipwreck that carried the type of items we had recovered, it always carried ballast—but strangely we found not a single ballast rock. For a while I thought that the artifacts might have come from a ships' chandlery, but this theory would not hold water. All the wooden sheaves and most of the metal artifacts were marked with the English broad arrow, proof that they were Crown property. For many years before and after the earthquake all items carried on English ships of war, from cannon down to pots and pans, carried this mark of ownership. I ruled out the possibility that the artifacts came from a ships' chandlery, for no shop would have been permitted to sell Crown property.

It was a mystery all right, and it remained one until the fourth week. Then, finished with operations on one square of our grid chart, we set out buoys for the adjoining square and began excavating. Almost at once we discovered one end of a shipwreck lying about six feet under the surface of the sea floor. Further excavation revealed that only the keel, ribs, and part of the lower deck remained of the ship. Atop the lower deck we found a large brick wall, and directly underneath the keel was a wall of similar construction that appeared to be part of the same building. Artifacts found under and around the wreck, many of them duplicates of those we had uncovered the preceding three weeks, clearly belonged to it.

Now the detective work began, to identify her. From the size of her surviving timbers I knew that she was a ship of at least 250 tons, and her construction indicated a warship rather than a merchant ship, a conclusion borne out by the great size of the cannon found near the wreck. The English broad-arrow markings clearly pointed toward her being an English warship, and the walls and artifacts found above and below the wreck indicated that she had been lost during the earthquake. Contemporary accounts revealed that there was only one English warship lost during the earthquake—H.M.S. *Swan*. Now what had seemed the most baffling thing about the wreck, the absence of ballast, became the most important piece of evidence for establishing the ship's identity. All of her ballast had been removed so she could be careened and had not been replaced, as she was lost during the earthquake.

The complete story of how the *Swan* actually met her end was not easy to piece together, for at first glance contemporary accounts seem to contradict one another. While all agree that she was flung amid the ruins of the town by the tidal wave, some state she was totally lost and others declare she merely lost her guns. After extensive correspondence with the British Admiralty, I was able to learn the history of the *Swan*, from the time of her construction to the time she was lost, and what I learned proved conclusively that we had found her.

Constructed in 1673, she measured seventy-four feet in length (which tallied with our measurement of her keel), had a beam of twenty-five feet, weighed 305 tons, and drew ten feet of water. She was originally built as a fire ship, but in 1688 she was converted to be a warship of thirty-two guns, and the following year she was sent to Jamaica, where she shared duties with her sister frigate H.M.S. *Guernsey*. As we know, she was being careened at the time of the earthquake; the job must have been completed when the upheaval occurred, for her guns were back in place. Probably she was waiting for fresh ballast rocks to be brought from the nearby hills before joining the *Guernsey* in the crucial task of routing the French invaders from the north coast. Without her ballast—at least one hundred tons for a ship of her size—she was relatively light in the water, and this is the reason the tidal wave threw her so far from her original position. She landed upright atop some buildings, and the force of the collision was great enough to dislodge almost everything above the water line; masts, rigging, and cannon were thrown farther to the southwest. The great weight of the cannon caused them to sink deep in the soft sediment almost at once, and thus the contemporary accounts stating that the *Swan* lost all her guns are correct. Yet the conflicting accounts, stating that she was totally lost, are also correct. Although she did not disappear beneath the sea immediately (the more than two hundred people who survived by clinging to her had reasons to be grateful for that), because she was resting on top of several buildings, her keel was broken in several places and she was deemed beyond salvaging. As a useless derelict, she was left to rot away: her wooden hull fell prey to teredos (a type of marine worm similar to land termites in that they subsist on wood), and gradually all traces of her disappeared beneath the sediment of the sea floor.

By this time we had also uncovered a substantial amount of information indicating that this section of the town had been violently thrown into the sea, rather than sliding in gently, as I had first thought. We had found one half of a pewter spoon six feet deep in the sediment and then two months later found the other half of the spoon ninety-five feet away under a fallen wall. During the first week of excavation we found a few shards of a large Dutch bellarmine jug and it took us three months to find all the pieces to reconstruct it; some of them were as much as one hundred feet away from where we had found the first pieces. On another occasion, more than a year passed before I discovered the second half of a beautiful delftware plate, which lay four hundred feet from where the first half was discovered. There is also the possibility that, like the *Swan*, many items could have been broken and carried some distance by the tidal wave.

AUGUST

The new month began with warnings of a hurricane approaching the island, and I was torn between stopping the operation and towing the barge to a safe haven, and neglecting to take any precautions and hoping that the storm might change course. I decided to take the risk, and fortunately the hurricane veered away and we suffered only several days of heavy rains from it. We were still excavating the forward section of the wreck and making a lot of progress despite the presence of several visitors on the site. One was almost an old friend, one we had come to know well: a beautiful bat ray six feet wide. Since we had begun working in the area, we had seen it leap out of the water and land with a splash at ten-minute intervals for several hours every day around midday. The local fishermen told us that it had been there, playfully jumping and splashing daily, for more than five years. Although it was jumping about quite close to where we were working, we never saw it underwater, probably because of the poor visibility. We didn't mind having it around, for it had squatter's rights to the site and clearly meant no harm.

Another visitor was not so welcome: a manta ray more than twelve feet wide. Manta rays, also called devilfish, are a forbidding sight, mainly because of their enormous mouths (one twelve feet wide normally has a mouth at least three feet wide), which contain, in place of teeth, long filaments to filter the plankton they eat from the sea water. Like bat rays, they mean no harm and are fond of jumping. However, they can be dangerous, for they grow as large as twenty feet wide, and their playful leaps have carried them onto the decks of boats and their great weight has occasionally killed people who happened to be under them when they landed. Our particular manta ray demonstrated a desire to play with Kelly, and nudged him one day when he was surfacing with a bucket of artifacts. Before Kelly knew what was happening, his new friend had embraced him with its wings. I knew nothing of the drama, since I was busy with the air lift at the bottom, but the boys on the barge were so panic-stricken that they jumped overboard and swam for shore. Kelly, keeping his head as usual, did nothing to antagonize his captor. He remained perfectly still until the manta ray, probably deciding that Kelly wasn't much fun as a playmate, unfolded its wings and swam away.

On the first Sunday of the month a thing I had almost given up hope for finally occurred. After spending several hours with volunteer assistants preserving artifacts, I decided to take a swim. Plunging into the sea, I opened my eyes underwater and was astonished to find I could see objects a considerable distance away—even without a face mask. It was the day I had been anticipating for months, one with water clear enough to permit underwater photography. Everyone quickly donned diving gear, I grabbed my camera, and we swam out to the *Swan*. Visibility was about twenty feet; it seemed like a miracle. I took a number of shots of my wife working around the wreck, the most interesting ones showing her discovering a human jawbone and silver plate, which she found under a section of the keel. Then, out of film, I had to race all the way to Kingston for more. When I returned, I found the tide had changed and visibility was back to normal, or about two feet. From then on I kept enough film on hand to stock a camera shop—hoping that the miracle might occur again.

The next two weeks were really rugged: Wayne, who was still unable to dive, took two weeks of sick leave; and Kelly, who was like my right arm, was selected to serve as a swimming official for the Eighth British Commonwealth Games, which Jamaica was hosting. Trying to do a job that really required three men was a real challenge, but I had no other choice; the representatives of the Port Royal Company of Merchants had already submitted numerous complaints to Seaga since we started the excavation, claiming that I was deliberately trying to hold up their development plans by working at a slow pace. This was ludicrous, for I had been working at the pace of a madman. I couldn't carry the artifacts or bricks to the surface while air lifting, so this was done during the times when the boys were emptying the barge.

Some of the original boys I had hired at the start of the excavation had quit for various reasons, but I had no difficulty replacing them, for everyone was anxious to work for "the slave driver," as they would call me behind my back. I was never really able to get across the reasons why I and everyone on the project should work so hard. As the boss of the project, they thought I should sit ashore under a shady tree, drink cold beer, and let others do the work, rather than break my back on the bottom all day long. One of the new boys I hired was called Money, and I soon learned the reason why he was so named: he enjoyed a reputation for stealing everything he could lay his hands on. During this period when I was working alone, a small silver coin got caught on the screen on the bottom of the air lift, and while I was trying to pry it loose, it got sucked up the tube and deposited on the barge. I gave the signal that an important item, or a "goody" as we called them, had gone up, and then forgot about the matter. The next time that I had to stop air lifting, while the barge was unloaded, I surfaced and asked to see the coin. At first the boys all denied seeing it and then one of them pointed Money out and said he had taken it. After getting the coin back, I fired Money on the spot, and he left making threats that he would kill me when I came ashore.

I promptly forgot about the matter until the end of the day, when we came ashore. Money, filled with potent rum, was prancing around waving a machete and screaming that he would chop my head off to a small crowd that had gathered. Several times he came up to me swinging the machete almost in my face, and I pretended that I didn't even see him, which only increased his fury. Ivan the Terrible appeared with a machete and asked me if he should fight Money for me, to which I replied that it was my own battle. I ordered several of my boys to start digging a hole. Money soon took great interest in this event and finally demanded to know why they were digging the hole, to which I replied: "They're digging your grave, Mon, because I'm going to take that machete from you and chop your head off." Money's rage quickly turned to fear, and he threw the machete at my feet, fell to the ground on his knees, and began crying and begging me not to kill him. I not only forgave him the following day but hired him back, and he turned out to be one of the best workers I had: on two occasions he actually reported two boys who had tried to steal artifacts off the barge.

Around this same time another amusing incident occurred. A report reached the government that some Americans had located a treasure buried by none other than Henry Morgan on Goat Island, about twenty miles west of Port Royal. I was ordered to go there with several armed policemen to apprehend the Americans and seize the treasure. We went by helicopter to surprise them, but when we arrived we didn't find a single soul on the deserted island and I assumed that the matter was closed. Not so. Someone notified the government that the Americans had reburied the treasure before fleeing and I was ordered to go back and locate it with my metal detector. I spent a day on this wild-goose chase and then put Wayne, who had just returned from sick leave, in charge of the search. With about fifty unhappy soldiers, he spent a week digging holes all over the island, but their only finds were beer and soft-drink bottles.

By the time Kelly returned, about a third of the *Swan* had been uncovered, and I decided to postpone excavating any more of it for the time being. It was a decision I made with regret, but a necessary one, for I didn't have the means to preserve the wood remaining on the wreck, which was in a remarkable state of preservation, and I had hopes that all of it could eventually be raised and placed on exhibition in a large tank. After covering the parts of the wreck we had excavated, to prevent them from being attacked by teredos, we moved our dig to the northwest section of our large hole—which was already about one hundred fifty feet in diameter.

In this area we uncovered some new walls, much to Kelly's delight. As usual, many beautiful pieces of pewter and silverware turned up, several of which furnished us with new mysteries to solve. Under one wall we found a pewter spoon stamped with the initials E.P. Property records showed two landowners with

those initials in old Port Royal: Edward Pinhorn and Edward
Payston. Since Pinhorn's residence was closer to where we found
the spoon, in all likelihood it belonged to him. The second artifact with owner's initials was a pewter plate with the initials A.B.,
found under another wall. The only possibility among property
owners was one Adam Brewen, whose property lay some distance
from where we found the plate. Had his house, like the *Swan*,
been lifted by the tidal wave and deposited in another spot?
Or was it only the plate that had been flung a great distance,
landing near a wall that later fell on top of it? Or was the plate
the property of someone who wasn't a landowner? If we had
found numerous artifacts with the same initials in one spot, it
would have been safe to assume that the objects were associated
with the walls under which they were found.

My disappointment over failing to unravel these mysteries
soon gave way to excitement over some new finds. Among several
standing and fallen walls, I first found a brass apothecary's
pestle, and began to suspect that we might be working in the
site of an apothecary's shop. Then, a few days later, we discovered a wooden chest buried four feet deep in the sediment
beneath one of the fallen walls. Its dimensions were 3 feet 2
inches by 2 feet 4 inches by 9 inches. Was it a treasure chest?
My heart pounded as I touched the top gingerly, and as the
fragile wood began to crumble in my hands, I realized that it
would be impossible to bring the chest to the surface intact.
Using a small knife I succeeded in removing the top, seeing
to my surprise that the inside of the chest contained straw. So
much for the resurgence of my childhood dream of finding
treasure at Port Royal! I had to laugh at myself. What I found
amid the straw was a different kind of treasure: twenty-one small
glass medicine bottles and two ceramic medicine jars filled with
salve. Other finds in the same area also substantiated the fact
that we were on the site of an apothecary's shop.

Our next discovery was even more fascinating—one I never
expected to make. Old documents revealed that turtle meat was
one of the main staples in Port Royal and that most of the
turtles were caught in the nearby Cayman Islands, then brought

to town and placed in turtle crawls to await slaughter. The crawls were located close to the beach in about a foot of water, so the turtles could survive for long periods of time. Though I knew from the documents that the area we were working in contained several turtle crawls, I had not expected to find any traces of them, for I assumed that during the disaster the wood of the fences would have floated away and the turtles would have swum to freedom.

I was proved wrong on both counts. During the last week of the month, we found not one but two turtle crawls, side by side. Approximately thirty-two feet long by nineteen feet wide, each was fenced with about two dozen vertical wooden posts, four to five feet high and four to five inches thick. Some of the posts still had the original cross boards between them. How the posts remained standing upright during the upheaval is a mystery; perhaps they were driven very deeply into the sand. Why there should have been thousands of turtle bones in and around both crawls is also puzzling; perhaps the turtles were quickly covered over or prevented from swimming away because their flippers were bound together, a not uncommon practice. Whatever the reason for the remarkable survival of the crawls and the turtle bones, there they were, and I was delighted. In a few cases we found the bones of an entire turtle laid out to form a skeleton, and from these we were able to estimate that the average turtle's weight was about three hundred pounds. From the number of skulls we found, we knew that at least four hundred turtles had been lost in the disaster.

Throughout the course of our dig we had been finding bones daily—some of which were human. We received a visit from Dr. Lucille Hoyme of the Smithsonian Institution, a noted anthropologist, who specializes in the study of old bones. After a week spent examining our collection of over a ton of bones, she reported that neither man nor beast of old Port Royal showed any signs of disease; none had died a natural death, but all were victims of the earthquake or a butcher's block.

Rarely a day passed that we didn't recover at least one new type of artifact that we hadn't seen before. During this month some of the unusual items found were a brass ring with two naked women on it, a frying pan with pork rib bones in it, a ceramic jar containing honey, two glass bottles containing olive oil, a piece of canvas with the initials R.J. on it, a part of a wig made from human hair, and a pewter plate with arithmetic computations scratched on its bottom. In addition we also found thousands of other artifacts. Those made of iron being the most numerous, we filled ten of the 55-gallon fuel drums just with iron artifacts.

After waiting more than four months, I finally got a sink and a water supply installed in the room I began using exclusively for preservation work. Many more months were to pass before I received many other things I badly needed for preservation work, and many items, including electricity, I never got at all.

SEPTEMBER

September was Kelly's month, since I was out of action for most of it. On the very first day of the month, I was pumping with the air lift when suddenly I felt something on the top of my head. Then I felt things begin to slither around my head and neck—the tentacles of a small octopus, evidently feeling sportive. Not in a corresponding mood myself, I attempted to pull it off, but it merely tightened its grip. Kelly joined in the tug of war, without success. The situation became dangerous, for the suction of the embrace threatened to pull off my mask. Then I had an inspiration. I raised the air-lift tube over my head, turned the pressure on full blast, and the octopus, refusing to loosen its hold, was sucked up the tube, piece by piece by piece, giving the boys on the barge a real surprise. I had a surprise, too—finding the tube stuck fast to the top of my head. Quickly I shut off the air pressure, and Kelly doubled over with laughter.

In retrospect the contretemps was amusing, though not while it was happening. I soon discovered that it portended worse to come. For the first week, the troubles did not amount to more than nuisances, albeit painful ones, such as having my fingers mistaken for food by the small fish and crabs that hovered around the mouth of the tube to pounce on the worms un-covered by the air lift; the fish were no problem, but the crabs, ranging from six to twelve inches in size, could give nasty bites. Three mornings in succession we arrived to find that all our buoys were missing: some fishermen had found the line we used a good source of fishing line, so I began using light wire instead and the problem ended.

Early in the second week the real misfortunes occurred. A hurricane passing close to Jamaica created strong winds that made the water in the harbor so rough we couldn't use the air lift: the high waves washed the sediment off the barge and right back down on top of us. Instead we used the air hose as a jet and excavated by hand, finding a considerable number of im-portant artifacts. We had been employing these emergency measures for several days when in the course of groping in the sediment I cut my hand deeply on a piece of glass. I gave myself the proper first-aid treatment, sure that I had extracted all the slivers of glass from the wound. Within two days my hand swelled to twice its normal size and I had to visit a doctor, who informed me that I had blood poisoning. He reopened the wound, removed some glass I had missed, and told me I would have to stay out of the dirty water for three weeks.

I was staggered. The only consolation I had was that Wayne was finally able to dive again and, though he had to take things a bit easy for a while, he could help Kelly carry on the dig without me. The very first day that Kelly took over command of the air-lift tube he uncovered a wall and under it found a pewter tankard and half of another (both relics badly crushed by the wall), two pewter spoons, half a pewter fork, another handful of human hair from a wig, a ceramic wig curler, an iron buckle from a horse's harness, two porcelain cups, a sword, and a beautifully ornamented brass scabbard tip. It was a good day's work.

Early the second day they found fourteen complete onion bottles (several still corked and with brandy in them), another pewter spoon, a pewter plate, a pewter bowl, and a lovely blue-and-white-delftware figurine, four inches high, of a young boy. Then Kelly found that further excavation under the wall would be unsafe. Madly in love with the air lift, he didn't want to stop using it for the time-consuming chore of disassembling the wall, so he elected to move on to another area. For the rest of the day he and Wayne found nothing except a few clay pipes and some pottery fragments.

At the end of the day Kelly brought his haul into the lab, where my wife and I were doing preservation work, and gave me a summary of the day's events. I was convinced he had made a mistake in abandoning the wall, but said nothing to him; he had to learn for himself, and he did. For the next ten days he found no walls and very few interesting artifacts, and was becoming so depressed that not even the joy of handling the air lift could cheer him up. Then I suggested that he go back to the wall and take it apart, and reluctantly he agreed.

It took Kelly and Wayne all the next morning and the better part of the afternoon to take the wall apart and send the bricks to the surface, but before the day was over Kelly ceased to regret his long separation from the air lift. In a mere two hours he and Wayne recovered several pewter plates, two pewter candlesticks, a large brass plate, two ornate brass scabbard tips, a brass button decorated with three cannon, an intact medicine bottle, and the most exciting find of all: a brass still, probably used for distilling rum. For the rest of the week they continued to find many artifacts, the most interesting among them being several earthenware plates and bowls, six multi-colored slipware cups, another pewter candlestick, a silver wedding band, and a brass colander.

If there was one thing that made my enforced sojourn ashore at all tolerable, it was the knowledge that my team was doing such a good job without me. I utilized all of the time ashore doing preservation work—except for a few days when I was sent on another wild-goose chase: An American yacht had made a brief stop in Kingston and obtained the services of two fishermen who claimed they knew of an old wreck on a reef off Morant

Key, which is located off the southwest coast of Jamaica. A week later the fishermen, in miserable condition, were rescued by a fishing boat, having been without food or water for four days. They claimed that after they had showed the wreck to the Americans, divers recovered a number of gold bars and then abandoned them on the deserted cay. I was ordered to go back to the cay, despite the fact that the fishermen said the yacht had already left, to search for it, on the assumption that it might have returned to salvage more from the wreck. Naturally I saw no signs of the yacht, but I did inspect the wreck and found that it was a seventeenth-century English merchantman and that there were still a vast number of artifacts from it embedded in the coral bottom.

By this time we had recovered more than three hundred intact onion bottles, which I hadn't attempted to preserve, having been told by various experts that there was no known method for their preservation. If removed from the water, the onion bottles begin shedding thin flakes of glass, and within twenty-four hours nothing remains of them but a pile of glass chips. Why this happens no one has yet been able to determine. It seems to be only the onion bottles, and primarily the ones found at Port Royal, that suffer so badly; the rest of the glassware found there and on other sites presents few preservation problems. Was it something in the bottom sediment that caused a chemical reaction, or the sea water itself? During the mapping operation, when I recovered a number of these bottles, I had sent them to different preservation experts, who reported they could not find any means of preserving them. Then I contacted several glass experts at the Corning Glass Museum in Corning, New York, and asked them to assist me. Daily for months I had been taking samples of the bottom sediment and sea water, and temperature and salinity measurements of the water, which I sent to them. Finally they determined that the large amount of bauxite (a mineral from which aluminum is made) in the Port Royal sediment might be responsible for causing a destructive chemical reaction with the lead used in the composition of the glass—but they were unable to develop a means by which the bottles could be preserved. I began experimenting on my own, and with the assistance of Alan Albright, a preservation expert with the Smithsonian Institution, finally found a solution. Nitric and sulfuric acid baths were used to remove calcareous deposits and lead-oxide coating, which were followed by a number of baths in distilled water until the glass was free of alkalis. Next the bottles were dried in several baths of alcohol and then covered with several coats of polyvinyl acetate. The preservation of the onion bottles was finally solved, but we still had that of the iron and wood objects, which proved even more challenging.

OCTOBER

On the first of the month I was back in the water, though technically the three weeks I was supposed to stay out were short a couple of days. In this case, being an early bird had happy consequences. Almost at once I located a fallen wall sixteen feet four inches long, eleven feet three inches wide, and the width of four bricks thick. Rather than wait until Kelly and Wayne had completely disassembled it, I was hard on their heels with the air lift, excavating under each new section the moment they had taken it apart. There was good cause for this eagerness in addition to the joy of being in the water again: under the wall lay a wealth of artifacts. Among our finds were a pewter mirror frame with pieces of glass still stuck to it, three pewter plates, three pewter spoons, a pewter funnel, two large pewter tankards, two pewter measures (small tankards used in taverns to dispense liquor), a silver winetaster, several dozen broken wineglasses, and thousands of ceramic shards from drinking mugs. Also present were clay pipes and onion bottles in quantities almost comparable to those found under the first wall we had excavated, in May. On the strength of these artifacts, I concluded tentatively that we had located our second tavern.

Two days later I was stuck ashore: Seaga had notified me that he was bringing a number of important government officials out to inspect our operation around nine in the morning. However, they didn't arrive until four that afternoon and I spent the day pacing up and down the beach, while Kelly and Wayne were enjoying the most successful day of the excavation thus far. Besides finding twenty-two pewter objects, they brought up a 16-inch silver flagon, an exquisite silver mug, two brass serving bowls, and a large number of intact ceramic plates and cups. These artifacts belong to the same tavern, and I was becoming quite fond of taverns, since they produced such interesting finds. When the VIPs arrived I called a halt to the day's dig and everyone was suitably impressed by the artifacts Kelly and Wayne proudly brought ashore. I took advantage of the opportunity to approach Seaga for more funds, stating that it would enable me to hire more divers and increase the amount of artifacts we could discover. He agreed with my logic, but said that nothing could be done until the following summer, when our new budget would be debated in Parliament.

With the group of visitors was an American industrial designer, Sergio Dello Strologo, who had recently arrived on the island as a consultant from the International Labor Office of the United Nations to help the Jamaicans establish a profitable handicraft industry. Sergio, who was also a diver, took an immediate interest in my project, and during the two years he spent in Jamaica, he helped me in many ways. He felt that the best way to convince the government to provide more funds for the project was to show them that our work was actually profitable. Since our finds were to all eventually end up in museums and would not be sold, he decided to make replicas of the most interesting items, which could be sold to tourists. He did such a good job of making the replicas that there was also a great demand for them off the island and they were soon being sold in the Abercrombie & Fitch chain of stores across the United States and elsewhere. The replicas in greatest demand were pewter plates, tankards, spoons, forks, knives, ceramic plates, cups, mugs, onion bottles, coins, and many items of jewelry. His silver coins were so perfect that we soon received complaints from numismatists claiming that they were being sold as real coins in the States. To eliminate this problem, he had the word REPLICA stamped on the edge of the coins.

Early in the second week of October, hurricane Inez, which passed near Jamaica, unleashed a torrent of rain that plagued the island for the next two weeks. Our usual few inches of underwater visibility was reduced to zero and we were again forced to work by touch alone. When the rains began, we were excavating in and around a large pile of ballast rock and I was happily anticipating another wreck. We dug and dug without finding signs of any. Then, just as I decided that the ballast had probably been discarded by a ship, we uncovered parts of a ship's keel and ribs nearby. Not long afterward we amassed a collection of ships' fittings (smaller than those found around the *Swan* and not marked with the broad arrow), spikes, nails, a key, two padlocks, two small iron cannon (one three feet long and the other four and a half), cannon balls, musket balls, a sword blade, and numerous shards from Spanish olive jars (amphora-like earthenware vessels).

What kind of ship was it? Most of the artifacts recovered provided no clues, for they were the kind that had been common to ships of all nations for a century before and a century after the earthquake. I had some hope of eventually identifying the cannon, a type I had never seen before (nor, as it turned out, had any of the cannon experts I later consulted). The shards from the olive jars, though manufactured in Spain, were no real help, since the jars were used by ships of all nations to carry everything from water to gold dust. I abandoned work for the day acutely disappointed at having to let the ship's identity remain a mystery overnight.

It remained a mystery longer than that. The next day, one on which I was especially eager to get into the water to hunt for clues, turned out to be the worst day we had yet had during the excavation in terms of misfortune and sheer frustration. I had a blowout on the way to Port Royal and crashed into a telephone pole, but fortunately no one was injured. Arriving at the Naval Hospital, we found that while Ivan the Terrible was out fishing during the night, someone had broken into the room where we kept our fuel and made off with all of our gasoline. That meant we couldn't use the Aquanaut apparatus and would have to wear the cumbersome aqualung tanks. Next, one of the boys, trying to place the outboard motor on the skiff, dropped it into the sea, so instead of using the skiff to tow the barge out to the wreck area that day, we had to swim out, pushing both skiff and barge. At the site, I discovered that someone had robbed all our marker buoys, and it took us almost an hour in the black water to find the same areas they had been positioned in and to place new ones. Once underwater, I discovered that the heavy rains and high winds of the night had deposited more than three feet of mud in the hole. I had no more than a minute to brood over that before one of the boys on the barge accidentally dropped the heavy air-lift tube. It sank like a stone, striking the regulator of my aqualung with enough force to break it in two. Air began to rush out of the valve on my tank, and I reached the surface without breath to express my feelings about almost being decapitated. A moment after I descended with new equipment and began excavating, a boat passed over the floating hose of the air lift, cutting it in two. Assuring my team (and myself) that it was all in a day's work, I replaced the hose and began excavating again. Next, it fell to the compressor feeding the air lift to join the conspiracy against us: it developed a leak in the oil filter. While Wayne repaired it, Kelly and I returned below to dig by hand. In the blackness I caught hold of a large moray eel, which twisted around, sank its fangs into my rubber face mask, and ripped it off. Surfacing to get another one, I bumped my head on the bottom of the skiff. That was the last straw. I suspended operations and sent everyone home. I spent the rest of the day doing preservation work, hoping the day's curse would spare the artifacts. It did, and I took that as a good sign.

The following day everything was back to normal, with only a few minor problems. We continued to locate artifacts from the wreck, but none that helped identify it. Then, late in the afternoon, Kelly discovered a pair of brass ships' navigational dividers. Cleaning revealed they were marked with a fleur-de-lis, evidence that they were of French manufacture. On the basis of the find, I couldn't reach a definite conclusion about the nationality of the wreck, for any ship might have been carrying dividers made in France, but the possibility that the wreck was French seemed a good one. Contemporary accounts of the earthquake stated that a ship captured from the French, at anchor near Port Royal's fish and meat markets, had sunk during the disaster. Was that French prize our wreck? We were excavating in the general area of the markets, so it was more than likely. However, I had no conclusive evidence as yet. The following week, when we located the fish and meat markets close to the site of the wreck, I became convinced that we had found the French prize.

The first indication of the markets was an area about forty by fifteen feet covered with bones piled two to three feet deep. The southern half of the area contained the fish bones, and the northern half contained the bones of cows, horses, pigs, goats, and wild boars. There was a clear line of demarcation between the fish and the animal bones, but not much distance: evidently the fish and meat markets had stood side by side. Between them we found two standing walls (the first we had found still upright) that formed a right angle and were part of the same building. Disassembling the walls, we found artifacts that could have come from either market. Among them were an iron balance bar belonging to a large scale; two brass pans with three holes near the rim of each, indicating that they, too, had belonged to a scale; and a piece of brass chain that had very likely attached one of the weighing pans to the scale. We also found a round lead weight with a woman, a dagger, and a bell stamped on it (possibly the identifying marks of the maker); several knives; an ax; two sharpening stones, and half of a large grinding stone.

The month was a good one for us, producing the tavern, the French prize, and the fish and meat markets. During the final week we were deprived of the large air compressor that fed the air lift (the Public Works Department needed it to clear a major road blocked by a landslide that had followed the heavy rains), but we continued excavating by hand. Recoveries for October were unusually varied, and in quantity equaled those of any previous month. We filled six 55-gallon oil drums with coral-encrusted objects including nails, tacks, spikes, padlocks, hinges, hammers, adzes, saws, knives, a pitchfork, cannon balls, ships' fittings, buckles, two kettles, a skillet, and a large cooking caldron. In lead, besides the scale weight, we found bottle stoppers, musket balls, and a sounding weight. In copper and bronze, besides the items already mentioned there were pins, needles, thimbles, nails, tacks, handles of knives and of pots, buttons, buckles, part of the inside of a pocket watch, a candlestick, small weights for weighing precious metals, and diverse ships' fittings. In addition to the numerous items of pewter found around the tavern site, we also found a pewter snuff box, and a complete cross and half of another (perhaps old Port Royal had not been quite as godless as it was reputed to be).

In addition to metal artifacts we located and recovered about ten thousand wall bricks, some fireplace bricks, roof tiles, and floor tiles. In wood there were fragments of chair and table legs and woodwork from buildings, knife handles, a small measuring cup, three lignum-vitae sheaves, and a round dish probably for playing draughts (checkers). In bone there were cutlery handles, buttons, and what may have been a container for pins or needles, with a screw-on top. In glass there were more than one hundred fifty onion bottles, a few medicine bottles, many wineglasses, and a beautifully etched glass tumbler. Our total of clay smoking pipes was almost four hundred, and we found various other items such as leather, cloth, and even a few nuts. We collected about ten bushels of pottery shards and found a good collection of complete ceramic cups, mugs, plates, bowls, jars, a jug, and half of a candlestick. The ceramic ware included more than twenty different types, mostly of European origin but also a few shards of Chinese export porcelain.

I speculated a great deal on the pieces from China, especially after we discovered a brass Chinese coin dating from the sixteenth century. Was it possible that a Chinese resided in Port Royal at the time of the earthquake? The property records revealed a landowner named Chin John May, but there is no way of being sure whether he was my man or whether he was even Chinese. It is more likely that the chinaware and the coin arrived on a trading ship, either via Europe or via the Philippines and Mexico (the Manila Galleon route). Whatever their history, they ranked high among October's most interesting finds. Another interesting recovery, made by Kelly, was the half of the Arawak metate that made me wonder whether the Arawaks once had a settlement on the cay. The most fascinating find of all was a large ceramic jar that contained a petrified chunk of butter weighing several pounds. It was not the oldest butter ever found under the sea—a cask of butter dating from 1628 was found on the *Vasa,* a wreck raised in Stockholm Harbor in 1962—but it was certainly the oldest butter I ever found.

NOVEMBER

We were faced with one problem after another during November, and foremost was the weather. Rain fell almost continuously, flooding many parts of the island and on one occasion causing a landslide that blocked the road to Port Royal, preventing us from reaching it for three days. The boys on the barge were constantly deluged, with the result that by the middle of the month three of them had come down with the flu and were out of action. The strong north winds accompanying the rain made the sea so rough that we frequently found it difficult to use the barge, and sometimes impossible. We had to cope with mechanical as well as natural difficulties, for the air compressor we received to replace the one taken from us in October showed signs of temperament: on some days it worked like a charm; on others it worked sporadically; on still others it refused to work at all. November had the dubious distinction of being the month work came to a standstill more often than in any other and, to complete the catalogue of disaster, the month I came as close to death as I've ever been.

On the credit side, November was also the month we found

our first standing building. We found it early in the first week, far different from those described in the romantic Port Royal tales I had read as a boy. At the start we had no idea we had found a house at all. There was no roof; either it had been swept off by the tidal wave or removed by salvors. The first sign of the house was a standing wall about a foot under the bottom sediment. I used the air lift to excavate a section sufficiently large to enable Kelly and Wayne to begin taking the wall apart and moved to an area about fifteen feet away. Excavating there, I uncovered another wall, which seemed to be standing at a right angle to the first. Quickly I told Kelly and Wayne to stop what they were doing, and I continued excavating the second wall. Exploring with my finger tips (visibility was nil, as usual), I discovered that the walls were attached. I moved along the second wall, much shorter than the first, and came upon another wall adjoining it. I used the air lift to remove the sediment covering the top of it and a few minutes later came upon a fourth wall, joining the third to the first. It was a complete standing building, and although I didn't expect to find any skeletons sitting at a table inside, I was quite elated.

Since the first wall was almost completely excavated, I decided to explore that before doing anything else. Our probing disclosed a doorway with a wooden lintel to support the bricks. The door itself was gone, but we did find a brass hinge. Using the air lift to excavate part of the interior, we discovered that the floor consisted of squares of flat basalt rock; that the building had been divided, by a brick wall with a doorway, into two separate rooms; and that the insides of the walls had been plastered. On top of the first wall were three indentations, corresponding to another three on the top of the opposite wall, and I had no doubt that they once supported roof beams.

So far we had found no windows, nor did the excavation of the short end walls reveal any. I concluded that they must have been in the long wall opposite the one with the main door, but before excavating further I wanted to get the dimensions of the building, for I feared that any or all of the walls might suddenly collapse. By placing buoys at regular distances on top of the walls, we were able to determine from the surface the length and width of the building: 21 feet by 15 feet 4 inches. The height (nine feet) and the thickness (two feet) of the walls we ascertained by using ropes as tape measures, tying knots in them, and later measuring the distances between the knots.

We never did find out about those windows. Right after measuring the building we quit work for the day, and the next morning we found that all the walls had collapsed during the night. I was extremely disappointed, having had hopes that the building would remain standing long enough for me either to make a drawing of it or to photograph it (the latter was never more than a slim hope). Kelly and Wayne did not share my disappointment, but set to work with a will removing the bricks and pumping debris from the inside of the house in anticipation of finding a wealth of artifacts underneath. Knowing that a standing building would certainly have been salvaged soon after the earthquake, I warned them not to expect too much, and I was right. The only artifact we found was a small, four-pronged harpoon, probably lost by a salvor who was attempting to spear something from the surface.

That building failed to come up to the expectations of any of us. If I had known from the beginning that it was a standing one, I would have attempted to excavate differently, pumping inside and outside the walls alternately so no excess pressure would be placed on any part of them and they might remain upright. I made up my mind that the next time I found a standing wall I would check for others before digging any further. My chance came almost at once. No sooner had I finished excavating the area of the first fallen building and moved to another area, leaving Kelly and Wayne to raise the bricks, than I discovered another standing wall. I moved along the length of it, making a trench two feet deep, and found that it was attached to another wall. That in turn was attached to another, and the other to still another; I had found my second standing building. Resolved to do all I could to keep it that way, I excavated the inside of the building to a depth corresponding to that of the trench outside. Then I worked carefully, removing no more than a foot of sediment outside the building before doing the same on the inside, thus keeping external and internal pressure on the walls as nearly equal as possible. It was a slow, time-consuming process, but the building remained standing.

When about five feet of the walls was exposed, I decided to get a profile of the building and conduct some preliminary mapping: the afternoon was waning, and I knew that despite all my precautions some disturbance during the night could easily cause the walls to collapse. Again using the buoys and knotted ropes, we established that the building was 32 feet long, 17 feet wide, and had walls 2 feet thick and between 7 and 8 feet high (the last had to be estimated, both because we hadn't excavated down below the floor level and because we could find no indication that the bricks on the top of the walls had been the topmost layer). Much larger than the first building, the second was also more interesting to explore. One of the long walls possessed both a doorway and a window, the other had two windows, and there was still another window, a small one, in an end wall. Time did not permit a thorough exploration of the fourth wall, which might have had a window too. The interior, divided into two rooms like the first building, also had plastered walls; in one spot the plaster was very black, a sign that a fire had been habitually lit near it. The floor was cement, and we deduced the composition of the roof from black slate tiles we found inside the house. We also found pieces of lead window grills as well as fragments of the opaque glass they had once held. Before suspending operations for the day I made a sketch of the entire building, including the several different brick patterns used in the walls. It was my intention to brace the walls with wooden beams both inside and out as soon as we had finished excavating, in the hope that we could keep the building standing on a permanent basis.

The next morning began badly: our trustworthy Aquanaut apparatus, which had never failed us, refused to start. Normally we had to use two of them at once, because only two divers can breathe from each unit, but I had loaned one of them just that morning to the Police Department for use in searching for the body of a young boy drowned the day before. So we descended with aqualungs, half expecting to see our building reduced to rubble (our misfortunes never came singly), but it was still standing, much to our delight. Not long after we began work, Kelly cut his hand on a piece of glass. Remembering what had happened the last time I applied amateur first aid to a cut, I sent him off to a doctor in Kingston, where he received fifteen stitches. With Wayne's assistance I kept working for more than five hours without mishap. Then Wayne complained of a severe sinus headache, so I sent him to the surface. I stopped using the air lift, for with the building almost completely excavated I thought it unwise to proceed further by myself. I considered calling it a day (as a rule we never dived alone, for reasons of safety), but then I decided to take the opportunity to explore the end wall I had bypassed the day before. I persuaded myself that a simple task such as that couldn't possibly lead to trouble. Famous last words—or nearly.

I began groping along the wall, and the next thing I knew I woke up to find myself pinned under it, my mask gone and my eyes smarting from the irritation of the salt and dirt in the water. Later I calculated that I had been knocked unconscious for at least five minutes, long enough for water to flood my lungs and drown me. Fortunately I had fallen face downward, pushing against the purge button on my single-hose regulator, with the result that I received the air I needed, so much of it that it was a wonder I wasn't blown up like a balloon.

As soon as I realized where I was, I attempted to push the wall off me, but it wouldn't budge. Though it was more than likely that other parts of the wall had been broken by the fall, it was just my luck that the part on top of me was still a solid mass; it must have weighed a ton. I knew that I couldn't count on being rescued, for how could anyone on the surface know what had happened? The only thing for me to do was to try to dig my way out. Not knowing in what direction I had fallen and consequently without any idea of the shortest way out, I decided to dig straight ahead. Later I estimated that it must have been forty minutes (it seemed like forty years at the time) before my fingers touched the edge of the wall. I crawled through the handmade tunnel until my arms and head were clear of the wall. I could see a pale glimmer of sunlight filtering down through the murky water as I crawled out a little farther, when suddenly part of my regulator got caught between two bricks in the wall. I wasted several precious minutes of my rapidly dwindling air supply trying to free it, but couldn't. Since most of my body was still pinned to the bottom, I couldn't maneuver well enough to ditch the entire aqualung. Every second, it became harder and harder to breathe. I knew that I had only one chance: to try to break off the part of the regulator wedged in the wall and blast off for the surface on my own breath. Jerking my body forward with every ounce of strength I could muster, I felt the regulator snap and found my torso clear of the wall. Another jerk, and I knew a moment of panic as I felt myself caught again. However, it was only my ankle, which had been wedged by my movement into a spot where the wall almost touched the sea bottom. I had no trouble extricating it, and very little reaching the surface. When I arrived —breathless, without a face mask, and bleeding from cuts on my face and head—one of the boys on the barge asked me what had become of the carpenter's level and tape measure I had taken below. I burst into hysterical laughter. To this day I don't know whether he was trying to be witty or whether he was really concerned about the tools, but at the time it seemed like the funniest remark I'd ever heard.

The laughter drained whatever strength I had left, and I had to be pulled into the skiff. After seeing a doctor to make sure my skull hadn't been fractured, I went home and slept for eighteen hours. When I awoke I promised my wife that I would shun all walls until they had been taken apart, and I promised myself that the rule about not diving alone would be a hard and fast one from then on. Returning to the job, I was saddened to see that all four walls were down and my dream of preserving the building intact was over. There was some consolation in the fact that I had succeeded in measuring and drawing it before it fell into rubble, but none in what we found under it when all the bricks had been raised: one small grappling hook most likely lost by a salvor who had used it to fish for valuables soon after the earthquake.

On my second morning back in the water I exposed another standing wall, and with the use of a metal probe established that it wasn't part of a building. Remembering the promise to my wife, I first decided to wait until the divers disassembled it before proceeding with the excavation. I moved to another area, finding no walls and no artifacts, and gradually my resolution crumbled. I had assigned Kelly and Wayne to other tasks, and it would be hours before they could get to work on the wall. Could I wait that long, knowing as I did how valuable a source of artifacts any wall was? No, I couldn't. I convinced myself that the chances of coming to any harm were slight, since the wall was only eight feet long, and began excavating on both sides of the wall. For a change, being an eager beaver paid off in something other than aches and pains. Under the base of the wall I found a round object resembling a duck's egg, so thickly encrusted with coral that I had no idea what it was. My metal detector indicated that it was composed of non-ferrous metal, which convinced me it was worth investigating further.

An X ray made later that day revealed the outline of a man's pocket watch. It was unquestionably the most important and interesting single artifact we had uncovered, and everyone concerned with the excavation became ecstatic and rumor flew over the island that I had found Henry Morgan's own watch. The exact nature of the find was not to be known to us for some time. For two weeks Mr. Purnell and I worked late into the night, and in that time all we accomplished was the removal of the coral covering the silver watch case. Then Mr. Purnell was transferred to the United States Embassy in Tokyo, leaving me the responsibility of opening, cleaning, and preserving the watch. Stan Judge, who was devoting many of his evenings to preserving artifacts, offered to take charge of it. Since he was an expert mechanic, I had no hesitation about turning it over to him. At once he set up a special workbench in his house, complete with jewelers' tools, a watchmakers' magnifying glass, an electrolytic bath, and other delicate professional equipment. In light of such dedication, I knew I couldn't have entrusted the watch to better hands.

For the next two weeks I saw neither hide nor hair of Stan: my only communication with his house was an occasional telephone call from his wife, who complained that he was ruining his eyes and health by sitting up nights over the watch. Finally Stan telephoned and asked if I wanted to see what he had done. I raced over to his house the moment I put down the receiver, expecting to see the watch completely cleaned. Such was not the case. To my amazement, I learned that it had taken all that time simply to open the case. At that stage, all we could say with any certainty about the watch inside was that it was definitely made of silver. Although parts of the face were visible, the Roman numerals on it could barely be discerned. Both hands, in all probability made of iron, had long since disintegrated. In the hope that the hands had left an impression on the corroded face of the watch, as had the hands on the watch found by the Link team, I took a number of infrared photographs, but the results were negative.

As time passed, my impatience knew no bounds. I was aware how conscientiously Stan was devoting himself to the job (I was still getting the telephone calls from his wife), and I didn't want to hound him. At last, after six weeks, I received the long-awaited instructions to bring my camera over to his house. I arrived with film enough to photograph a dozen watches, but for almost an hour I was too overwhelmed by what he had accomplished to think about the camera. He had taken the watch completely apart, and each of the tiny brass movements was in a perfect state of preservation. As for the watch itself, the silver face shone as brightly as a mirror. On it the maker's name, Gibbs, and the place of origin, London, were clearly marked, and inside was the maker's full name, Aron Gibbs.

The discovery of the watch gave us all a tremendous lift. We needed it, for the finds of November, both in quantity and in quality, were negligible compared with those of other months. The reason we came up empty-handed so often was that we were working in an area of standing buildings, where much salvaging had taken place right after the earthquake, but knowing the reason didn't make us feel any better. The small number of interesting artifacts we did manage to discover were located at some distance from the standing buildings. A few days after I found the watch, Kelly found three silver Spanish coins; the only one with a legible date was minted in 1687. Among the pewter objects recovered were three silver spoons bearing the initials ME, RS, and MF. I could find no trace of an M.E. in the property records. For RS, I found a Richard Sudbury; and for MF, a Mark Fowler and a Morris Flenn, the latter the more likely owner because his property was located very near where we had found the spoon. As had been the case with the pewter plate and spoon recovered in August, it was impossible to ascribe ownership with any certainty; the evidence was too inconclusive. Except for the watch, November was a frustrating month all around.

DECEMBER

Matters went from bad to worse for us in December. By then our hole had reached enormous proportions, with diameters of almost 250 feet and 150 feet at its longest and widest points—probably the largest hole ever excavated on any marine archaeological site. We could move only to the north in enlarging the hole: shallow water prevented us from working closer to shore, the amount of hose available from the shore-based air compressor to the air lift prevented our working farther offshore, and the nearness of the marine laboratory prevented us from working on the southern edge of the hole. So we pushed on excavating to the north—in the direction of Fort James—but no matter where we dug on the north side of the hole, we found nothing. Not a single wall, either standing or fallen, and of course none of the artifacts we generally located under walls. Even the supply of onion bottles, clay smoking pipes, and pottery shards—things we were accustomed to bringing up by the hundreds—ran out. In two weeks of excavating we found less than we had up to then on an average day. The only finds of interest we made during this period were three pewter spoons, a brass candlestick, and a copper pan, which we had actually found under a small wall on the southern edge of the hole while excavating one day by hand when strong north winds prevented us from using the air lift.

I just couldn't understand what had happened, unless it was just plain bad luck. Later I learned from historical documents that the new area we were working in was an area where small boats that brought fish and meat products to the markets were pulled ashore and kept when not in use. Naturally there would be few artifacts to find in such an area, where there were no buildings erected, but I didn't know this at the time, and even if I had, I doubt it would have made me feel any better. The sadness and frustration showed on all our faces, including the boys on the barge. During the second week we increased our working schedule by two hours each day, hoping that the additional time on the bottom would speed up the process of making some good finds. My wife, seeing me more and more dejected each evening, suggest that I make a jump farther to the north, in an area where my preliminary explorations with the metal probe had located many walls—to start digging a new hole. I was reluctant to do this, since I was determined to finish excavating the section that would be endangered by the proposed dredging operation. Then, like a sign from the gods, I received news that the government had notified the Port Royal Company of Merchants that no dredging could begin for at least another full year. Still I hesitated to abandon my systematic, inch-by-inch excavation.

Two things overcame my reluctance: the approach of Christmas and a dream my wife had one night. I knew that if our dig continued in the same rut my team would be assured a far from merry holiday, and I seriously considered moving to a new spot for one day, if only to excavate around and under one wall to bring up some nice "goodies," as my boys called all artifacts. Then, on the morning of December 19, my wife mentioned at breakfast that she had had a dream the night before, the first she ever had in color, of us finding a chest full of treasure at Port Royal. I laughed at first and said that with the luck we were then having, I doubted if we would even find a Coke bottle that day. Knowing full well all we were likely to find in the area we were working was a coral-encrusted piece of iron or a few ceramic shards, I decided this was the day to take some drastic action. I asked my wife to choose a location on the chart and I would move the dig there. She placed her finger on a spot about a hundred feet north of the hole and said she really had a good feeling that we would strike it rich this day. All the way to Port Royal I kept thinking about her dream of the treasure chest, but I felt too foolish to mention it to Kelly or Wayne, for fear that they might think their boss had gone off his rocker.

Everyone was overjoyed when I informed them we were moving for the day. In my excitement I had forgotten that the day before, when things were going badly, I had taken both Aquanaut units into Kingston for cleaning and servicing, and only three aqualung tanks were filled (with no high-pressure air compressor in Port Royal we had to take the tanks all the way into Kingston to be refilled each time they were empty). The plan called for me to use the tanks and run the air lift, while Kelly and Wayne assisted me by descending on their own breath to take up the buckets containing artifacts and debris too large to go through the air-lift tube.

At first things went as disappointingly as they had all month. After pumping away about two feet of fine silt held together by long blades of eel grass, instead of encountering the level of hard-packed mud I reached a solid mass of pieces of sharp coral. I had to dig them out by hand, since they were too large to go up the air lift, and place them in the buckets that Kelly and Wayne grabbed and dumped on the barge. Breathing very slowly to conserve air, I succeeded in stretching the air supply in two tanks, normally a two-and-a-half-hour supply, to four hours, but I accomplished very little else. In all that time I had penetrated to a depth of only six feet below the surface of the bottom sediment, and the hole I had excavated was scarcely wider than my body. Still more galling was the fact that I had not uncovered a single artifact, not even a small fragment of pottery—a record for the dig, and certainly not one that I was eager to set.

The moment the second tank was empty I took off for the surface, unpleasant thoughts about men who rely on the dreams of women buzzing through my head. When I reached the barge I was informed that I had had an urgent telephone call. Turning the third tank over to Kelly and instructing him to go down and pump, I swam ashore to the telephone. I had been on the phone hardly longer than a minute when one of the barge boys came up to me at a run, shouting that Kelly had found something great. I hung up, raced to the shore, and saw Kelly and Wayne aboard the skiff, their ear-to-ear grins visible even at a distance. Seeing me, Kelly waved a hand: it was the gesture of someone who had just won the heavyweight championship of the world. I must have broken all swimming records in getting out to the skiff.

Kelly stuck out his hand and showed me four silver Spanish pieces of eight in a remarkable state of preservation. Usually coins found under water are very badly sulfated, and even after cleaning, most of their impressions are barely visible, with the result that discerning the date on one coin in a hundred is a cause for rejoicing among numismatists. On these pieces of eight not only were the dates visible but all the other markings as well. I couldn't believe my eyes. I asked Kelly if there were any more coins below. He said he thought so, but had not investigated further because of my instructions to notify me at once of any important finds made in my absence.

Grabbing a face mask, I gulped air into my lungs and plunged to the bottom. There I found that Kelly had deepened the hole by a foot: he had hit soft sand below the coral I had removed so painstakingly. I squeezed myself down into the hole, reached into the sand, and felt nothing but coins everywhere. Making a pocket of my hands, I scooped up coins and tried to inch my way out of the narrow hole. It wasn't easy without the use of my hands (I wasn't going to let any of the treasure slip though my fingers) and it was even more difficult to reach the surface without the fins I had been in too much of a hurry to put on.

I deposited my precious burden on the skiff, and a cursory examination of the fifty or so coins assured me they were as well preserved as the four Kelly had found. I seized the tank Kelly had been using in preparation for another descent and a resumption of the excavation, but quickly decided I would be better advised to remain on the surface. Fishing boats were crowding around, lured by the excitement we had not been prudent enough to conceal, and I wanted to make sure the coins were safe, so I sent Kelly down instead. Much smaller than I, he could maneuver better in the narrow hole, and besides it was really his part. Wrapping the coins in cloth so the spectators wouldn't have their suspicions confirmed, I took them aboard the barge.

Wayne and I stationed ourselves there like sentinels, watching for any coins that might pass through the screen on the bottom of the air-lift tube (about a dozen did). The air lift was turned down to low pressure, just enough to send up the silt and sand falling into the hole: the coins were in a heap and it wasn't necessary to dig them out of the sediment. For me, sitting there and feeling as useless as I've ever felt in my life, the moments Kelly remained below took on the quality of a slow-motion film. A few times I made quick dives to see if he needed me, reaching down and tugging on his leg to let him know I was there. Each time, he filled my hands with coins and I took them up to the barge, happy to be doing something. After what seemed hours (it couldn't have been more than forty-five minutes) Kelly surfaced and informed me that his bucket was completely filled with coins. I went down to help him raise it, and he returned back to the bottom of the hole.

More slow motion. Fifteen minutes of it. Then, out of air, Kelly came up with both hands full of coins. He said he was sure there were more, so I dived down into the hole. It was a tight fit, but I managed to squeeze myself in and grab a few coins. Suddenly I felt the sides of the hole giving way. Surfacing in a hurry, I placed the coins in the skiff and shouted for a bucket. Wayne tossed me one and I took it down, throwing it into the hole seconds before the sides collapsed completely. Soon there was merely a hollow where the hole had been. I knew that by the next morning not even the hollow would remain. Currents stirred by the night offshore wind invariably deposited silt and sediment on the site. At sunrise, when the wind generally changes direction, most of the night's accumulation is carried away again, except for the silt and mud deposited in any holes or hollows on the sea floor. However, I had taken bearings on the trove and was confident that I could find the bucket again with the metal detector. To be absolutely sure of finding the spot again, the best plan would have been to tie a buoy to the bucket, but a buoy would have revealed the location of the treasure to everyone and his cousin.

I surfaced to face an awesome sight: what must have been all the inhabitants of Port Royal lined up on shore, their eyes glued to the barge. I sent Wayne ashore to ask for police protection. It arrived at once, doubtless because news of the treasure had already reached Police Headquarters. Then we rushed to Kingston and presented our find to Mr. Seaga, who was then in the middle of an important meeting with a number of government officials. Overjoyed, he immediately called an end to the meeting and took us over to see the acting Prime Minister, Mr. Donald Sangster, who offered warm congratulations to all of us, and later that evening had us come to his home for a cocktail party. After turning over the find—499 silver coins—to the Institute of Jamaica for safekeeping, I rushed home to tell my wife the great news, but she had already heard it on the radio.

The next morning, we were on the site at least an hour before our usual time. Both Aquanaut units were back for use and I had the metal detector ready for the bucket hunt. As I had foreseen, the entire bottom was as smooth as silt. I turned on the metal detector and got a big reading within seconds. Sure it was going to be easy, we began excavating. Half an hour later we turned up the object that caused the metal detector reading: a cannon ball. With more than a dozen members of the press ashore, as well as almost five hundred spectators, I felt a bit of pressure on myself and tried to locate the bucket again. In fact I tried for twelve straight hours that day, finding three more cannon balls and various iron objects, but no bucket. I feared that in the excitement of the day before, I might not have correctly recorded the compass bearings I had shot on the new area. When we finally had to quit because of darkness, I sent the barge to be emptied, and Kelly and I remained below to dig by hand. Lying very close to the surface of the bottom sediment and in the same general area I had searched all day, we found eleven pieces of eight, probably dropped by us the day before.

The discovery proved we were in the right area. This time, because there was a police boat guarding the site around the clock, I thought it safe to leave a buoy. I took quite a lot of ribbing from several members of the press when I got ashore, who were far from happy after spending the whole day anxiously waiting on the beach. The amounts of treasure we had recovered had been exaggerated beyond belief: some rumors stating that we had actually recovered more than three hundred bars of gold. From that time on I was dubbed "Mr. Goldfingers" and very few Jamaicans would believe that we had not discovered any gold—only silver. I began receiving so many telephone calls from crackpots who thought I had become a millionaire from the find, wanting me to give them "some of the gold," that I had to have my home phone number changed to an unlisted one.

The following day we resumed the search for the elusive bucket, and around noon the police launch and the two policemen on shore took off for lunch, leaving us unguarded. I was on the bottom with Kelly while Wayne supervised operations aboard the barge. A dugout canoe with six mean-looking drunks arrived and tied up to the barge. Seeing trouble in the offing, all the boys dived overboard and headed for shore, leaving Wayne alone. Wayne ordered them to move off and they responded by threatening to kill him with the machetes they all carried if he didn't "give them some of the pirate gold we had found." Then two climbed aboard the barge, armed with their menacing machetes, and Wayne grabbed a shovel and knocked both of them overboard into the water. Wayne began pounding furiously on the airlift tube, and Kelly and I knew there was trouble and shot up for the surface. The four others had by this time boarded the barge and Wayne was finally having the opportunity to put his karate training to use. While Wayne was battling with two of them, the other two were leaning over the side of the barge and swinging their machetes at us, so we quickly climbed aboard the skiff, ripped off our diving gear, and grabbed crowbars to aid Wayne.

Just then the police launch came into view, with sirens blaring away (our boys had rushed to notify the police of the problem), and the attackers began scurrying back into their canoe, which Kelly and I quickly overturned. Wayne was so mad that he jumped into the water and grabbed two of them by the head and was attempting to drown them, until we pulled him away and the police yanked them all out of the water. They later received sentences to six months in prison at hard labor, to our great delight.

Wayne had a small gash on his right arm, so I sent him to see a doctor while Kelly and I got back to work. We found eight more coins close to the surface of the sediment that day, and the following day only a large pewter shoe buckle. There was no sign of the bucket, though we had dug quite a good-sized hole by then, excavating mainly by hand to remove the large, solid chunks of coral below the sediment. The next two days we found only a few onion bottles and several dozen clay pipes. The following day was Christmas (a happy one after the treasure find), and my wife, Stan and Louise Judge, and I celebrated the holiday underwater at Port Royal by clearing more coral out of the hole.

In spite of our industry, we found no more coins during the next week. Then, just before calling a halt to the operations on New Year's Eve, I found the bucket. It was sitting upright on top of the remains of a wooden chest, the wood so badly eaten by worms that it crumbled to pieces from the slightest movements near it. Nevertheless, I saw that it had been quite large. If it was the chest that had contained the coins—a piece of eight located inches away persuaded me that it was—its capacity was great enough to hold many more than we had found. Nearby I found a large brass keyhole plaque engraved with the coat of arms of the Spanish Crown and half of a brass key. Buried about a foot below the chest I found ten other silver coins, which had fallen out of the bottom as it decayed.

That the chest should have survived all this time, in an area accessible to salvors for years after the cataclysm, struck me as little short of miraculous. How had the salvors overlooked it? Possibly a wall—like one of the many disassembled early in the eighteenth century to provide bricks for the Naval Hospital—had once covered the chest and concealed the treasure trove. Or maybe it had been concealed by some type of perishable material such as tobacco leaves or canvas that had long since disappeared. Still another plausible explanation is that it was actually buried under ground before the earthquake occurred and consequently not visible to the salvors.

How it actually got to Port Royal presents still another mystery, for the coat of arms on the plaque clearly indicates it was property of the Spanish Crown. Possibly it was plunder brought into Port Royal by pirates or privateers. However, the property records of old Port Royal revealed that a Spaniard named Benjamin Buenedo Musqueta owned property very near the place where we found the chest. If it belonged to him, perhaps he was in the employ of the Spanish Government and had come by the hoard legitimately. We know that at this time there were several Spaniards residing in Port Royal who were factors in the slave trade, and possibly Musqueta was one of them.

Months went by before I accidentally discovered what I now believe is the answer to the origin of the treasure chest. During August of 1691 four Spanish treasure galleons in the fleet of the Marqués de Vado, sailing between Cartagena, Colombia, and Havana, Cuba, on the return voyage to Spain, were wrecked on Pedro Shoals, and about four million pesos in treasure was lost with them. Fishing boats from Port Royal rescued a large number of the survivors and about half of the treasure. As soon as the wrecks were abandoned by the Spaniards, a large number of salvage sloops from Port Royal descended upon them and began salvage operations. England and Spain were then at peace, and the Spaniards demanded all of the treasure recovered—offering to pay a fee to the salvors. The English Government agreed that the treasure rightfully belonged to the Spaniards and ordered the Admiralty officials at Port Royal to have all of it seized and returned to the Spaniards. However, it was well known at the time that many chests of treasure were concealed by the salvors. The one we found most likely came off one of those four lost ships on Pedro Shoals.

I convinced Edward Seaga to enlist the services of Mr. Robert Nesmith, curator of the Foul Anchor Archives, in Rye, New York, and a specialist in Spanish colonial coinage. Together we spent several interesting days identifying and cataloguing the coins. The majority came from the mints of Lima, Peru, and Potosí (at that time part of Peru, but today in Bolivia), and a few originated in Mexico City. Most of the coins were dated in the 1680s—the earliest dated 1653 and the latest 1690. All the coins looked as though they had just come from the mints, a circumstance that made Mr. Nesmith even more excited about the find than I was: he claimed he had never seen coins of the period in so perfect a state of preservation. Since almost every one of the coins was dated and they were all from a period in which good coins are quite scarce, Nesmith wrote a report to Seaga on his investigation of the coins and said that at a minimum, any of the coins could be sold for at least three hundred dollars and many were worth as much as one thousand dollars. This meant that our hoard was valued at at least $150,000. In his report Nesmith recommended that a limited number, say around fifty coins, be selected for museum display on the island and that the rest be auctioned off in the near future.

This was too unique an opportunity to let slip by, so as soon as I knew that Seaga had read Nesmith's report, I asked him to have a meeting with me and others in the government who were connected with my project. Seaga started the meeting by saying, "No doubt our famous archaeologist has requested this meeting so he can demand a higher salary, in view of his recent find at Port Royal." This got a good laugh all around, and I then took the floor assuring everyone that I didn't want a raise, but since the subject was brought up, after working more than a year on the project, I would like the employment contract I had never received. (Two days later I finally had it.) My main reason for requesting the meeting was to raise more funds for the project, as we were still working on a shoestring: in fact, I was still depending on donations of equipment and supplies from many sources to keep the operation going. I pointed out the value placed on the coins, plus the fact that three different experts on antiquities had inspected all the artifacts we had recovered throughout the year and valued them at between one hundred and one hundred twenty thousand dollars. I then mentioned the fact that we had recovered all these items at a cost of less than ten thousand dollars to the government. I requested that our budget be at least doubled so I could hire more personnel—divers, a preservationist, an artist, and an artifacts officer—and buy many badly needed items, especially those needed for preservation work. To my astonishment, no one disagreed with my request and Seaga promised that when the next fiscal year began, on April 1, my annual budget would be at least twice the amount it was for the past year, and maybe even three times as much. I should have known better than to believe a politician. When April rolled around the next year, I found myself struggling with the same budget I had had the previous year.

The year produced treasure and a vast collection of artifacts, as well as knowledge, in quantities that had surpassed my wildest expectations. Still, there was so much more I wanted to know about old Port Royal, and I was sure that many of these questions would be answered in the course of our work during the following year.

Chapter Eight

YEAR 1967 JANUARY

The new year really started off promisingly. On New Year's Day I gave my team the day off, but, as usual, I couldn't stay away from Port Royal and took my wife and a group of friends out to sort and piece together pottery. My wife had given me a land metal detector for Christmas to use around the old Naval Hospital. To check the unit's sensitivity, I took it over to the shed where we kept the 55-gallon drums containing iron artifacts from the sunken city and grabbed a small conglomerate about the size of an orange and the shape of a small cannon ball. I got a non-ferrous reading on the detector, which greatly surprised me, and I at first thought that the detector wasn't working properly. But after testing it on other pieces of both ferrous and non-ferrous metals and getting the right readings on the detector, I decided to break the clump apart and see what was inside of it. Using a rubber mallet I gently tapped on it until it broke in two and out fell a gold wedding band, four plain silver buttons, and two brass buttons with anchors embossed on them. There were also several fragments of canvas in the clump; apparently these items had been stored in a small pouch.

We had finally found our first piece of gold on the site, and I wondered how many other important artifacts were concealed in the thousands of coral-encrusted conglomerates in the fifty or so drums already filled in that shed. The majority of these conglomerates consisted of iron objects, and since I had neither the personnel nor the equipment to clean and preserve iron, I was forced to just store them in water for the time being.

Alan Albright, the preservation expert at the Smithsonian Institution, had perfected a method of treating iron objects recovered from the sea, but it was long and complicated. Each piece requires careful examination by an expert before any attempt to preserve it can be undertaken, for the nature of the treatment varies with the size and thickness of the pieces and with their component elements. As a rule, the larger the object, the better the chances of preserving it. A large cannon, for example, usually requires nothing more than tapping with a hammer to remove the coral encrustation, placing it in a running bath of fresh water for several weeks to leach out the salts, then putting it in an electrolytic bath for about a month, and finally covering it with a coating of plastic or clear resin to prevent it from rusting. Smaller objects, which are generally more fragile than a heavy cannon, require more delicate treatment. Usually various types of chemicals are used in removing the coral growth and the iron-oxide coating on the artifacts before the salts can be leached from them and they can be placed in the electrolytic baths. The smallest objects, such as nails and tacks, present much greater difficulties. In many instances all of the metal of the object may have been converted to iron oxide, with the result that the only thing left inside the conglomerate is a hollow impression in the shape of the original object. When this occurs, no preservation is possible and a record of the object can be obtained by two different methods: either by X-ray photograph or by making a replica of the original object. When the latter method is used, a hole is usually drilled into the conglomerate and the hollow is filled with plaster of Paris or other materials, and, after hardening, the conglomerate is broken apart and a replica of the object is obtained.

Ever since the project began, I had been pressing the Jamaican Government to provide me with either a fluoroscope or an X-ray machine so I could at least determine the contents of the hundreds of coral-encrusted conglomerates we were bringing up each day. Less than 5 per cent of these objects were identifiable, and I was losing very valuable archaeological information by not being able to determine the exact nature of every item we recovered in each area. In desperation I finally wrote to the archaeological division of UNESCO in Paris and requested that they find some means to help me cope with this problem.

From the tag marking the conglomerate containing the ring and buttons, I knew that it was one of the objects we had picked up the week before while searching for the area of the coin hoard. I also realized that the size of the chest indicated that it could hold a great deal more coins than we had found, and I had great hopes that we would be finding many more in the days to come.

During the first few days of the month, Kelly and Wayne seemed to be acting moody and not working as hard as they usually did, and I urged them to tell me why. The curse of the treasure was the problem. They felt that they were entitled to a bonus for making the find, or at least one of the coins as a souvenir. I explained to them that although I agreed with their feelings, it was our job to find treasure, and not just artifacts, and I knew that it would just cause us all trouble if I asked for a bonus or coins for them. The next day I gave each of them a silver coin I had found years before on a shipwreck in the Bahamas, and this appeared to have solved the problem—or so I thought.

The boys on the barge really had it easy this month. Usually we would fill the barge with sediment six to ten times a day, but in this new area we were fortunate if we even filled it once—and most of that consisted of chunks of coral, which we brought to the surface by hand. Below the first two feet of silt and down to a depth of about ten feet, there was a solid mass of dead coral, most of which consisted of staghorn and elkhorn coral—long, sharp pieces that intertwined and had to be separated by hand.

Our fingers and hands suffered terribly: my fingers were so lacerated that I was unable to use a typewriter or hold a pencil. Gloves would have helped a great deal, but then we would not have been able to differentiate between artifacts and coral. By the end of the month we had excavated a hole with a radius of only fifteen feet around the area of the original coin hoard.

My hope of finding the rest of the coins I believe had been in that chest never materialized. On the fifth of the month we found four more, then another on the ninth, and then none until the twenty-seventh, when three more were found, and another the following day. All nine of these coins were heavily sulfated and had to be cleaned in the electrolytic bath Stan Judge had built to clean the silver watch. Those we had found in December were in such an excellent state of preservation they had required only rubbing with baking soda and water to remove a thin black patina of silver sulfide.

For the second month in a row we found no walls; in fact we didn't find a solitary brick during the whole month. According to contemporary charts of the old town, we were working either on the northern edge of the area where the small boats were stored ashore or near the site of the small jail, called the "lockup," where lawbreakers were kept during the night until tried the following morning and usually sent to one of the two prisons. On the seaward side of our hole, only about a foot under the silt, we discovered one end of a cobblestone street, sixteen feet wide. Using the hose connected to the air-lift tube as an air jet, we blew away the silt covering it and found that it was sixty-eight feet in length. Buried in the silt on top of the street we discovered hundreds of pieces of burnt wood, most of which were once parts of houses. No doubt they were remnants of the dreadful fire that devastated Port Royal in 1702 or from one of the other fires that afflicted the town.

This new area yielded fewer artifacts than any we had excavated previously; it was even more barren than that which had prompted me to make the big jump to the north. On the average day in the past we generally found about twenty clay pipes, about half a bushel of ceramic shards, and several hundred coral-encrusted conglomerates. This whole month netted fewer of these items than we usually brought up each day. The only pewter we recovered were a crushed tankard and a spoon, both found under the landward end of the cobblestone street. The only really interesting find in January was a large three-legged cooking caldron filled with beef bones and with a brass ladle still in it.

By the middle of the month, when it appeared that we were not going to find another hoard of coins and the number of curious spectators had dwindled to only a few each day, I asked the police to stop guarding the area. Ironically, during the period they were present we had more thefts than usual. Three times gas was siphoned from my car, twice the battery was taken, and a number of other things also disappeared. One Sunday when I had brought about a dozen friends out to smash sea urchins in the water and to work in the preservation laboratory, the large lunch my wife had made and a cooler of beer and soft drinks disappeared without a trace. Ivan the Terrible was furious when we told him of the theft and threatened to murder the culprits, but they were never identified.

During the first year of operations my project had been under the direct control of the Institute of Jamaica—specifically under its director, Bernard Lewis—but things didn't work out as well as they should have. Lewis served on numerous committees on the island—some of which met weekly—in addition to running the Institute, and he had very little time to attend to the details associated with my project. Bills went unpaid for months, and when I put in a request for simple items such as stationery supplies, these, too, took months to get. For months I tried to ignore the problems, but when I realized how they were slowing down my work at Port Royal, I brought the matter to the attention of Seaga and demanded some action be taken. Early in the month he transferred our whole operation to the Jamaica National Trust Commission, the body responsible for the maintenance and preservation of all historical sites on the island.

The commission was headed by a chairman, Mr. Frank Hill, who was a newscaster on the government-owned radio station, but the actual running of it was in the hands of Mrs. Pansy

Rae Hart, a very dynamic and understanding person. Although we were still working on a very meager budget, Pansy managed to make ends meet, and went out of her way to do everything she could to keep the project on an even keel. One of her first tasks was to enlist the services of an Englishwoman, Mrs. Gloria Gilchrist, who had had previous training in museum restoration work, to work full time as my assistant. Unable to pay her from the funds we had available, Pansy took the money needed to pay her salary out of some other, undisclosed budget, that wasn't being used.

I had planned that Gloria would fill the role of artifacts officer, draftsman, and artist, and also do some preservation work in the Port Royal laboratory, but it didn't work out. From the start she felt that the people around the Naval Hospital were hostile toward her, and she feared bodily harm. In turn the same Jamaicans complained of her superior attitude, which they greatly resented. After a week of this, Pansy obtained space in the basement of the Institute of Jamaica and we set up a reservation laboratory for Gloria there. Her chief task, which lasted throughout the year she worked under me, was to sort, identify, catalogue, and try to piece together the hundreds of thousands of ceramic shards we had recovered. She did wonders at this arduous work and reassembled hundreds of items we had no idea even existed. On several occasions Dr. Ivor Noel Hume, the Director of Archaeology at Colonial Williamsburg, in Virginia, came to visit and assisted her a great deal in identifying the ceramic and other types of artifacts we had recovered.

A number of times since the beginning of the project, editorials in the island's newspapers had criticized the fact that although we had been making fantastic discoveries at Port Royal, the people of Jamaica were being deprived of the opportunity to view our finds, since none had been put on display in a museum. The main museum on the island was a part of the Institute of Jamaica, but it had been closed for many years, ostensibly "for repairs." Shortly after I was placed under the control of the National Trust, I convinced Pansy that something should be done to rectify this situation. She obtained the use of a large room in the library building of the Institute, and Gloria and I soon had a very impressive display set up. So many people came to view the display that Seaga held a meeting to suggest that funds be raised to build a museum at Port Royal devoted entirely to the sunken city.

FEBRUARY

My plan was to continue enlarging our new hole, mainly excavating on its southern extremity, so it would eventually be connected to the larger hole we had excavated the previous year. During the first three days of the month our only recoveries were two small iron cannon balls and several clay pipestems, and Kelly and Wayne urged me to make another jump to the north in hope of finding a better area—both from the standpoint of abundance of artifacts to be found and easier sediment to work in. By this time our hands were so badly lacerated that we were forced to wear a glove on one hand, which we used for pulling and tugging on the pieces of coral, using the other to identify objects by touch.

Landslides were a continual source of trouble, and rarely a day went by when one or all of us didn't suffer some cuts or bruises from the larger objects that tumbled out of the sides of the hole when a landslide occurred. Early on the morning of the fourth a large coral head—about eight feet in diameter—fell out of the side of the wall and struck my right foot. The pain was excruciating and I knew it was serious. Kelly and Wayne swam me ashore and then carried me into my office, while one of the boys from the barge ran over to the Police Training School for help. Fortunately a government helicopter had just landed on the parade grounds there, bringing some VIPs for an inspection, and the director of the academy had it fly me to the Kingston hospital. X rays disclosed a broken ankle and two broken toes, which were reset, and a cast was placed on my leg and foot. When I notified Pansy what had happened, she said it couldn't have happened at a better time. The Jamaican Government Tourist Board was having a big tourism-promotion display in New York City at Abercrombie &

Fitch's department store, and as a result of the display of Port Royal artifacts we had just opened in the Institute of Jamaica, it had been decided that a similar display should be exhibited at Abercrombie's. Just that morning Seaga had phoned and ordered her to have me select some one thousand items for the exhibit and take them to New York. As it turned out, the Port Royal exhibit was an astonishing success in the show.

The show lasted for ten days, and even though the city was immobilized for most of that period by a terrible blizzard, more than a hundred thousand people visited the Port Royal exhibit. Along with Frank Hill, the Chairman of the Jamaican National Trust Commission, I spent eight hours each day dressed in a suit (I hadn't worn much more than a swim suit for more than a year, nor worn shoes) answering myriad questions about our project, sunken treasure, and related topics. Treasure fever was sweeping New York at this time, because in addition to our exhibit, another was being held, at the Parke-Bernet Galleries, an exhibition of the treasure and artifacts recovered by the Real Eight Company from several of the 1,715 fleet shipwrecks off the east coast of Florida. On the last day of the show, Hill notified me that because the exhibit had been so well received in New York, it was going to travel to Chicago next and then on to six other Abercrombie & Fitch stores across the country, and that Seaga had ordered both of us to travel with it. The tour was going to take two months, and I had no intention of spending such a long period of time away from work in Port Royal. Rebelling, I threatened to quit unless I was excused from a task I didn't really enjoy in the first place. As a substitute, I made two hours of tape recordings recounting the history of old Port Royal and our work on the site, and these were played on a continuous basis at each of the places the exhibit was shown.

A number of surprises awaited me when I returned on the fifteenth of the month, not all of them pleasant. The cast had been taken off while I was in New York and I was anxious to get back into the water, especially since I had lost so much time. I had given the whole team a vacation while I was away, and they, too, were ready to get back to work.

The Jamaican branch of the British Sub-Aqua Club had been quiet for months and I had thought I had heard the last of them. However, taking advantage of my absence, on two occasions the club went en masse to the site and attempted to dive there, in flagrant violation of the law. Both times Ivan the Terrible notified the police and they were prevented from entering the water. One of the club's leaders then wrote a lengthy letter to the editor, which was published in the Kingston newspaper, accusing me of many unjust things and demanding that the club be permitted not only to dive at Port Royal but also to participate in my project. He also insinuated that the government had lied about the exact nature and size of our coin find, and suggested that members of the club be assigned on a volunteer basis to oversee our work, reporting all our finds as they were made. In plain words, we were being accused of stealing some of the treasure we had found. Part of the blame lay with Seaga, for he prevented us both from revealing to the press the exact amount of coins we had found and from combating the rumors and articles stating we had found an enormous treasure. Not until February 2, six weeks after the main hoard was recovered, did the government officially announce the exact number of coins found. As soon as I read this item in the newspaper, I phoned the man who had written it and challenged him to a duel with spearguns underwater at Port Royal the next morning. He never showed up.

Rumors were also circulating at this time that I was planning to sue the government for half of the treasure, because I had not been on an employment contract at the time it had been found, and, according to the laws of "treasure-trove," was entitled to half of it. Apparently someone in the government actually believed this rumor, as I was summoned to the office of the Attorney General's office and asked to sign a document relinquishing all claim to the treasure, which I did with a good laugh.

The Port Royal Company of Merchants also came out of the woodwork while I was away, and Sir Anthony Jenkinson threw a party at his beach club for more than two hundred stockholders of the company and other prominent persons in the community. He made several announcements in the press stating that his group was more determined than ever to get their development of Port Royal underway and demanded that the government give them immediate permission, without making any specific reference to the proposed dredging operation, which was to be the first phase of the development scheme.

The government had announced that general elections were to be held that month, and "election fever" gripped the island. To win the election, the opposition party, the People's National Party, used every means possible in trying to convince the Jamaican electorate that the party then in power was bad for the island. It was only natural that they would take the side of the Port Royal Company of Merchants and try to prove that the Jamaican Labor Party had erred in not permitting them to develop Port Royal, and a number of articles to this effect appeared in the press.

Major E. H. Marley, the chairman of the company, was waiting for me the first morning I returned to work at the site, and asked to have a chat in private. Even before he opened his mouth I had a good idea what the gist of our conversation would be about. He merely took up where Jenkinson had left off over a year before, offering me a fantastically large salary if I would terminate my work for the Jamaican Government and join his group. As politely as it was possible for me under the circumstances, I told him to go to hell and to remove his chubby body from the premises. His parting words were: "You'll be begging to work for us after the elections, when we take over your project." Apparently he was convinced that the PNP would win, and he had some kind of arrangement with someone in that party relevant to getting their scheme underway. Fortunately, the JLP won the election by a landslide, silencing the Port Royal Company of Merchants for a long period.

After Marley's hasty departure, I was happy to get into the water—an environment I have always found more pleasing to be in than the land, even the dirty waters of Port Royal—and away from the everyday problems of mankind. Fortunately all my marker buoys were still in place; otherwise it would have taken some time to find our new hole, which had completely filled in with sediment during the period I was away. The whole day was lost just removing this sediment and getting back to the condition we had left the hole in. The following day we found four pieces of eight and then five more the next day, all of which were in an excellent state of preservation, like those we had discovered in the hoard. The team members were excited again and believed that we would soon make another big find. Then things slid back to the unrewarding level they had been in at the beginning of February, and for the next two days we didn't find a single artifact—not even a fragment of a pipestem or a ceramic shard.

Besides the discovery of the coins this week, I had some other, unwanted excitement. Jamaicans take a fierce interest in elections, especially the general elections, which are held every five years. Early in the week several disturbances between rival party members had taken place and people had been injured. The situation became increasingly serious, with gangs of ruffians attacking the headquarters of both parties in various precincts in Kingston. Violence broke out on a major scale, and the government announced in the press that a number of persons had been killed. The matter escalated daily, and by the time elections were finally held, more than fifty persons were unofficially reported dead. To make matters worse, the government had evicted the main body of the Rastafarians from Dunghill, their traditional camping grounds, and these normally peaceable men joined in the violence, and riots erupted all over the island. The Rastafarian cult originated some sixty-five years ago, and its members wish for "repatriation" to Africa (Ethiopia) and revere Haile Selassie, Emperor of Ethiopia, as a god. Sporting bushy hairdos with plaited locks which are sometimes stiffened with cow manure, religiously smoking as much marijuana as they can get, and squatting on other people's land, the members of this sect are usually docile and gentle, preaching peace and love—but they were now on the warpath.

On Saturday, the day of the elections, riots in Kingston were so bad that I was unable to safely reach the area of town where I normally picked Kelly and Wayne up, so I telephoned them to take the day off and decided to drive to Port Royal and work alone in my preservation laboratory. The radio was blaring away and telling all law-abiding citizens to stay at home, as I rounded a corner in the road and had to slam on the brakes to avoid hitting a roadblock of garbage cans set up by a group of about twelve Rastafarians, who appeared to be out of their minds from marijuana, liquor, or both. Before I could turn the car around and make a fast getaway, two of them yanked the car door open and pulled me out. All of them were carrying machetes, knives, and pistols, and I knew I was in big trouble. After I received a bloody nose from several fists smashing into my face, the leader of the group announced that he would have to kill me because I was white and an enemy of the black people of the world. Just when I was about to close my eyes and wait for the fatal blow to fall, one of them recognized me and screamed, "Don't mash dat mon up. He Mr. Goldfingers, bringing up all the gold from Morgan's city, for the poor people of Jamaica." Suddenly I found myself being patted on the back as a bottle of powerful white rum was thrust into my hand and I was ordered to take a few healthy swigs. The leader of the group then told me that I was free to go and ordered two of his men to sit on the hood of the car and escort me out of that area, where he said I might run into more trouble. Two of my windows were broken by flying stones, but I finally reached the outskirts of the city, where my two escorts jumped off, and once on the open road I broke my old record for getting out to Port Royal. Once there, I phoned my wife and had her move in with friends for a few days, and I stayed at Port Royal for two days until the island got back to normal.

Wayne and Kelly took the ferryboat out to Port Royal the following Monday and we got back to work on schedule. During the week we located five fallen walls and recovered a considerable number of artifacts, including many items of pewter and two silver spoons from under them. Under one we found a large number of tools—two shovels, a rake, a hoe, two pitchforks, two pick-axes, four saw blades, five hammers, an adze, two axes, and a grinding stone—indication that we were probably on the site of a tool shed.

Throughout the course of the excavation, many of the onion bottles we brought up still had corks in them and held their original contents. On a number of occasions I had the contents of these sealed bottles analyzed by the Chemistry Department of the University of the West Indies. During the week we found several more sealed bottles, and on Friday when one came up, the boys on the barge decided to open and drink the contents. About an hour later, unaware they had done this, I was summoned to the surface and found four of the five (one had had the sense not to sample the vintage) doubled up with pain and rolling around on the deck of the barge. We got them all into the skiff, and I rushed them over to the infirmary at the Police Training School, where they were given a drug to induce vomiting, and the next day they returned soberly to the job again. They had polished off the whole bottle, so we couldn't analyze the contents, but I was sure of one thing: They wouldn't try to drink any more of old Port Royal's liquor.

MARCH

Early in the first week of March we located a large section of a fallen wall, above which were several large pieces of wood I first thought to be roof beams. There were fewer pieces of dead coral in the sediment in this new area, which made our work much easier. As Kelly and Wayne took the wall apart and carried the bricks to the surface, I kept pace with them excavating with the air lift. As we had expected, the wall was a good source of interesting artifacts, and we recovered more during this week than we had in the three previous months combined. After completely removing the wall, which was at a depth of about six feet below the surface of the bottom sediment, I began excavating deeper, and at a depth of ten feet we found another, smaller fallen wall. Beneath this wall we found the remains of a complete human skeleton, which an anthropologist was able to determine as that of a male around thirty years old. Scattered among the bones were a number of personal effects, which probably belonged to the victim: fragments of a pair of shoes (the soles indicated that the man wore a size 10), a leather belt with a pewter buckle (the belt had only one hole in it and this indicated that the man had a 37-inch waist), a brass religious medallion (indicating that the man was probably a Catholic), a brass watch case, an ivory double-edged comb, and a small onyx Brazilian talisman, or good-luck charm, in the form of a fist (I had found similar ones on several shipwrecks in Mexican waters).

As soon as we had found the first traces of "John," as we called him, I turned off the air lift and continued excavating by hand, using a brush to clean the bones off and a ping-pong paddle to fan the sediment away. When we had started that morning, I noticed that two boats of fishermen were setting up fish nets quite close to us, and I asked them to move farther away, but they refused and I dropped the matter. About the time that I had "John" completely uncovered and was trying to make a drawing on a plastic slate of the arrangement of the bones, a tremendous explosion occurred, which nearly knocked the three of us unconscious. The fishermen had thrown in a stick of dynamite—either to kill or scare a school of fish into their nets—about fifty feet from where we were diving. The concussion from the blast was so great that I felt as if my chest had been crushed. The three of us rushed to the surface with bleeding ears and quite dizzy. After roundly cussing out the fishermen, I suspended operations for the day, and we went to see a doctor in Kingston. Kelly and I were fine (although we suffered from severe headaches and had difficulty hearing for a few days), but Wayne had a broken eardrum and was told he couldn't dive until it was healed. I gave him a week's sick leave. When he returned to work and was put in charge of supervising the topside operation, he complained of continuous severe headaches, and after about a week he quit. This left the burden of all the diving on Kelly and me. During the month, I hired seven divers in succession to replace Wayne, but none lasted more than a few hours before quitting.

The explosion had precipitated a massive landslide in the hole, and when we got back down on the bottom the day after the accident, "John" was nowhere to be found, and I discovered that what I had mistaken for roof beams were actually the ribs of a large shipwreck. Using the air hose to blow the silt off the wreck

—the top of it was only about a foot below the surface of the bottom sediment—we found that it was about fifty-five feet long, and only the keel, keelson, and lower ribs of the wreck remained. Months later I was able to establish that this was only the forward section of a much larger ship. Over the remaining wooden parts of the wreck was a great pile of ballast rock, on top of which were hundreds of 150-pound iron mortar balls, all cemented together by coral growth. We spent several days using large crowbars to pry the mortar balls and ballast rock apart, and dug a hole down to the keelson about ten feet in diameter, where we found numerous artifacts, including a French silver coin dated 1721—indicating that the wreck had sunk after that date. Later, through research, I was able to learn that it was one of about a dozen that had sunk during a hurricane in 1722. In a small hole we made on another section of the wreck we discovered four well-preserved whale teeth and several handfuls of lead musket balls.

The wreck was lying at a right angle—east and west—to the shore and right in the path we were following to connect the two holes together. Realizing that it would take quite a long time to pry all the mortar balls and ballast rock loose from the coral, and still faced with no means to preserve the wood from the wreck, I decided to bypass it. First we tried to excavate around the western, or seaward, side of it. There we encountered what appeared to be part of the ship's cargo: a massive mound of tree trunks and branches of logwood, which was used as a dyestuff. The air lift was of no use and we spent a week with saws and axes trying to cut our way through that jungle of timber but made very little progress. Mixed in with the logwood we did find many artifacts, including a small pewter teapot, a pewter tankard, and most of the pieces of a large stoneware Dutch bellarmine jug—which made Gloria Gilchrist quite happy.

I then decided that we would attempt to go around the eastern, or shoreward, side of the wreck—which turned out to be a good move. About this time I had two visitors, who spent a week working with us. Alan Albright, the preservation expert from the Smithsonian Institution, had come obstensibly to help me with some preservation work, but after an exploratory dive the first morning, when he found a plate and a large tankard, both made of pewter, he decided to spend all of his time diving. The other visitor was Dr. Colin Jack-Hinton, Curator of the Western Australia Museum, in Perth, who had come to learn more about marine archaeological techniques. Several valuable shipwrecks had been found off Western Australia, and he was in charge of excavating them, despite the fact that he didn't even know how to dive. When he first arrived I tried to convince him that he should learn to dive, because he couldn't really supervise the salvage of the wrecks from the surface, but he claimed he had no desire to learn. The moment that Alan popped up to the surface with his finds, Colin quickly changed his mind, and after several hours of training in a swimming pool that evening, he was on the bottom the following morning and worked like a professional for the rest of the week.

Near the shoreward end of the wreck we located four fallen walls, and each of them produced a good collection of artifacts; the most interesting, again, all made of pewter—three large chargers, seven plates, a bowl, three spoons, a mustard pot, two bottle stoppers, and what appeared to be a pastry baster. Later I learned that my pastry baster was actually a urethra syringe, which created quite a stir among the experts at the British Museum, who correctly identified it from photographs I sent them. Syphilis was a major problem in old Port Royal, and syringes of this type were used to treat it, by injecting a mixture of molasses and several drugs into the sexual organs of both males and females. According to the experts, ours was the oldest one extant.

We also discovered a substantial number of other artifacts, which indicated that we were working in an area where a dining room or a cookhouse must have stood: twenty-six onion bottles, many items of ceramic and glassware including two exquisite pieces of Chinese porcelain—a saucer and a cup; bone knife handles (the iron blades long since disintegrated); a copper pan; two iron cooking caldrons; and a brass skimmer. Under one of the walls we also found several human bones and one tooth, a brooch made of agate, and the fragments of a pair of women's shoes. Did these items belong to another victim of the earthquake who had been trapped under a fallen wall? It appeared so, even though we found only enough human bones to account for about one fourth of a skeleton.

All four walls were of the same type of construction and appeared to have been part of the same building. All the items of pewter contained the maker's touch marks—which I was able to identify easily—and four of them (three plates and one tankard) had the owner's initials, PF, on them; however, I was unable to find anybody with a name corresponding to these initials in the property records.

Under the shoreward tip of the shipwreck Colin and Alan, who were digging by hand, discovered the remains of a wooden chest or box, which had probably been the ship's tool chest. On top of the wooden fragments of the chest and around it we found two brass hinges, a padlock and key, and several dozen tools; hammer heads, ax heads, knives (one with a wooden handle), adzes, wedges, a pair of scissors, and several types of ships' calking tools. Beneath the remains of the chest and its contents they found other objects, which possibly belonged to someone who had served on the ship: a copper snuff box, a brass pipe tamper with the Tudor rose seal on one end of it, two brass buttons (each with three anchors on them), a copper cane handle, and several dozen copper straight pins.

One morning when I felt confident that Colin and Alan could handle the air lift, I took Kelly for a brief trip to inspect an area where Ivan had reported finding a shipwreck while fishing one day around the small cays lying off the south side of Port Royal. From Ivan's directions we easily spotted an area where a large number of ballast rocks were embedded in the coral-covered sea floor. Kelly and I took off in different directions, armed with crowbars to pry loose any interesting items we might locate. After some time I, hearing Kelly banging away on something, scurried over to where he was and found that he was working at something shiny on a long cylindrical object that looked like a small cannon. On closer inspection it turned out to be a large bomb, and I quickly stopped him. During World War II the Americans had used the area as a bombing test range, and there are many unexploded projectiles lying all over the bottom. Ours turned out to be a 500-pound bomb, and Kelly had actually been chipping the coral off the brass detonating head. He was damned lucky it hadn't gone off. I reported his find to the harbor master, and several days later it was raised and exploded. With the exception of the ballast rocks and a few coral-encrusted iron fittings from the wreck, we found nothing more to identify or date it.

On another day, Kelly and I went to investigate another shipwreck, reported to be in shallow water near Harbour Head, the eastern end of Kingston Harbour. From various fishermen I had received reports that it had recently been located by divers who were reported to have raised a considerable number of artifacts from it. Although a salvage lease is needed for anyone to excavate a wreck in Jamaican waters, these divers, who I later discovered were members of the local diving club, were excavating the wreck illegally, without a permit. Apparently they had used some type of excavation tool, because all the sand had been removed from the wreck and they had dug a number of holes around it. They had also chipped all the coral off four large cannon and a ten-foot-long anchor, which were lying amidship over the keel of the shipwreck. The cannon were of Spanish origin, and from the thousands of fragments of Spanish olive jars and other ceramic ware I deduced that it was probably a Spanish merchantman dating around 1600 to 1650. I later learned that my identification was quite correct: She was a 200-ton Spanish merchantman named *La Familia Santa*, which arrived from Spain with a general cargo of merchandise in 1625, but she was leaking so badly that she had to be run aground to prevent her from sinking. The Spaniards had salvaged all of her cargo and then left her there to rot away. Kelly and I returned to the shipwreck the following day with a small portable water jet and used it to move the sand and cover the wreck over again. I also notified the authorities to take action to prevent pirate divers from working the site again. Two months later I returned to the site to make certain that it had been properly protected and was shocked to find nothing left of the wreck but a large deep hole, with the wooden remains of the wreck ripped apart and strewn all over the place. The four cannon and the anchor had been dragged close to shore, probably to be raised and taken away. How had the pirates managed to work right under the noses of the police? A police harbor launch had been watching the area periodically ever since I had reported finding the site plundered. I later learned from fishermen that the pirates had actually worked on the site at night using underwater lights. From other sources I learned the identity of the culprits, but they were never prosecuted, because the father of one of them turned out to have plenty of political pull.

Ever since the project was initiated I had been writing a monthly archaeological report, which I had been told must remain confidential—for some unknown reason. One of the main objectives of my work, as I saw it, was to obtain all the archaeological data possible and publish it for the benefit of others in the field. I was asked to write and present a detailed report on the first year's work on my project at the Third Underwater Archaeological Conference, which was to be held in Miami on March 29, and when I notified Mrs. Hart that I would write the report and wanted to attend the meeting, she informed me that she thought it was a good idea and would have it cleared with Seaga. I was furious when she later told me that the Minister had no objections to my attending the meeting, but he did not want me to present a paper on Port Royal. This brought on another of the many arguments I had with Seaga while my project was underway. It turned out that he feared that I might severely criticize the government's inability to provide me with the funds, personnel, and equipment I really needed. Only after I promised not to mention these facts and permit him to censor the report, did I receive permission to write it. My report was very well received at the conference and everyone showed a great interest in our work at Port Royal.

APRIL

Confident that Edward Seaga, true to his word, would have our annual budget at least doubled for the new fiscal year, which officially started on the first of April, I had several advertisements placed in the press and on the radio for new divers, but I didn't get a single query from anyone. I also purchased a 16-foot aluminum skiff and a water pump, which I converted into an underwater jet. I planned to divide the operation up into two separate teams: one of the two new divers I would hire would work with me on the air lift; and Kelly would have another as his assistant and use the jet in other areas, when they weren't busy disassembling walls and raising bricks. In this manner we could speed up the excavation and cover more ground. I had also planned to hire several other people to work ashore as artists, draftsmen, and preservationists, but before I got around to doing this, I learned that I would be receiving the same budget as I had the previous year. Mrs. Hart said that since I had already bought the skiff and water pump, I should try to find two more divers and she would find the money somewhere to pay them.

After my advertisements failed to raise any divers, I decided to train two of the young boys who worked on the barge. After trying all five of them out one afternoon, I selected two: Alphonso, who was sixteen, and Vincent, who was only fifteen. Because of their ages I had to get their parents' permission to use them as divers, but this was no problem, especially since they would receive a considerable increase in salary. Both started out very enthusiastically at the task, but after a few days they were complaining that the work was too difficult and dangerous. To prevent them from quitting I finally had to use them only on a half-day basis—one in the morning and the other in the afternoon. Vincent gave up after three weeks and got his job back on the barge, but Alphonso stuck with it, and when he would work, which wasn't all the time, he was a better worker and diver than Wayne had been. For unknown reasons, Alphonso would develop all kinds of mysterious ailments—usually claiming his stomach hurt or he "had bells ringing" in his head—and he would not dive about one or two days each week. However, I needed him badly, so I kept him on.

Early in the month an editorial appeared in the local paper about what a hazardous occupation divers around the world engaged in and compared their work to the work we were doing at Port Royal, which the author considered more dangerous than any other. The editorial made a big point of the fact that divers working for an oil exploration firm off the coast of Alaska, who dived only one or two hours daily, were being paid a salary of $3,700 a month, while my divers were working as much as fifty hours a week and receiving very small salaries. Armed with the article, Kelly approached me and demanded a raise in salary. At the time, he was making only $220 a month before taxes and other deductions were taken out, and I couldn't really blame him for wanting more money. I promised to try to get him a raise.

During the first ten days of April we continued excavating around the shoreward and the south sides of the shipwreck, but it was slow going, because the sediment was composed of about 50 per cent pieces of dead coral—most of which had to be excavated by hand. In addition to the usual cuts and bruises we generally suffered from, we had a number of other problems: On two occasions 150-pound mortar balls fell either off the wreck or out of the side of the hole—lack of visibility prevented us from ever seeing them falling—and struck me on the head. Both times, my head was split open and I had several stitches. I didn't mind the cuts as much as the two bald spots where the doctor had to shave my head before sewing. We also had a miserable time with crabs: hundreds of them had moved into the area and made their home in the cave-like area around the perimeter of the shipwreck, which we had made by excavating under it, and their main pastime seemed to be pinching our fingers and other exposed parts of our bodies. Each morning we devoted about half an hour to killing as many as we could before starting the day's excavation, but they seemed to increase in number anyhow.

Sharks were another hazard. We had just gone through a period of about four months without seeing a single one—either underwater or on the surface. Then suddenly they appeared again, and at times there were as many as six or eight around on the surface at one time. At first they didn't bother us at all, until one day a small one made a pass at Alphonso as he was surfacing with a bucket of artifacts and gave him a nasty bruise on the leg bumping against him with its sandpaper-like hide. That evening

24. Pewter tankard with name William Deaven inscribed on it. *Photo by Marx.*

25. Sir Henry Morgan. *Photo courtesy of Jamaica Tourist Board.*

26. Grinding stone found on site of the meat market. *Photo by Marx.*

27. Marx and Kelly with artifacts found on the site of one private dwelling. *Photo courtesy of Jamaica Tourist Board.*

28. A typical day's find, which includes silver and pewter plates and chargers, clay pipes, a ceramic chamber pot, shards, bones, an iron object, etc. *Photo by Marx.*

29. Silver and pewter objects found on the site of one private home. *Photo by Marx.*

30. Arawak Indian metate, used for grinding corn and other grains. *Photo by Marx.*

31. Ceramic Arawak Indian bowls found on the site. *Photo by Marx.*

32. Combination brass pipe tamper and wax seal for letters. *Photo by Marx.*

33. Wayne Roosevelt and Kenute Kelly
with small iron cannon. *Photo by Marx.*

34. Artifacts found on the site of a tavern:
onion bottles, clay pipes, pewter tankards,
brass candle holder, and lead ash tray. *Photo by Marx.*

35. The Roman inscribed stone found i Kingston Harbour. *Photo by Marx.*

36. Copper scale pans before cleanir *Photo by Marx.*

37. Copper scale pans after cleaning. *Photo by Marx.*

38. Parts of the brass movement from the gold pocket watch. *Photo by Marx.*

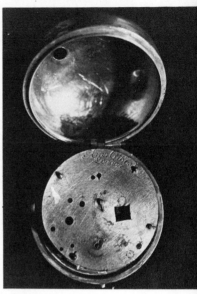

39. Inside of the watch and case, with maker's name *Aron Gibbs* and *London* inscribed. *Photo by Marx.*

40. Gold pocket watch, with maker's name *GIBBS* and *LONDON* showing on the face. *Photo by Marx.*

41. Section of brick wall with plaster still clinging to it. *Photo by Marx.*

42. Brass and silver buckles. *Photo by Marx.*

43. Maker's touch marks on a pewter plate. *Photo by Marx.*

44. Obverse of a Spanish silver piece of eight. *Photo by Marx.*

. Reverse of a Spanish silver piece of
ght. *Photo by Marx.*

46. Chart showing the area excavated during the first eight months of the excavation
—May to December 1966. The dark objects
are all walls of buildings. *Photo by Marx.*

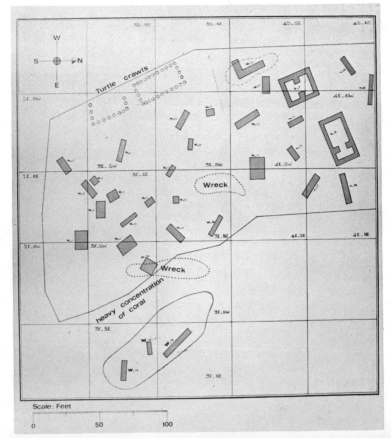

I put Ivan the Terrible and several of his cronies to work. The next morning they proudly displayed seven sharks they had caught on lines during the night, one of which was a fourteen-foot hammerhead, a type considered to be a man-eater. Two hours later another shark—estimated between four and ten feet, depending on who told the story—attacked Kelly's air hose on the surface and bit it in two. I decided to hold a shark-fishing tournament, with a case of beer for a prize for whoever caught the most sharks. During the rest of the day and during the night, a total of seventeen sharks were caught, and Peanuts, one of the boys who worked on the barge, won the contest by catching four. During the afternoon session I finally learned the reason for the sudden appearance of so many sharks in our area: the new cook at the Police Training School had been throwing into the water all the scraps and garbage from the kitchen after each meal, instead of into garbage cans as his predecessor had done. Once he was restrained, all the sharks disappeared as fast as they had arrived.

As a joke, Kelly and Alphonso had raised one of the 150-pound mortar balls that had clobbered me, and said I might want to keep it as a souvenir. What appeared to be a small fragment of rope was embedded in the coral covering it, and I began chipping it loose. Sparks began flying as I reached the solid metal, and I began smelling something burning. Suddenly I realized that what I had thought was rope was actually the fuse of the mortar ball, which I knew was hollow inside and filled with gunpowder, and it was actually burning. Fearing that the ball might explode, I quickly rolled it back into the sea. Just as someone was saying, "The chief is really a scaredy-cat," the ball exploded and sent a geyser of water twenty feet high into the air. Apparently the powder and lower end of the fuse had remained dry over the years under the protective coral growth covering it.

Our April finds were as numerous and exciting as those of the previous month. Under a small pile of loose bricks we found a large cutlass still covered by its leather scabbard, and pieces of four large muskets. Nearby, where we found about thirty intact onion bottles, I found a wedding band of 22-carat gold and a small brass cannon, only three and a half inches long. At first I thought it might be a toy, or off a ship model, but I later learned that it was actually used as a timepiece. Mounted with a magnifying glass above in a special case, which was set on gimbals so it would work well despite the movements of a ship, the cannon was filled with a small charge of powder. When the sun was at its zenith—at noon each day—the sun's rays would strike through the magnifying glass and ignite the powder in the touchhole, causing the piece to fire. This was the signal for the ship's navigator to shoot the sun with his astrolabe or other instruments to compute the ship's latitude. Other unusual artifacts found were several children's marbles, an Indian arrowhead made of flint, the bottom or top of a small wooden cask with the initials PR (probably for Port Royal) burned into it, a fragment of a leather shoe with a pewter buckle still attached, a seventeen-inch-long meat cleaver made of iron with a wooden handle, and a fragment of window glass on which someone had scratched a crude sketch of a horse. There was also the usual collection of pewter ware, the most interesting piece a porringer with a handle in the shape of two sea serpents.

A new wharf had been constructed on the other side of Port Royal, away from the area we were excavating, so that the Port Royal ferryboat would no longer interfere with our operation. On numerous occasions our air hoses or anchor lines from the barge and skiff had been cut by the passing ferryboat, and at times when the captain was in a hurry the boat created a big wake and the sediment would be accidentally washed off the barge and back into our hole, so we lost precious time having to pump it up again. April 11 was the first day the ferryboat began using the new wharf and should have been a day of rejoicing for us—but it wasn't.

Late in the afternoon I was excavating in an area where there seemed to be an unusual amount of ceramic shards and fragments of broken glassware. Earlier Kelly had discovered that there was a large coral head—which we later found to be about twelve feet in diameter—protruding from the side of the hole. I made a mental note to move it at the close of the day's operation, and I moved about ten feet away from the area I figured it might fall into.

Somehow I unknowingly worked my way back to the dangerous area, and the next thing I knew I was under the massive coral head. Fortunately I was lying flat on the bottom and had a pile of loose bricks piled up on both sides of my body—waiting to be taken up to the barge—and they took the full shock of the coral when it tumbled out of the side of the wall; otherwise my back would probably have been broken. Kelly was about twenty feet away at the time and unaware of what had happened. I gave the emergency signal on the air lift and someone pulled him to the surface and told him to check on me. I felt Kelly trying to move the coral head off me, but it wouldn't budge an inch. I had previously worked out several precautionary measures, which the surface crew was to carry out in the event of an emergency. The main thing was to start up the second Aquanaut unit, if it wasn't already running (I still had horrible memories of being trapped under that brick wall the year before and running out of air). That way, if the unit supplying me with air below happened to stop for any reason, the boys could quicky unscrew my air hose and attach it to the other unit. Kelly got the second Aquanaut started quickly and then sent one of the boys after Vincent and Alphonso, both of whom had quit for the day. About fifteen minutes after I had first been trapped, all three of them were on the bottom trying to move the coral head, but it still wouldn't budge. Ivan the Terrible then arrived with two dugout canoes full of fishermen and ordered the divers to sling ropes under the coral head, so they could try to lift it. I felt the divers frantically working with the ropes and knew that they were doing everything they possibly could. Even with the fishermen pulling and the three divers on the bottom pushing, the coral head would not move. Ivan then swam ashore and rushed over to the marine laboratory and asked them to bring their research boat, which had a large lifting boom and winch on it, to move the coral head off my back. While several students were scurrying about trying to find the keys to start the boat's engine, Kelly got four fishermen who could dive a little and three of the boys off the barge, and gave them all diving face masks. After a few practice dives, in which Kelly tried to make them all dive at the same time, since they had to hold their breaths underwater and couldn't stay down long, all ten of them attacked the coral head. On about their tenth dive, I felt the coral head moving and I tried to arch my back to help them a bit. I felt the head roll off my body, but I also felt a terrible pain in my back: I had slipped a disk when I arched my back.

Kelly and Alphonso, grabbing me under the arms, dragged me up to the surface, but the pain in my back was so excruciating that I couldn't climb aboard the skiff, so they swam me ashore and carried me into the laboratory. All three telephones in Port Royal were out of order, which was a common occurrence, so they couldn't call for an ambulance. Kelly couldn't drive an automobile, nor could anyone else who was around, for that matter, so I foolishly decided to try to drive to the hospital in Kingston. I was paralyzed from the waist down, so Kelly sat in the driver's seat and manipulated the clutch, brake, and gas pedals from my instructions, while I controlled the steering wheel and gear shift. I was really in bad pain, and about five miles outside of Port Royal, while still on the desolate Palisadoes road, I blacked out. Kelly got confused with the pedals and hit the clutch instead of the brakes and the car careened off into a sand dune but wasn't damaged at all. Fortunately a beer delivery truck appeared, and Kelly stopped it and had it carry me to the hospital.

The hospital staff was so used to seeing me appear with various injuries that I was already considered their most popular patient. When the doctor informed me that I had a slipped disk and would have to stay in traction for several weeks, I convinced him to let me do so at home. The press played my accident up in a big way and I became a hero overnight. Among the numerous "Get Well" cards I received, there was one from the members of the local diving club, which said: "Hope the hell you get killed the next time." I made good use of the time in bed catching up on my reading, and writing several archaeological reports about the Port Royal operation with the use of a tape recorder.

While I was convalescing, Kelly took charge of the project and did a very creditable job. Although the doctor was against my moving around, I convinced him to let me out of bed on the twenty-second of the month so I could get back to Port Royal. During the rest of the month I had someone drive Kelly and me to and from Port Royal each day, and I hobbled about on crutches supervising the topside operation and working in my preservation laboratory.

MAY

Not knowing how long it would be before I could dive again —if I'd taken the doctor's advice it would have been months—I decided to find another diver. Kelly had a close friend, a good diver, who worked as a seaman on a small freighter plying between Kingston and Miami. The vessel happened to be in port at the time and I executed a brilliant job of salesmanship and convinced his friend, named Coral Morgan (both appropriate names for the job), to work with us. Quickly dubbed Henry Morgan by everyone at Port Royal, he was quiet, hard-working, and a good diver. He had worked as a professional diver for several years in the construction of docks in Kingston Harbour, and also as a commercial spearfisherman, supplying hotels on the island's north coast with fish and lobsters. He had been making more than four hundred dollars a month as a seaman, yet he was willing to give up that job and join my team for a salary of only $168 a month. The question is, why? It must have been because of the aura of excitement that our project created.

During the first week of May I was still ashore hobbling around on crutches and going out of my mind from not being able to dive. My accident had been a lot more serious than I first realized. Since it occurred, I have had constant back trouble, and at the time of writing this book (which is six years later) I have been told by doctors that I have three deteriorated disks and must undergo surgery to have them removed. For months I had been hounded by members of the American press who wanted to write articles on our project, so during my enforced time ashore I invited them all to come down at the same time to get it over with. Journalists and photographers descended en masse on Port Royal from *National Geographic Magazine, The Saturday Evening Post, Argosy, Venture,* the New York *Times,* and the Miami *Herald.* I felt a bit silly playing hero when I was barely able to walk, but they were all satisfied and wrote flattering articles.

Meanwhile Kelly was "riding" (as he called it) the air lift, using Coral and Alphonso as his assistants. For the first few days they were working in good sediment, which was easy to pump up the air lift, but then they located the edge of a large fallen wall covered by between five and ten tons of ballast rock, which had probably fallen off the new shipwreck we had located. Before they could get under the wall, where they knew they would find many important artifacts, all the ballast had to be removed and the wall torn apart. They first tried to send the ballast up to the surface in buckets, but it was such a slow process that I finally told them to move the ballast into a spot we had already excavated in the new hole. Even so, this procedure took ten full working days and was a lot more tedious than just excavating. Mixed in with the ballast they found a wide variety of artifacts: cannon and musket balls, many types of ships' fittings, brass buttons, pewter and brass buckles, tools, bottles, crockery, and a lead packing seal with a nice design on it.

I had spent the second week of the month doing preservation work ashore and using a metal detector, with two helpers doing the digging, on various parts of the shore where the land had covered the sunken city over the centuries. It was just like in the water: everywhere that I got a good metallic reading and the boys dug, we found artifacts from the old town and later periods. The only problem with digging on land was that when we dug down only two feet, we hit salt water and had great difficulty going deeper. The fact that many artifacts from the time of the earthquake were so close to the surface was most interesting and convinced me that a large-scale land excavation of Port Royal should be undertaken. I passed this information on to Dr. Ivor Noel Hume of Colonial Williamsburg. He came down to visit sometime after and made a number of test holes in the area. In one test hole he discovered a three-inch ceramic figurine of a gentleman, dating from the time of the earthquake, which closely re-

sembled Henry Morgan. He then backed me up and wrote a
lengthy report to the Jamaican Government stressing the importance of a land excavation of Port Royal. For the time being, the
government had its hands full keeping my project going and
could do nothing about the land dig.

On the first morning of the third working week, the diving
team began disassembling the large brick wall, which measured
fifteen by nine and a half feet and was twenty inches thick.
Around noon Kelly came out of the water with blood gushing out
of his hand: he had cut it on a large piece of glass and it took
about twenty stitches to be closed up. Since neither Coral nor
Alphonso had experience using the air lift, I knew I would have
to disobey my doctor and start diving again. Actually, it turned
out that I felt less pain when I was underwater than I did on land
—probably because my body was weightless in the water and
there wasn't any pressure on the disks and nerves. I continued to
use the crutches for another month to get around on land, but
underwater I was working at my old pace, except that I couldn't
lift anything heavy.

It took the rest of the day to finish removing the wall. Most of
the bottom side was smoke-blackened and I conjectured that we
might be on the site of another cookhouse, which turned out to
be correct. During the rest of the week we recovered what may
have been the complete contents of an old Port Royal cookhouse,
including the remains of the fireplace, with several burnt logs
mixed among the firebricks. In pewter there were ten spoons, two
bottle stoppers, eleven plates (and pieces of three others), pieces
of two large chargers, a serving bowl, a porringer, a mustard pot,
and two tankards; in brass and copper we brought up a tea
strainer, a colander, several buckles, a door handle, a five-inch-
high mortar (the pestle was fashioned of stone), several pans, a
candlestick, a cooking pot (twenty-one inches in diameter and
twelve and one half inches high, with turtle and fish bones in it),
two skimmers, a ladle, a sewing thimble, several sewing needles,
and five buttons; in iron there were a pair of scissors, numerous
knives of different sizes, a large spoon, two keys, a padlock, a candle snuffer, four large cooking caldrons, two smaller three-legged

kettles, and several lengths of chain (probably for hanging caldrons in the fireplace); in glass there were various types and sizes
of bottles (including seven onion bottles), fragments of window
glass, wineglasses, tumblers, a linen smoother, pieces of a large
pitcher, and a red bead; in wood we found a bucket, a large stir-
ring spoon, and numerous fragments from a table; and we recovered dozens of ceramic items such as plates, jars, cups, bowls, plat-
ters, mugs, floor tiles, and also a chamber pot, a pitcher, a candle
holder, a flower vase, and a saltcellar. In addition to these items
we found several striking flints, two human teeth, three ivory cutlery handles, a walnut, a handful of chickpeas, and a six-inch-long
bone brush with horsehair bristles still on it. We had really hit the
jackpot. The strange thing was that on the various types of pewter
we found eight different sets of owners' initials—for all of which
I found corresponding property owners listed—so I couldn't really
determine whose cookhouse we had excavated.

There was other excitement that week in Port Royal. Several
high-ranking government officials, who were Blacks and not
members of the Morgan's Harbour Beach Club, had been refused
admission to the club, and they created quite a stir on the island,
claiming that they had been refused admission because of their
color. In fact, although about 95 per cent of the island's population was colored, there were very few colored members of the
club. Rumors were circulating around the island that the club
would be closed and Jenkinson would be deported, but after a
while the clamor died down and everything returned to normal.

About this same time Ed Link wrote a letter to Bernard Lewis
saying that he was hoping to return to work at Port Royal in the
near future and that he was willing to work together with me,
rather than independently—a prospect that pleased me. To my
surprise, Seaga told Lewis to tell Link that my team and I were
doing such an outstanding job that we did not require any outside
help. Our excavation was a "Jamaican project," and Seaga and
others in the government were proud that their newly independent nation could undertake such an important project on
its own.

During the last week of the month we continued to make good finds, although not as many as the previous week. We found two smaller walls, which were of different construction than that of the cookhouse. Under one of them we found an undated Spanish copper maravedi coin and a Spanish silver one-real coin dated 1662. Then, under the other, to my great astonishment, among many artifacts dating from the period of the earthquake, we discovered a silver fork with PORT ROYAL and the date 1864 engraved on it. How had it gotten under the fallen wall and mixed into the same stratigraphical level as the other artifacts? It was found nine feet below the surface of the bottom sediment. The only explanation I could come up with was that it had been accidentally dropped on the sea floor and dragged down into the sediment by the anchor of a ship.

I was constantly hearing vague rumors that one or more of the boys on the barge were stealing artifacts that were either brought up by the divers or landed on the screen aboard the barge. I decided to test the boys' honesty one day and hid a replica gold coin in my diving suit and then sent it up the air lift to land on the barge. At the end of the day I asked all of the boys if anything interesting had landed on the screen and they all answered that nothing had, with nervous looks that betrayed their guilt. I noticed that one of the five boys who alternated between working on the barge and on the skiff was gone, and the others told me he had gotten sick and gone home. I found the boy and told him a lie, stating that the other boys had confessed that he had robbed the coin. He broke into tears, admitted the theft, and said he had sold the coin to an American tourist for twenty dollars. I combed every hotel in Kingston that evening trying to find the tourist to buy back the phony coin, but had no luck. I fired the boy next day and mistakenly considered the matter finished. Trade unions on the island are very powerful, and although no one on my project was in a union, the boy's father went to a union official and complained that I had fired his son. The official appeared and demanded, even after I told him why I had fired the boy, that I either rehire him or pay him three months' wages. When I refused to do either, he approached all of my workers and asked them to go on strike. Taking about all the guff I could, I told Ivan to remove him from the premises, which he did in not too gentlemanly a fashion. The following morning two police officers appeared with a warrant to arrest Ivan for assault. An urgent telephone call to Seaga got us out of this mess and I had no further problems with union officials.

JUNE

June proved as exciting and productive as May had been. With three divers now on the payroll besides myself, I hoped to finally get two excavation teams working simultaneously, but it never happened. During the month, I always had at least one diver working with me, on a few occasions two, but never three so that I could split them up into two separate teams. Kelly was finally able to dive on the tenth of the month, but he seemed very low in spirits, and when I asked what the problem was, he announced that since I had been unable to get the raise in his salary, he was quitting at the end of the month, which he did to my great regret. Alphonso was out of action more than half of June with numerous ailments: various cuts and bruises, the flu, and an ear infection. Coral appeared with a note from a doctor at the beginning of the month stating that he had a serious ear infection and should stay out of the water for at least three weeks. A large hole was being dug in the middle of modern Port Royal for a water cistern, and I assigned Coral to recover every single artifact that was uncovered in the hole. From the hole, which was about twenty feet in diameter and dug to a depth of six feet with the use of several water pumps to keep out the sea water, he recovered twelve bushels of ceramic shards, pieces of glassware, iron objects, and clay pipes. In addition he found a pewter toy lamb, a lead spigot, two silver spoons, and two nineteenth-century British halfpennies.

We were plagued with an epidemic of stinging jellyfish for most of the month, and all suffered from stinging burns on our heads, necks, and hands. Around the middle of the month we had a problem with a very inquisitive eight-and-a-half-foot hammer-head shark, who hung around for the greater part of one day repeatedly butting us with his snout. Finally Kelly borrowed a speargun and killed the shark with a well-placed shot in his brain.

I had feared that the closer we got to joining the two holes together, the less chance we would have of locating walls, and consequently would be finding fewer artifacts, but this was not the case. During the month, we located thirteen fallen and standing walls, and because the sediment was chiefly composed of silt, mud, and gravel, we excavated an area greater than we had in the four previous months combined. From the dimensions and the type of construction (the pattern in which the bricks were arranged in the walls), I was able to determine that the walls belonged to four different buildings.

Early in the month we located a standing L-shaped wall eight and a half feet high; one section of it was fifteen feet six inches long and the other eleven feet long. In the middle of the longer wall was a space for a window (the glass and frame were missing), which measured three feet by three feet. Then, a few days later, about twenty feet from one end of this wall, we found another standing L-shaped wall, with the exact dimensions of the first and the same construction pattern, so I had little doubt that it was the other half of the same building. About midway in the longer wall was a doorway slightly over six feet high, with the wooden lintel still in place over the door. All four walls were coated with white plaster inside. In the area between both sections of the building we found seven oak roof beams, of the right length to have been used on the same building, and thousands of fragments of black slate roof tiles. The only artifact of any significance found in the same general area was an ornate brass slave collar with "EG 87" engraved on it. The two ends formed a hasp, and the collar was probably kept secured to the slave's neck with a small padlock, which we didn't find. I can only surmise that the initials belonged to the slave's owner and the numerals were the identification number of the slave. If this is in fact so, then the slave could have belonged to either Edmond

Grimston or Elizabeth Gooding—both of whom were property owners at Port Royal.

Nearby we located three other sections of walls, all belonging to the same building, and I believe we were in the dining room of a house belonging to either a man named William Morris or one named William Murro, according to the owner's initials we found on several pieces of pewter ware. We found seven plates and a charger stacked up neatly in a pile, another charger, four complete spoons and pieces of eleven others, a porringer, a tankard, a measure, two bottle stoppers, and the lower half of a watch case, all of pewter; we found a small gold toothpick; three silver spoons; of copper or brass items we recovered two large bowls, a door handle, several drawer handles, four hinges, a six-inch door lock, several small rings (probably used for hanging curtains) four buckles, five buttons, three small weights (the type used for weighing precious metals), and several straight pins; we brought up several onion bottles, an ink well, one button in the shape of a rose, and various types of glassware; three iron knives (one with a wooden handle) and a large lock for a door; and a wide variety of crockery, several nice pieces of Chinese porcelain, and a multicolored delftware chamber pot. Although many of these items were identical to those we had found in the two cookhouses, the absence of any cooking implements or firebricks ruled out the possibility of excavating a cookhouse.

We then ran into an area of loose bricks—3,984, to be exact—which I believe might have been ripped off different walls by divers in the past century for use on the Naval Hospital and for some unknown reason never raised. After we had sent them all to the surface and excavated under them, we discovered a number of artifacts that led me to believe that we had reached the area where the old "lock-up" had once stood. We found one almost complete six-foot-long musket (only a part of the wooden butt was missing) and pieces of six others, 190 lead musket balls, half of a powder horn made from the horn of a cow, six iron knife blades, and fragments of three different swords or cutlasses.

Next, for almost a week we worked in a barren area without any walls, and our only finds were a few iron cannon balls and numerous ceramic shards and broken onion bottles. Our luck changed at the beginning of the last week of June, and we located five different sections of fallen walls from one building: a cobbler's shop. In the area we found two cobblers' awls, a hammer, several of the curved knives used for cutting leather, half of an earthenware pattern in the shape of a shoe sole, a sharpening stone, twelve complete shoe heels and ten soles, and fragments of leather from at least several dozen pairs of shoes or boots. Scattered all over the area were thousands of small iron and copper shoe tacks and numerous wooden fragments of a workbench or table.

As soon as we had completed the excavation around the cobbler's shop, we located three sections of walls and numerous artifacts belonging to a carpenter's or cabinetmaker's shop. Among the numerous iron objects we identified (the majority were too thickly covered by coral to identify) were two axes, two hatchets, two hammers, a large sledge hammer, two wedges, two augers (for drilling holes), a file, a four-foot-long saw with its wooden handle still attached, an adze, a pair of scissors, a penknife, a large L-shaped carpenter's square, and thousands of tacks, nails, and spikes. In addition to these items we recovered a whetstone, a lead plumb bob, a fragment of a lead pencil, the head of a large wooden mallet, hundreds of brass tacks and nails, several dozen sheets of copper, a roll of copper wire, a six-pound chunk of beeswax, about thirty pounds of lead in sheets, four brass hinges, and six brass drawer handles. We also miraculously found all the pieces of a large workbench and a stool—both of which bore marks of long use—and the pieces of a large bed—which showed no signs of use—which perhaps the carpenter had been making or had just finished at the time of the disaster. About a week later, when we were working nearby we also discovered a foot-long folding carpenter's rule, half of which was made of brass and the rest of a hard wood. It was in such a perfect state of preservation that the brass part could move and be folded into the center of the wooden portion. It was graduated in quarters of an inch, but I found that the foot calibrated on the ruler was three eighths of an inch less than the foot measurement we use today.

During the month, we found a large number of artifacts in other areas: among the most interesting were a copper fishhook, a brass weight in the shape of a bell used on grandfather clocks, parts of another scale (the four-foot-long balance bar and two fourteen-inch-diameter copper scale pans), twelve lead scale weights of different sizes and shapes, seven small packing seals (one had LEYDEN stamped on it and the others all had different initials or markings), an iron (for ironing clothes), a sounding lead (probably off our new wreck), several black glass beads (the type used on rosaries), a ten-inch-long tusk from an unidentified animal, a bone double-edged comb, and a beautifully carved ivory cane or parasol handle.

On the last day of the month we at last excavated our way into the old hole, which we had abandoned six months before, and thus joined both holes, but it took us almost three more months before we had made the new hole the same width as the old one. June would have been almost perfect if only Kelly had not had to seek a higher-paying job.

JULY

July was another fabulous month, although it started out slowly. On the first working day, our only interesting recovery was a large coral-encrusted conglomerate weighing around a hundred fifty pounds. For some reason the members of my team were convinced that there was gold in some form inside the conglomerate, which was about four feet in diameter, so I gently began taking it apart. There wasn't any gold in it, but it did contain seventy-three carpenters' tools and thousands of nails and tacks, and from fragments of wood on the outer edges of the conglomerate I was able to determine that they had all been stored in a wooden chest and no doubt belonged to the carpenter whose shop we had just finished excavating. Because they had not lain loose on the bottom, but were packed tightly together, electrolytic action between the different objects gave them cathodic protection, and with the exception of several tools on the outer edges of the conglomerate, they were all in a remarkable state of preservation. After a bath of running water for several weeks, they needed only a coating of paraffin wax to preserve them.

The following day we located a small fallen wall—only three by four feet—and packed tightly under it were twenty-six onion bottles, a brass candle holder, two pewter plates, another brass bell-shaped grandfather-clock weight like that we had found the month before, and six broken ceramic plates—one with a beautiful frigate under sail painted on it. Then, late in the afternoon, the shore-based compressor that supplied the air lift broke down and we were without the use of it for the next six days. It took a mechanic from the Public Works Department only an hour to make the repair, but he couldn't come any sooner.

During the period that the compressor was broken, a number of interesting things occurred. I had detailed Alphonso and Coral to spend several days smashing sea urchins, picking up loose bricks we had overlooked in the hole, and removing a number of large coral heads that were projecting above the surface of the sea floor. Kelly appeared one morning and I was happy, thinking that he had decided to return to work again. Unfortunately he had come only to pose for some photographs for a journalist from *Ebony* magazine who was doing an article on him.

I had hired a good artist named Walter McFarlane, a resident of Port Royal who had just graduated from the Jamaican School of Art. By this time we had recovered over six thousand clay smoking pipes, and at the instigation of Adrian Oswald, an Englishman who was considered the leading expert on pipes of the period we were recovering, I was then working on an archaeological report about the pipes each night at home. Louise Judge had already spent a considerable amount of time making drawings of the more than one hundred different pipe shapes and five hundred makers' marks, so I had Walter take over and complete the task working on a full-time basis. The university had closed for the summer, and my wife came to work as a volunteer and measured the bore diameters of this overwhelming number of pipes—a very tedious job.

One morning a man appeared carrying a heavy bag, which

contained 376 Spanish eight- and four-real silver coins, all dated between 1721 and 1785. He had been bulldozing on his property near Old Harbour and had accidentally uncovered the hoard. By the time he had spotted the coins being pushed along in front of the bulldozer blade, he found that they also extended for about two hundred yards behind him. Mixed in with the coins were hundreds of ceramic shards, and he figured that they had been stored in ceramic vessels, which I later identified as Spanish olive jars. I spent the rest of the day using a metal detector on his property and we found fifty-four more coins. During the next few weeks, using my detector, he recovered 119 more, including three of gold. This find was exciting and I felt it was about time we made another big coin find at Port Royal.

Sergio Dello Strologo had been involved the past few months in restoring a Kingston "great house" (the main residence on the old plantations) that was to be made into a museum, and also in constructing a bar and restaurant on the lines of a seventeenth-century Port Royal grogshop. Since Seaga had been unable to raise any funds to build a museum at Port Royal to display some of the items we had recovered, Sergio got permission to use the "silver house" (a small building adjacent to the "great house" where the silver service and other valuable items were stored in the old days) as a Port Royal museum. I spent several days helping him set up the display in it; then he suggested that it would enhance the display if we had a few old cannons and an anchor to place outside the building.

Unable to get the use of a large boat with a lifting boom to raise these items from an old shipwreck located in the harbor, we devised another system. After attaching several fifty-five-gallon fuel drums to them, we filled the drums with air from the Aquanaut units and thus raised them to the surface. Then we towed them to a beach and Stan Judge provided a wrecker truck to lift them and place them on a truck, which he also loaned us. It seemed that everything I ever did on Jamaica had to be done the hard way.

After the air compressor was repaired, we started excavating again, but had four bad days in a row, finding practically nothing.

Then, late on the afternoon of the last working day of the second week, we located a large fallen wall, and in a matter of only a few minutes I found a gold soupspoon, a beautiful silver porringer, three pewter plates and three spoons, several small ink bottles (with ink still in them), a small vial of mercury, a pistol, and several dozen lead pistol balls. I wanted to keep going and pump as much as I could under the wall, but mindful of the accidents I had already had from walls falling on top of me, prudence won out and we reluctantly stopped for the day. It was payday for my team and they were all anxious to rush to Kingston and spend their money after a hard week at Port Royal. I wanted to come back out the following day, which was Sunday, and begin tearing the wall apart, but I was committed to give a lecture to the Jamaican Historical Society, so I just had to wait until Monday.

As I was driving Coral to Port Royal on Monday morning, he surprised me by saying (he rarely spoke at all) he had a feeling that we would make a fantastic find that week, and I tended to agree with him. The three of us went to work on the wall, and by noon we had completely taken it apart and had a nice large pile of loose bricks stacked up behind us. While Coral and Alphonso were sending the bricks up to the surface, I went to work with the air lift. Until that time I had never been able to pump more than seven full barge loads in a full working day. However, in the next five hours, because the sediment consisted of only sand, I was able to pump eight full barge loads, and the boys on the barge were all complaining about the extra hard work. Disappointingly the only artifacts I had found during this whole time were a few more pistol balls and a knife with a bone handle. It was already an hour past usual quitting time and I had to let the boys go home, but Coral and Alphonso were willing to stay longer.

The three of us brought out the water jet, and our persistence finally paid off. In a matter of minutes we found another wall of the same construction as the one we had taken apart earlier in the day and only a few feet from it. With the jet I began blowing away sand from under the edges of the wall and suddenly heard someone let out a loud howl. Coral appeared with two

Spanish silver eight-real (pieces-of-eight) coins, pressing them against my face mask so I could see them. During the next two hours, we found nine more of the same type of coins and two silver spoons. Hunger pains (I hadn't eaten in twenty-four hours) finally forced me to call it a day. The coins were in an excellent state of preservation, like those we had found the year before, and I knew they must be part of a hoard. As tired as I was that night, I had difficulty sleeping for more than an hour at a time: I kept waking up and thinking about what else might be under that wall.

When I started the air-lift compressor the next morning, the fan belt flew off, broken in two pieces, and we didn't have a spare available, so I sent Ivan to Kingston to buy another. On the bottom I found that there wasn't even an inch of visibility. This ruled out using the water jet, which might blow more coins away than we would find. Vincent, who had once worked as diver for me and was then working on the barge, joined us as a diver this particular day, and the four of us worked side by side digging under the wall by hand. By two in the afternoon, when Ivan got back with the fan belt, we had found only three more pieces of eight.

I got the air lift into action while the other three began taking the wall apart. Less than ten minutes had passed when I felt a round object caught on the bottom of the air-lift screen. After reducing the pressure a bit, I extracted the object, which was shining bright as the sun: it was a Spanish four-escudo gold coin. I quickly took it to the surface and told the boys on the barge to watch the screen very carefully, because I felt other coins would be going up the air lift. When I got down to the bottom, Vincent was holding two silver spoons he had just found. Minutes later a minor landslide occurred, and in the gloom I found the whole bottom in front of me covered with hundreds of silver coins—most were eight reals, but others were of the smaller denominations; fours, twos, and ones. I knew that the ones and twos were too small to be caught on the screen on the bottom of the air lift, so I turned it off and surfaced. I had my wife, Ivan, and Walter join the boys on the barge to grab any coins landing on the screen and went back down again with a bucket full of glass jars, which I distributed to each of the divers to hold the coins they found. With the pressure turned on as low as possible, I used the air lift to gently suck up the sand around the coins, as we tried to pick them all up by hand. By the end of the day we had recovered 439 silver and the one gold coin, and only about ten had gotten past us and gone up the air lift to land on the barge.

The expected crowd, numbering about two hundred persons, were waiting when we got ashore, shouting things like: "Old Goldfingers done it again" and "Mon, how about buying all of us a few drinks at the Buccaneers Roost." My wife drove over to the Police Training School and asked for several policemen to escort us into town, where I planned to deposit the coins in a safe in Seaga's office. All she could get was one unarmed policeman who offered to follow us in his car, as he was off duty and on his way home. I made a brief stop at the Custom House, in the town, to phone Seaga's office and alert them that I was on my way in with the coins, fearing that the office might be closed when I got there. I certainly didn't want to keep such a valuable treasure at home. When I got back out, my wife told me that the impatient policeman had taken off for town without us. In Kingston, Seaga was waiting for us with three bottles of champagne and we had a nice celebration in his office.

Kelly appeared the next morning, but since he was no longer covered by insurance, I couldn't permit him to dive, so he took command of running the barge operation. I also hired two more boys to work on the barge, so there were a total of ten persons carefully watching the barge. To be extra cautious, after the barge was loaded each time and ready to be emptied, I had them sift through all the sediment, using fine-mesh screens set up on the shore, and this really paid off: during the next two weeks they found about sixty small coins missed when they were pumped up on the barge. During the first half of the day we found about thirty silver coins and another silver spoon; then we hit another hot spot where the boys had removed a section of the wall. Our day's total was 353 silver coins—again, all of them in an excellent state of preservation and fully dated.

During the next six days we found only eight more silver coins, and it looked as if we had found the main bulk of the hoard. Then, on the morning of July 26, we found still another wall of the same construction as the other two, about five feet from where the edge of the last one had been, and I was sure we would hit it big again. Coral and Alphonso began taking one end of the wall apart, as I pumped the sand off the top of it. Soon the bucket was full of artifacts: a pewter candlestick, two pewter plates, two silver belt buckles, eleven pewter and brass buttons, a handsome brass protractor, and a penknife with mother-of-pearl inlaid on the handle. I decided to take the bucket up to see if any coins had landed on the screen and found that three small, one-real coins had been sucked up.

As soon as I reached the bottom, Coral grabbed me and dragged me quickly over to the section of wall they had just begun to take apart. Because I had turned off the air lift for a few minutes, visibility was better than usual—about six inches. Coral guided my head close to the wall and I could scarcely believe what confronted me. Stacked in neat rows of about twenty coins each were hundreds of silver coins. I grabbed Coral and Alphonso and we went up to the surface. I wanted the water to clear up better because it was a sight I wanted everyone on the team to enjoy. After waiting an hour I went down and saw that visibility was about three feet, so I brought down every man on the team, including Walter, who had never been underwater before, and gave them the opportunity to see that beautiful sight. How the coins had remained in such neat piles was a real mystery.

For the next two hours I gingerly extracted the coins, handing them to Alphonso and Coral, who were peering over my shoulder, until we had filled all the jars we had. As those two began kicking to the surface with the treasure, the downward thrust from their fins caused a minor landslide and the remaining rows of coins slid down from under the wall, deeper into the hole. After finding all we could locate visually, I brought the air lift back into action and began digging in the area they had fallen into. While I was doing this, Alphonso went back up the same section of the wall where the coins had been and began digging around by hand. He found several silver coins and then once again I heard a tremendous howl. He had found three gold wedding bands stacked neatly on top of one another. After shoving them on one of his fingers, he swam over and placed them against my face mask. By the end of the day we had recovered 557 silver coins—the most we had ever found in a single day.

All three of the gold rings were intricately fashioned, and one of them consisted of two hands clasped together. Engraved on the inner side was the inscription "When this you see remember me." Another one had "Continue Constant" inscribed on it.

During the next four days, while Alphonso and Coral carefully took the the large wall apart, I kept excavating with the air lift in the same general area. In one spot I found 513 lead musket balls, most of which were sucked up the air lift and deposited on the barge. Near them I also found the rear half of a large musket with beautiful silver inlay work on the butt and the initials MC scratched onto the brass butt plate. A number of other interesting artifacts also turned up: three pewter spoons, a keyhole plate with a coat of arms embossed on it, much of the movement of a large clock, a spoon, two candlesticks, the lid of a snuff box, a small precious-metal-scale weight, several small links of a chain (the kind used on a small scale), and one third of a British coin —all made of brass. During this time we didn't find another coin on the bottom, but twenty-six small ones and two reals were found on the barge, having gone up the air lift.

Then, on the last of the month, we made our greatest find of the whole excavation. The day actually started off badly. Alphonso and Morgan were raising the last of the bricks they had pried from the wall, but during the night a small moray eel had apparently found a home among the pile of bricks and, annoyed at being disturbed, he bit the end of one of Alphonso's fingers off. After applying a tourniquet, I had Walter drive him in to the hospital. The rest of the day went slowly, and my only finds were a few onion bottles and a modern beer bottle someone had dropped into the hole. Then suddenly I heard the signal on the air-lift tube that something special had gone up the tube. I hadn't seen a single coin because of the water's extreme murkiness: I had excavated to a depth of more than twenty feet, below the sand and into a level of mud. I went to the surface and saw everyone crawling around on the deck of the barge picking up coins. I had hit another hot spot on the bottom, and in a matter of only a few seconds, 173 small one- and two-real silver coins had gone up the air lift and sprayed out all over the barge. One of the boys said, "Boss, it's the first time I've ever seen it raining coins."

I went back down again and pumped for another hour, until I got the signal that it was time to quit, but we didn't find any more coins. Before surfacing I decided to make a thorough inspection of the hole after lying motionless for about twenty minutes to give the water some time to settle. I first found a few pipe-stem fragments, and then with eyes glued to the bottom I spotted something white barely sticking out of the side of the hole. Using my callus-covered fingers, I began digging the object out of the hole. It turned out to be an exquisitely beautiful ten-inch-high Chinese porcelain figurine of a woman holding a baby—like the Madonna and Child. Later I learned that it dated from the Ming or the Ch'ing dynasty, had probably been made in Te-hua, a town in Fukien Province, China, and was a representation of the Goddess of Fertility and Childbirth. The figurine, although quite fragile, had not been damaged save for the missing head of the infant. Search as we did for the next month, we never found the lost head. To me, the figurine was more precious than all the 1,536 silver coins and other artifacts we had found that month.

AUGUST

There's an old saying that "treasure brings trouble," and I really believe that there's a great deal of truth to it. As soon as we began finding the coins of the new hoard, Seaga had the police post a launch over the site around the clock and also stationed two policemen ashore. The curious spectators and the members of the press appeared, as they had when we made our first big coin find. Again I was ordered by Seaga, who had since become the deputy prime minister, to keep our find a secret, a tactic

I knew would certainly cause trouble. Keeping anything a secret at Port Royal is nearly impossible, especially with a team who were only too willing to tell anyone anything for a few beers. The inevitable rumors started right away, and again our find was magnified beyond belief. To make matters worse, a rumor was circulating that I had discovered a four-foot-high statue of Henry Morgan made out of solid gold and had smuggled it out of the country. I demanded almost daily that the truth about our finds be made public, but it never was—not even at the time I am writing this book. Whatever reasons Seaga had for keeping it a deep, dark secret remain unexplained.

When we arrived to start work on the morning of August 1, I spotted two men actually diving in the area where we had been finding the coins, and I quickly swam out. They turned out to be the two policemen who were running the launch, diving, as one of them explained to me, "to find a few coins for their children." It seemed incredible that policemen who had been sent to prevent our site from being plundered had the nerve to actually do it themselves. Several days later a police officer came to inspect the area, and he tried unsuccessfully to force one of the barge boys to give him a coin.

On the first day, we recovered thirty-one coins and another onyx Brazilian good-luck charm in the shape of a fist; the second day fifty-two coins, a pewter spoon, a brass shoe buckle, and a brass wedding band; and on the third day only seven coins and another pewter spoon. Early on the morning of the fourth day, after finding only another pewter spoon, I almost severed the thumb of my right hand when I attempted to extract a large piece of modern glass that had gotten caught on the air-lift screen. Since neither Alphonso nor Coral knew how to handle the air lift, I called it a day and rushed into Kingston to get eleven stitches.

The next three days were a national holiday on the island, Jamaica's Independence Day celebration, so I had to reluctantly suspend operations. One one of these three days, while catching up on preservation work in the laboratory, I was paid an unexpected visit by Prince Philip of England, who was on the island for the Independence Day celebrations. After giving him a complete tour of the place, in which he expressed a great interest, he shocked both me and the members of his party by expressing a desire to make a brief dive on the site. I tried to explain that the underwater visibility was quite bad and there really wasn't much to see on the bottom, but he insisted on going down anyway. After a few minutes of instructions in shallow water near the shore, I took him by the hand and we went down in the area where we had been finding the coins. It was almost as if I had planted the coin: lying right on the surface was a piece of eight. Visibility was only about four feet, so I swam him over the spot where the coin was lying several times before I finally gave up and picked it up myself. Later he said he had seen it and thought it was just a black sea shell. I was really a bit worried that something might happen to him, so after about ten minutes I dragged him to the surface, to the great relief of everyone present except the prince himself, who wanted to stay down longer. That evening Seaga phoned me and was furious, stating that I must be insane to risk the life of such an important person by permitting him to dive at Port Royal.

During the next week, we recovered only twenty-five silver coins, but we did find a good collection of interesting artifacts: another silver spoon, with the owner's initials MC on it; two spoons, a button, a porringer, a candlestick, and a chamber pot, all of pewter; more parts of a large clock, an apothecary's mortar, three shoe buckles, a salt or pepper shaker, four buttons, and two pans for a precious-metal scale, all of brass; a complete Spanish majolica plate with the number 9 painted on it; and fifteen onion bottles. All these items had come from under three small sections of walls of the same construction as those we had found everything under the month before.

Kelly had spent only the one day supervising the barge operation and had left before I even had a chance to talk with him. However, I knew that our treasure find had greatly excited him and he wanted to come back to work again. I spoke with him several days later and asked him to come back with us. He agreed, but it took almost three weeks before I could get the wheels turning and get him another employment contract. He started again at the beginning of the third week.

Things went rather slowly this week, and we found only nine silver coins: seven Spanish, one French, and one English. We also found a brass English counter, which looks just like a coin. Counters were used in accounting and sometimes as gambling chips. Artifacts were also scarce this week and it looked as if our bonanza was over.

From the nature of the finds we had made in the area of the coins, I decided we had to be on the site of a silversmith's shop. The coins didn't really offer any clues to this assumption, but all the items of silver and pewter ware did. With the exception of the owner's initials "MC" on the various pieces of silver we had brought up, none of them had any hallmarks or other markings on them. The same applied to all the pewter ware. According to law, all pewter ware and silverware made anywhere in continental Europe had to bear the makers' hallmarks or touch marks. Furthermore all the pieces looked as if they had never been used, and their shapes and styles were unlike any I was able to find in books on silver and pewter ware. Apparently they had just been made and were awaiting a buyer. The pieces with the initials "MC" on them might have belonged to the silversmith, or to a customer who had just purchased them. However, there were no property owners in Port Royal that these initials would fit. The precious-metal scale was another good clue: a device that every silversmith would have in his shop. In the old days many silversmiths also acted as coin changers and bankers as a side line. The brass English counter also indicated that our silversmith dealt with substantial sums of money, as did the large number of coins we found. The scarcity of many other items, such as ceramic ware and cooking implements, indicated that the shop was just used as a place of business and the proprietor probably lived elsewhere. The pistol and shot were probably kept by the smith as protection against anyone who might attempt to rob him.

Robert Nesmith, the coin expert who had helped with our first coin hoard, was unable to come back again because of sickness, so I invited Clyde Hubbard, another well-known expert on

Spanish colonial coinage, who lives in Mexico City. Clyde was as bug-eyed as Nesmith had been when he saw the remarkable state that our coins were found in. He spent a full week, working as much as eighteen hours a day, inspecting and cataloguing every single coin we had found. The majority of the coins were divided about evenly between the South American mints of Lima and Potosí, with the exception of about twenty, which were from the Mexico City mint. The date range of the coins was wider than the first hoard: these dated between 1552 and 1690, of which about 60 per cent were dated in the 1680s. Although some of these coins may have been salvaged from those Spanish ships that wrecked on Pedro Shoals in 1690, the early dates of many of them point to their having been in circulation for some time, and they probably reached Port Royal as plunder or through trade with the Spaniards. Of all the coins, Clyde was most excited over a solitary Spanish silver coin we had found earlier in the year. It had been minted in 1626 in Cartagena, Colombia, at a time when experts didn't even know that a mint in that city was operating.

During the last week of the month, while Clyde was still working on the coins, I had another visitor, who stayed for two weeks. After months of waiting, UNESCO had finally sent someone to look into the preservation problem, especially that of the iron objects. The expert they sent was a Mr. Garry Thompson, who was on the staff of the National Art Gallery in London. My excitement quickly died out after Garry informed me that his specialty was detecting fraudulent art treasures and that he had never worked in the field of preservation of any kind. During his stay I gave him a crash course in everything I knew about preservation and we conducted a number of tests and experiments together on iron objects, but learned little more than I already knew. Garry returned to London with several boxes full of iron artifacts and said he would do everything possible to solve the problem.

During the period that both Clyde and Garry were on the island, I gave a good tour of everything we had found. The majority of the artifacts that weren't then on display or awaiting preservation in my Port Royal laboratory had been turned over to the Institute of Jamaica for safekeeping—if you could call it that. While inspecting the various artifacts at the Institute, I noticed that a number of things such as the miniature brass cannon, the gold ring I had found in the coral-encrusted conglomerate, and other objects were missing. I demanded an investigation, but nothing came of it and the missing items were never found.

Since I had to spend most of my time with the two visitors during the last week of the month, I put Kelly in charge of the excavation, with orders to instruct the other two divers how to use the air lift. They had a discouraging week and found very little of interest. Kelly was so sad that he told me he was thinking of quitting again, but I convinced him once more to stay with the project.

SEPTEMBER

After spending most of the previous week ashore, I was anxious to get underwater again. I had a feeling that there were still more artifacts to be recovered from the silversmith's shop, and I was right. After one unsuccessful day of finding little, Kelly had jumped to the opposite side of the hole, where we already knew there were no walls. Once again back in the right area, I found several new brick wall sections of the silversmith's shop, and as I expected, some nice artifacts were uncovered. The most interesting were several chunks of iron pyrites (fool's gold), a set of brass navigational dividers (an identical set was recovered from a shipwreck lost in 1715 on the coast of Florida), more brass parts of a clock, the silver face of a pocket watch, three brass precious-metal-scale weights, a pewter ink well, and a Spanish one-real silver coin.

Coral was out of action this week and for the next two weeks, with an ear infection; and Alphonso also missed most of the week, suffering from an abscessed tooth, which he was too frightened to have pulled out. His jaw became so swollen that it looked like a balloon, so one day Ivan grabbed and held him while someone else extracted the tooth with a pair of pliers.

Early in the second week we were warned that Hurricane Beulah was expected to strike the island and to prepare for it. We towed the barge to a place called Hurricane Hole and tied it to several trees. Although the hurricane missed the island, we had four miserable days of torrential rains and very high winds. For two days Kelly and I tried to excavate with the small water jet, but the rains kept grounding out the gas engine and stopping the pump, and we were forced to give up. We had found a number of artifacts I was sure had no association with the silversmith's shop: a brass three-legged cooking kettle, a pitchfork, a meat cleaver, a handful of children's marbles, and an earthenware chamber pot.

Then we spent two days diving on and investigating a shipwreck located on "Wreck Reef," about four miles south of Port Royal. Ivan had also discovered this one on one of his fishing trips, and, as usual, he was sure that "dat one is just full of gold." The wreck was about sixty feet deep, so we weren't affected by the rough seas, but poor Alphonso, whom we left to watch the skiff above, became so violently seasick that he vowed never to go to sea again. The second day Ivan took his place in the skiff. The wreck had more than fifty large iron cannon and six anchors on it. It was a British warship dating from around the end of the eighteenth century. Instead of rocks, large bars of pig iron were used for ballast, and these bars, which Ivan had seen and thought were bars of gold, were scattered all over the bottom. So he wouldn't make the same mistake again, I gave Ivan a lesson in what happens to different metals underwater, making a big point of the fact that gold does not get discolored in any way and is always found with its bright, natural color shining. Save for a number of cannon balls, our only find was a crushed pewter powder bottle with a large British broad arrow stamped on it.

At the beginning of the third week we moved to the eastern, or shoreward, side of the hole, in an area we had not completely opened up, to join the two holes together. Here we soon found three large standing walls of a building, about twelve thousand bricks (probably from the same building), three oak roof beams, and hundreds of grayish-black slate roof tiles. Nearby was another standing wall, formed in a half moon, of a different type of construction from the others. I could never be sure of its use, but probably a house had a curved wall in it. Rather than waste time raising all the loose bricks to the surface, Kelly, Alphonso, and I formed a chain and moved them to an area in the hole we had already excavated, so that they could later be raised. Then, while the divers began taking the four standing walls apart, I went to work with the air lift and soon discovered that we were in the area of another private dwelling—probably a dining room. Besides a vast amount of crockery, ceramic ware, and glassware, we found three large chargers, one plate, nine spoons, and a belt buckle in pewter; five buckles and two curtain rings of brass; several bone- and wood-handled iron knives; nine leather shoe heels, and five soles. The week was marred by an accident in which Vincent slipped while jumping between the skiff and the barge and cut his chin badly, losing several teeth and requiring eight stitches.

During the last four working days of September we were without the air-lift compressor, which was broken again, and had to excavate with the water jet. Working in an area without any fallen or standing walls, our finds were rather meager. The only things of interest were all the components of a large scale, including its two brass pans and eight lead and six brass weights of different shapes and weights. One marked two pounds weighed out at only one pound nine ounces, and the one marked one pound weighed out at only thirteen and a half ounces. Whatever the scale was used for, it was apparent that people were being short-weighted in old Port Royal.

Jenkinson gave me another headache this month. He had a new wharf constructed in front of his beach club; and twenty-four 16-inch piles had been driven into the sea floor. This was done in one of the richest areas of the old town, and I felt certain that a great deal of damage had been done to buildings, which I knew to be in that area, as well as to countless artifacts. Unfortunately the deed had been done by the time I heard of it, so there was little I could do about it.

OCTOBER

The month started with a notice from the insurance company that covered me for accident and death informing me that my policy had been canceled because I was accident-prone and they were losing money on me. This was infuriating, because I was working for the government that owned the insurance company. Mrs. Hart tried in vain to have it reinstated; from then on, I had to pay my own medical bills and get reimbursed from my project budget.

The air-lift compressor, which had broken down during the previous month, was not repaired until the fourteenth of October. Why we had to wait almost three weeks for a two-hour repair job was one of the many things I could never quite get used to while working in Jamaica. If we had been able to get the necessary parts, we would have immediately repaired it ourselves. While Kelly, Alphonso, and Coral spent a number of days raising all the bricks from the big pile we had stacked the month before, I used the water jet first to blow away all the sea urchins around the perimeter and inside our hole, and then to clean off the shipwreck we had found in March. After the other divers had finished raising all the bricks, they joined me on the wreck and we began the tedious task of prying all those mortar balls and the ballast rock loose from the coral growth that cemented everything together in one solid mass. The vicious crabs were still around and we spent a great deal of time combating them.

With the use of a lifting bag we managed to remove almost eight hundred of the mortar balls from the wreck and placed them in a pile in the middle of our hole. It would have required about a hundred fifty-five-gallon fuel drums to store them in fresh water ashore if we had raised them all. Getting the fuel drums was not difficult, but I had no place to store them, for we had already taken over and filled all the rooms in the Naval Hospital. We made another neat pile in the hole with all the ballast rock we removed from the top of the wreck. Although we recovered several hundred ships' fittings—such as blocks, deadeyes, pulleys, and fastenings—other types of items I had expected to find were quite scarce. We did find various types of buttons and buckles, several intact post-earthquake bottles, a number of cooking utensils, and a few more tools—but nothing really spectacular such as navigational instruments or pewter or silverware. The timing was perfect: on the very afternoon that I had finished my measurements and drawings of the remaining wooden sections of the wreck, and we had covered it over again with sediment to protect it from marine borers, the compressor was repaired.

Coral was on the sick list once more: his ear infection had flared up and he was out of action from the tenth to the twenty-second of the month. Then, to make matters worse, Kelly quit again. During the first morning that we were able to use the air lift, a large coral head rolled out of the side of the hole and struck both Kelly and me. Kelly was knocked unconscious and received a bump on his head almost the size of a chicken egg. I got another open cut and received several more stitches. When I stopped to pick Kelly up the following morning, he handed me his resignation and said that the work was just too dangerous for the salary he was receiving. I had to agree with him, but I deeply regretted his leaving for the second time.

Still more problems were waiting for me when I arrived at Port Royal that morning. All six of the boys who worked on the barge and skiff and ran the shore-based compressor announced that they were on strike and demanded that their wages be doubled. Lack of funds prevented me from giving them even a small raise, so doubling their wages was certainly out of the question. After losing almost three weeks because of the broken compressor, I couldn't afford to lose any more excavation time and decided to work without them. I left Walter in charge of the compressor ashore and placed Ivan and Coral on the barge and skiff, while Alphonso dived with me. After about an hour Ivan signaled me to come to the surface: he and Coral simply couldn't cope with all the things that had to be done on both skiff and barge, which included the tagging and plotting of the position of all important artifacts that Alphonso brought up. The strikers watching us from shore were having the laugh of their lives, but I was determined to teach them a good lesson. I decided to dive alone and had Alphonso work on the barge, and we managed to get through the day.

The following morning, despite further explanations about the impossibility of a raise, the boys still refused to return to work. I fired them and hired three grown-up men who lived in Port Royal. Ivan took over running the compressor ashore in addition to his normal watchman's duties, and the three new men were able to do the job that the six boys had done in the past, so I was able to pay them double the amount that the boys had received. I was able to make their work easier and actually speeded up our excavation work on the bottom: a great deal of time—around two hours each day—had been spent throughout the course of our excavation each time the barge was full of heavy sediment and had to be moved close to shore and unloaded. By this time our hole was so large that I decided we could start depositing the sediment collected on the barge back into the hole. We would position the barge each morning so that the rear end of it was over an area of the hole we had already excavated, and as the heavy sediment accumulated on the deck of the barge, the men shoveled it overboard. With this system we were able to keep the air lift working for eight or nine hours continuously each day.

During the third week of the month we located several sections of fallen walls and recovered a typical collection of interesting artifacts: a gold cuff link; a silver wedding band and a silver spoon with the owner's initials ID on it; in pewter we found three plates, a tankard with the initials FHM on it, six spoons, and a porringer handle; in brass a candle holder, a spigot, two ladles, four buttons, two buckles, two drawer handles, a large scale weight, several hinges, and a colander; in iron two cooking kettles, a pair of scissors, a key, a door knocker, a knife, and a large spoon; in glass a large number of onion bottles and wineglasses; in ceramic a complete delftware plate, a complete slipware cup, several intact large jugs and vases, beads, and spice pots; and among the miscellaneous items we found were ten leather heels and six soles from shoes, six cutlery handles of bone and wood, a striking flint, two school writing slates, and three whetstones. The area produced an exceptional amount of ceramic shards—fourteen bushels full. The evidence pointed to another cookhouse.

During the following week we continued finding the same kinds of artifacts as well as several unusual ones: a 25-inch-high wooden mortar (probably used for grinding some kind of grain), a four-legged stone metate, a 12-by-12-inch fragment of straw matting, and the lower mandible of a human jaw. Nearby we located two standing brick structures that appeared to be water wells. They were almost four feet high, about the same diameter, with a hole two and a half feet across. According to all the old documents there wasn't any fresh water at Port Royal, so they were most likely salt-water wells used for household cleaning. At first I thought they might have been used as storage tanks for keeping marine products alive (the Romans had used this system), but the absence of a bottom to the wells ruled out this possibility.

A strong north wind blew during the last four days of October, so the air lift could not be used. With the water jet I continued excavating a large wall, and from under another small section of fallen wall I found a beautiful brass oil lamp with a three-foot section of chain attached to it. Experts of the London Museum identified it as being non-European and possibly Near Eastern in origin and the type of lamp used in a Jewish synagogue. Old documents related that the Jews of Port Royal did have a place of worship, and the property records show that a parcel of land in the same general area we were working was called "Jews Land" and had been owned jointly by a number of wealthy merchants. Had we located the site of the Jewish synagogue?

Very close to where I found the lamp I located six small opaque glass bottles that appeared to contain perfume. Using a hypodermic needle I extracted some of the fluid from one of the bottles. It was perfume indeed, and after centuries still retained the scent of roses.

On the next to last day of the month I suffered yet another bad bump on my head from a falling coral head, and the stitches from the cut I had received earlier that month broke apart and had to be restitched. When I returned to Port Royal the following morning, Ivan and the others presented me with a football helmet, which I proudly wore from that time onward to protect my poor head. Alphonso and I were on the bottom using the water jet, and after about an hour of work we both surfaced feeling very nauseous and dizzy. Coral had placed the Aquanaut in such a manner that the exhaust fumes from the engine floating on the water blew right into the air intake on the breathing apparatus. The insurance company had said that I was accident-prone, and it seemed that they were right.

NOVEMBER

The month got off to a distressing start, as October had, and I feared that I was becoming paranoid. Although I was under contract to the government, my wife and I had arrived on a two-year residence visa. Two immigration officers appeared early in November and told me that my visa had almost expired, that I was working illegally on a resident visa and should have obtained another type of visa, and that if it weren't obtained in forty-eight hours, my wife and I would be deported. It should have taken no more than a phone call to Seaga to solve the problem, but it didn't. I wasted two full days warming a bench in the immigration office waiting to see the head of the immigration department, and when I finally saw him, it took only a few minutes for him to read a note from Seaga and stamp our passports.

Then two government auditors appeared at Port Royal demanding that I help them make an inventory of every item we had out there and going over the hundreds of bills and vouchers related to the project during the past two years. Two of the boys who had worked for me, unable to write their names, signed the pay vouchers with an "X"; the auditors insinuated that I had pocketed their wages and signed the X's myself, until I produced the boys, who verified their X's. Two more days were wasted on this irksome business.

I had ample reason to be upset by a piece in the Kingston paper on the morning of November 10. The day before, a member of the opposition party in the House of Representatives, a Mr. Keble Munn, had demanded that Seaga investigate and answer several questions the next time the House convened. He accused me of illegally diving on shipwrecks, plundering artifacts from them, and smuggling them out of the country. He also stated that a large number of artifacts we had recovered from Port Royal were being sold in Nassau and claimed that this was being done by Things Jamaican, the government firm Sergio Dello Strologo had created to make, among other things, replicas of the Port Royal artifacts. Seaga came to my rescue at the next session of the House of Representatives and stated that I had dived on shipwrecks only at the orders of the government and that all artifacts I recovered had been turned over to the Institute of Jamaica. He also presented a number of the items being sold in Nassau; they were all replicas and not original artifacts. Not surprisingly it turned out that the Port Royal Company of Merchants had put Munn up to his false accusations.

Gloria Gilchrist had been doing a remarkable job restoring the ceramic ware and other types of artifacts. She had started with very low wages and a promise of a raise in the near future. She never received the raise and for months had been threatening to leave. I had arranged with Ivor Noel Hume of Colonial Williamsburg, early in the year, to have Gloria spend a month there learning new preservation and restoration techniques. Months passed while she anxiously waited to go to Williamsburg, but she was told that no funds were available. Then the final blow came. Early in November she was told that funds were finally available, but the very day before she was scheduled to depart, she was once again told that no funds could be provided.

In desperation she quit the same day and left for London, where she found a good job in a museum.

I did everything possible to replace Kelly, but could find no one who was willing to work for the wages the government would pay. Finally Ivan, renowned as the toughest man in Port Royal, offered to work as a diver. He lasted just ten minutes: a minor cave-in occurred, covering his head and shoulders with sediment for a few seconds, and he decided we were all crazy to work down there. Later in the month, we had a more serious landslide. A small standing wall fell out of the side of the hole and struck Coral and me. Coral was out of action for a week with a badly bruised shoulder and I had two toes broken on the same foot that had been injured in February, but I lost only a half day of work.

During the first week we located several more sections of fallen walls and still another intact standing well—no more than twenty feet from the other two. In this well we found the remains of a wooden bucket, so it seemed I was correct in thinking they had been used as a water source and not as storage tanks. Surprisingly the walls yielded a meager collection of artifacts: two badly sulfated two-real Spanish silver coins, several wineglasses, a copper pan, and several brass buttons. The following week things picked up, and from under two other fallen walls we recovered a nice assortment of artifacts. Among them were a gold wedding band and a gold cuff link (a match to the one we had found in October), two more two-real coins (in better condition than the other two), a copper Spanish maravedi coin, a pewter plate and two spoons, a pair of brass navigational dividers, a copper dinner bell, a complete delftware candle holder, a multicolored slipware cup (with tea leaves sticking to its bottom), and a life-size wooden hand and part of the arm (eleven inches long).

The third week in November things were slow again because we found ourselves in an area containing more than six thousand loose building bricks, which had to be raised. The main recoveries this week were coral-encrusted iron objects, and we filled ten of the fuel drums with these objects. Those of most interest were several door knockers, a large kettle, several broken swords, a two-pronged harpoon, and a grappling hook. The last two items may have been lost by seventeenth-century salvors. There was no way to determine whether the loose bricks had been taken apart by divers in the past or had crumbled apart from a building during the disaster.

The last week of the month produced more artifacts than the three previous weeks, and our spirits soared. During the first three weeks we had recovered only 376 items that were considered important enough to be tagged, but during the fourth week the surface crew tagged and plotted the positions of more than seven hundred objects. The most interesting were: four plates (found stacked together), two spoons, two bottle stoppers, and three tankards, made of pewter; a large plate with a mermaid and King Neptune embossed on it, two bowls, another bell, a large scale pan, several buckles and buttons, and an intricately engraved toothpick, made of brass and copper; two nice lead figurines—a child's toy of a man on a horse and a ten-inch-high maiden holding a dish in her hands; in ceramic there were two candle holders, three large mugs, seven plates, four cups, three vases, and four jars; and among the miscellaneous objects we had a wide variety of ships' fittings, six wild-boar fangs, several buttons of wood and glass, a bone-handled fork (one of the few forks we found), a tortoise-shell comb, an ivory brush handle, and the lower half of a wooden figurine of a knave (used in chess). There were three sets of pewter items found during the month: one initialed IP, for which initials there had been twelve different property owners in old Port Royal; IS, with nine different possible property owners to match with it, and LJ, for which there was only one possible match: a Leker Johnson.

Toward the end of the month we received a report from Garry Thompson, the preservation expert sent by UNESCO in August. Garry admitted that he had been unable to develop any method to preserve our iron objects, but said he would continue working on the problem and hoped to have some answers during the coming year. The main theme of his report was to recommend that a major preservation laboratory be set up at Port Royal and the necessary equipment and personnel be obtained. The equipment he believed we needed would alone cost well over fifty thousand dollars, and I knew nothing would be done about the problem for the time being. We didn't even have enough money to send Gloria to Williamsburg for a month.

DECEMBER

The first week of December we continued to make plentiful recoveries each day. No sooner would we locate, take apart, and excavate under a fallen wall than another would be found. The construction of the walls indicated that we were still on the site of the private dwelling we had located in November. Under a wall in an area no larger than a dining-room table we found three large chargers, ten plates, two spoons, a large two-handled pot, and a porringer—all of pewter; three candlesticks, a basin, a ruler, four buttons, a sixteenth-century Spanish maravedi coin, two buckles, a spigot, and four curtain rings—all of copper or brass; four jugs, three vases, two bowls, seven dishes, and a wig curler—all of ceramic; a silver Spanish two-real coin; and a large assortment of glassware, including a small ink well with ink still in it. This was the first area of this size in which the bulk of artifacts was actually greater in volume than the sediment.

The eighth of the month was my birthday, but not really a happy day for me. The feature article in the morning's paper was more than enough to start the day off badly. I had been the major topic debated the previous day in the House of Representatives, and much of the dialogue between Keble Munn, who was still hurling innuendo and accusations at me, and Minister Seaga, who was handling the rebuttals, was carried in the article. Once again Munn claimed that I was diving illegally on wrecks and smuggling treasure I had found on them out of the country, that artifacts found at Port Royal were being sold in other countries, that I was really unqualified for my position of directing the Port Royal excavation, that once I had worked for the government of Mexico and had been deported from that country for unspecified dastardly deeds, and that I was such a disreputable person that the National Geographic Society would have nothing to do with me. Seaga did a good job of defending me on all the points except the last two, which he said he would first have to investigate and would report on later. I settled the business of the National Geographic Society myself the same day. In that very month's issue of the *National Geographic Magazine* one of the feature articles was on Jamaica, and four pages of that article covered my work at Port Royal. Armed with a copy of that magazine and a letter from the Exploration and Research Committee of the National Geographic Society, in which they offered me a grant of money to be used on the Port Royal project, I descended on the editor of the newspaper, and the following morning he published a nice article clearing up this matter. Rather than wait for Seaga to make inquiries of the Mexican Government by mail, I wished to clear the charges immediately, so once again I contacted Pablo Bush Romero, under whose direction I had worked in Mexico, and two days later he arrived on the island. He was incensed that my reputation had been called into question and demanded to see the Prime Minister to clear the matter up. I convinced him that holding a press conference would be a better way to tackle the problem. In it he praised me and my past work so highly that I felt well vindicated. He demanded that Munn state his source for the lie that I had been deported from Mexico and stated that the government was trying to hire me to come back to Mexico when I finished at Port Royal to work as the Director of Underwater Archaeology for the Mexican Government. This time I thought we had silenced Keble Munn and the Port Royal Company of Merchants behind him, forever, in regards to my work, but I underestimated their venom once again. Several months later Munn was again casting aspersions on my character and reputation even more vehemently than before. I discussed the matter with Seaga on several occasions, but he didn't seem to think much of the whole matter, stating that the opposition party always went to the wildest extremes to discredit the party in power, and I just happened to be an unfortunate scapegoat. That may be the way in which politics are conducted on Jamaica, but I was to find that such unproved accusations have a long-lasting effect. Since leaving Jamaica I have had people all over the world ask me if I really did make off with a great deal of the things I had found at Port Royal.

When I arrrived at Port Royal my birthday morning, two other surprises were waiting for me. I was several hours late because of visiting the newspaper editor and expected to find everyone at work. Instead they were all sitting around idly, and Coral announced, as spokesman for the whole group, that I had been working them all too hard and that instead of starting work at seven each morning, they would not start until nine. I refused to give in and gave them a choice of continuing on the same schedule as before or quitting. They had a brief huddle and then got started for the day, several of them mumbling that I was a "bloody slave driver." The incident was soon forgotten and I couldn't have been such a hard bloke to work under, because they all chipped in and bought me a case of expensive whisky for a Christmas present.

Around noon on this eventful day I was summoned ashore to find the local Protestant minister and several of the elders of the town waiting with glum faces. The clergyman said that many of the people of Port Royal were distressed that the human bones we had recovered from the sunken city hadn't been given a decent Christian burial. He pointed to the human jaw I had been using on my desk as a paperweight. I had enough problems already that day, so I agreed to let them take all the bones stored in one of the rooms, where many human ones were mixed in with the more than six tons of animal bones. An hour later they reappeared with two large trucks and carried every single bone away and the next morning gave all the bones, in a mass grave, a decent Christian burial. From that time on, I kept all the bones we recovered stored in the basement of the Institute of Jamaica in Kingston.

As an anticlimax, my wife gave a surprise birthday party for me that night, but I was so tired that I fell asleep in a chair before dinner was served and never even got to blow the candles on the cake out.

The second week got off to a good start, and during the first three days we recovered about twice the amount of important artifacts we had found in the previous week. One of the most unusual was a complete sixty-five-inch-long musket, which weighed twenty-two pounds. I pitied the poor soldier or militiaman who had had to tote such a heavy weapon around. I also found a small lead British Government seal with the Tudor rose motif on it—the type that was used with a wire and bound around official mail packets. I placed it in the artifact bucket along with other items, but at the end of the day it wasn't in the skiff and everyone claimed he hadn't seen it. I knew it was possible that one of the divers might have accidentally dropped it while taking it to the surface, but one of the men who worked on the barge had a guilty look on his face. I said that I was going back down for five minutes, and when I came up, the seal had better be in one of the artifact buckets or I was closing down the whole project until I could hire a complete new team. When I came up, the seal was lying in one of the buckets. Several days later, someone informed me who had taken it and I replaced him immediately.

The last three days of the week were miserable. It rained torrentially. The seas were too rough to use the barge and air lift, so we spent the time raising bricks and killing sea urchins. Around this time there was a big earthquake scare on the island which lasted for several weeks. How it was started and who ever started it were never revealed, but many were sure a major quake would occur, and prepared for it. For days, trucks and automobiles with loudspeakers blaring roamed the streets warning the people and recommending precautions to be taken. The residents of Port Royal took the scare more seriously than most of the other inhabitants of the island, and many of the old people came to me and said they felt certain that the whole Palisadoes would sink into the sea. Alphonso, who hadn't been inside a church for years, started going to vespers every evening at Port Royal and even ceased to use his usual foul language during this period. As I had expected, nothing happened and things soon returned to normal.

The third week was a repetition of the first, and quite a few valuable artifacts were recovered: the two most interesting were a Chinese porcelain saucer with a beautiful garden scene painted on it, and a large German stoneware beer mug with a Spanish silver four-real coin, a 12-inch-long clay smoking pipe, and a silver spoon, all attached to it by coral growth. It was an item worthy of display in any museum. We also found a saw with a wooden handle, identical to the one we had found in the carpenter's shop.

I closed down the operation from the twenty-third of December to the second of January because of the Christmas holidays, which Jamaicans celebrate with great zest, but this didn't mean that I would finally get a badly needed vacation: there was a great deal of preservation work to catch up on and also a detailed annual report on the project to write. The year had been the most interesting and fantastic one of my life, and despite the irritating problems I'd had to confront almost daily I was anxious to start another year on the sunken city.

Chapter Nine

YEAR 1968 JANUARY

I started off the New Year with every intention of working at Port Royal for the whole year and for several more after that as well. Little did I know that I would be able to work only a few more months on the sunken city that had become like a second home to me. By this time the hole we had excavated was rectangular in shape and measured 420 by 200 feet and had an average depth of twenty feet below the surface of the sea floor. There was still a large area to be excavated that was threatened by the proposed dredging operation for the deepwater port.

We had excavated as far south as I dared go because of the proximity of the marine laboratory, as close to shore (east) as I could effectively work with an air lift, and as far seaward (west) as we could safely work because of the shipping channel. Consequently, I moved the excavation to the northern end of the hole and we began excavating to the north in the direction of Fort James and the richer section of the old town. I was sorry to leave the area we had been working, where the sediment consisted primarily of silt and mud, and move to where most of the sediment was composed of sharp pieces of dead coral, but I had no other choice.

The first eighteen days of January I excavated with the help of Alphonso and Coral during what turned out to be the longest period in the whole project in which we did not have even a minor accident, and the longest period that both Alphonso and Coral worked continuously without illness or injury. It was slow work pulling the large pieces of coral apart out of the sediment, and to speed up the operation we threw all the coral and other debris that was too large to go up the air lift, behind us in the hole rather than trying to carry it up to the barge. We managed to excavate an area extending the length of the hole another twenty feet to the north and located four sections of walls from separate buildings. We were working fairly close to the zone where we had found the first coin hoard, in December 1966, but the only silver we found was a fork. However, we did recover a considerable number of important artifacts: in pewter—six plates, three spoons, a mug, a bottle top, and a charger in three pieces; in copper and brass—a cooking kettle, a large platter, a set of navigational dividers, a knitting needle, an ornate door lock, a shoe buckle, a thimble, and a skillet; of the identifiable objects in iron we found a pair of scissors, a triangular scraper, three lifting hooks, a shovel, a large door lock with the key still stuck in it, a grappling hook, four horseshoes, a harness buckle, one padlock, a large cooking kettle, and a large number of other tools and ships' fittings; in glass—seventy-six onion bottles, several wineglasses, and three blue beads; and in ceramic ware we found an unusual number of intact items—plates, saucers, cups, mugs, vases, jars, bowls, and our first egg cup. One of the vases had three animal faces painted on it: a lion, a bear, and a wolf or fox. We also recovered a number of odd objects as well: a small ring made of jet, the top half of an ornately carved bone cane, a graphite pencil, two double-edged combs made of bone, several human teeth, and eleven pieces of carved wood that formed an almost complete chair.

The pewter ware bore six different sets of owners' initials, each of which could have belonged to two or more property owners.

About a year before, I had met Dr. Harold Edgerton, a famous physicist and electronic wizard of the Massachusetts Institute of Technology. He is internationally known as the inventor of the electronic strobe for photography and a large number of devices used in the field of oceanography including two different types of subbottom-penetrating sonar units called the "Boomer" and the "Pinger." In one of the lectures I gave about my work at Port Royal I covered the period that I had spent making a preliminary exploration with the metal probe and metal detector. After the lecture Dr. Edgerton, or "Doc" as he is known to friends, said that I really did it the hard way and should have used either his "Boomer" or his "Pinger." I explained that I had known of his equipment, but lack of money had prevented me from using them, and I had been begging for funds ever since to rent one of his units to make a complete survey of the whole underwater city. With the primitive method that I had to use at that time, I knew I must have missed many objects hidden beneath the sea floor and had not been able to plot those I did find as accurately as I should have. Doc handsomely offered to come at his own expense to make a complete sonar survey of the site, but it was almost a year before I could obtain permission from the Jamaican Government for him to do it.

Doc arrived with two assistants, Dr. Tsuneyoshi Uyemura of the University of Tokyo, and Dr. Louis Wolfson, a medical specialist from Boston, who had worked with Doc on a number of marine archaeological sites in the Mediterranean. The first two days were lost due to problems with customs officials concerning bringing his equipment into the island, this despite the fact that he was doing the survey for the government. From the nineteenth to the twenty-sixth we worked from sunrise to sunset each day and completed the survey sooner than planned. Fortunately one of the senior officials in the Survey Department was an active member of the Jamaican Historical Society and very interested in my work at Port Royal, and he was able to provide a team of surveyors to assist us, and he even provided us with a small survey boat named *Chart,* from which we operated. Ivan and another man worked from a skiff placing and picking up the buoys we required for the survey. I left Coral in charge of continuing the excavation, a move I was to regret.

Running between buoys offshore and markers set up by the surveyors ashore, we made more than three hundred runs at right angles to the shore, each spaced ten to fifteen feet apart, and each between five and eight hundred feet in length. The surveyors had the hardest job of all. In addition to plotting the position of each of the shore markers used on each run, they had to plot the position of each offshore buoy used on each run, so we would know the precise course we ran and the area surveyed on each run. Aboard the *Chart* I ran the vessel while Doc and his assistants operated the Boomer and recorded the exact time each run took, which was essential to establishing the precise position of each object we located.

Each run provided us with a graph showing the water depth, the bottom contours, and geological information to a depth of about a hundred fifty feet below the sea floor, and indicated the presence of the solid objects that were either protruding above or hidden beneath the sea floor. It did not identify the type of object; this would come later. By the time we had completed the survey we had located more than four thousand solid objects of considerable size on the site. The easier part of the survey was over, and the most difficult was still to come. All the data obtained on the sonar graphs now had to be transferred and plotted on four large charts of the site, which was a ticklish undertaking, because we had made the runs at varying speeds to counteract winds and currents, and the lengths of the runs also varied considerably. I put aside this task for the time being, because I had more important work to accomplish.

On the afternoon we finished the sonar survey, Doc said he still had several days left and wanted to know if I wanted any other sonar surveys made on the island. Immediately St. Ann's Bay, on the north coast of Jamaica, came into my mind, and after I told Doc what I hoped to find there, he was only too willing to help.

In April of 1502 Columbus set sail with four small caravels from Spain on his fourth and last voyage of discovery, and it turned out to be his most dangerous and least profitable voyage. After arriving in the Caribbean he spent almost a year cruising along the Central American coast, discovering very little of importance. Teredos caused such damage to the hulls of his small ships that two of them had to be stripped and scuttled off the coast of Panama. Then, with the two remaining ships—*Capitana* and *Santiago*—in deplorable condition, he finally had to admit failure and start for home, heading first for Santo Domingo, where he hoped to repair both vessels before making the long ocean crossing. By the time he was between Cuba and Jamaica, he was not only suffering from an acute shortage of water and food, but both vessels were leaking so badly and were so near sinking that Columbus' son Ferdinand, who chronicled the voyage, wrote: "Day and night we never ceased working three pumps on each ship, and if any broke down, we had to supply its place by bailing with kettles while it was being patched up."

The vessels were so full of water they made very slow progress, and when the wind swung around to the east, blowing from the direction they were heading, it proved too much. On June 25, 1503, they were forced to enter St. Ann's Bay, which Columbus had visited on his second voyage and named Santa Gloria, and run both vessels aground "about a bow-shot distance from shore." There were two fresh-water streams nearby and an Indian village from which Columbus hoped to obtain a steady source of victuals to feed the 116 hungry mouths on the two vessels. With only the fore and stern castles protruding above the water, there were insufficient accommodations aboard for all the men, so a large number of them were forced to live ashore.

Soon after his arrival Columbus purchased a dugout canoe from the Indians and sent it to Santo Domingo to notify the authorities there of his plight. However, due to the fact that the Governor of Santo Domingo was his enemy and delayed sending aid, Columbus and his men spent a year and five days before being rescued. Things went well during the first months of his enforced stay, and the Indians were happy to trade food for hawk bells, glass beads, and other items of barter. However, after the Indians had accumulated a large supply of these items, they began furnishing less and less food to the marooned Spaniards, and conditions deteriorated. When months passed and still no aid arrived, several of the expedition's leaders enlisted the majority of the men in a mutiny and plotted to assassinate Columbus, blaming him for all their miseries. But Columbus, though bedridden at the time with painful arthritis, was able to quell the mutiny in its early stages.

When the rescue vessel finally arrived and picked up the Spaniards, on June 29, 1504, leaving behind the two worthless hulks, Columbus was certainly a very discouraged and heartbroken man, and not long after his arrival in Spain he died.

From the book written by Ferdinand and other contemporary documents, the location of these two wrecks was quite well known, unlike that of other ships lost by the Spaniards in the West Indies over the centuries. In 1940 a Harvard University-sponsored expedition led by Admiral Samuel Eliot Morison, one of the world's leading experts on Columbus, used this same information and attempted to establish the precise location of the wrecks. In Morison's book, the Pulitzer-prize-winning *Admiral of the Ocean Sea*, is a chart of St. Ann's Bay marked where he believed both wrecks lay. He was almost right on the spot, for we found both wrecks within one hundred feet of where he estimated they were.

Aiding Morison when he visited St. Ann's Bay was a Jamaican plantation owner, Charles Cotter, who for the past forty years has been conducting land excavations on the site of New Seville, the first settlement founded by the Spaniards on the island, located on the shore near where Columbus' ships had been abandoned. For years Cotter had dreamed of someone being able to locate the site of the wrecks, but until I arrived on the island he had been unable to get anyone, including the Smithsonian Institution, interested in diving on the site. Cotter was overjoyed when we met and I told him that I was interested in searching for the wrecks.

I was especially fascinated by these two wrecks because I

knew that unless someone locates a Viking or Phoenician ship-wreck someday, these two are the oldest that will ever be found in this hemisphere. Although Columbus had lost other ships during his four voyages, they were all lost under conditions that make it very unlikely that any trace of them will ever be found. A good example was the *Santa Maria,* which was wrecked on his first voyage, off Cap-Haitien, Haiti. This wreck was completely stripped of all its timbers and other items and used to build a fort ashore for the men from this wreck who were left behind when Columbus sailed for home. On the other hand, I knew that because the two wrecks in St. Ann's Bay had been so heavy from the vast amount of water in them, most of the lower sections of their hulls were pushed deep into the silt and mud, thus preserving them from the ravages of the teredo. If I was right as to their degree of preservation, these wrecks could provide invaluable information concerning the construction of ships of that period, as well as other data.

Although my main work was at Port Royal, I considered these wrecks of even greater archaeological and historical importance, and repeatedly requested permission to mount a minor expedition to locate them. No interest was shown by the government, especially after I told them that there was no likelihood of finding any treasure or even any valuable artifacts on these wrecks. I finally convinced Seaga to permit me to spend one day searching, so I went up one Sunday in March of 1966 with my wife and Stan and Louise Judge. About a month earlier I had had a friend shoot aerial photographs of the bay, and I knew that even if Morison and Cotter were wrong in their location of the wrecks, there was an area only about the size of a football field in the entire bay that fit Ferdinand's description and where the water was deep enough for the ships to have been run aground. A series of charts of the bay dating as far back as the middle of the seventeenth century showed that the coastline and the shape of the bay, except where the massive landslide had occurred during the 1692 earthquake, which was at the opposite end of the bay from where I knew the wrecks lay, had not changed over the centuries.

As we were preparing to dive that Sunday, a number of

residents stood by claiming that this section of the bay was a mating ground for large sharks and it would be suicide to dive there. Just the night before, a fisherman had caught a fourteen-foot tiger shark and was there on the beach skinning it when we arrived.

With ten-foot-long metal probes, we swam along in a line forcing the rods down into the bottom sediment, trying to locate solid objects which might reveal the presence of a wreck. Using this method, by which we located several large dead coral heads, we spent five hours before we finally struck pay dirt. Nancy motioned to me underwater that she needed help. Her probe, which was down about eight feet in the sediment, was stuck in something solid and she couldn't pull it out. It took three of us to pull it out and six hours of excavating by hand and with buckets to reach the solid object, which turned out to be a wooden beam. When we relayed this information to Cotter, who was pacing up and down the beach in anticipation, he said that it was probably a piling from an old wharf that had sunk in a hurricane in that area over twenty years before. So I ordered everyone to forget about it and continue the search. However, my wife said that perhaps I was making a mistake and it might be part of a wreck. As usual, she was right. Feeling around in the pitch-black hole in the sediment, I discovered that there were treenails, or wooden pegs, in the beam, the method of fastening ships together in the old days and not one that would have been used on a modern wharf or ship. The hole was only large enough for one person to squeeze into, and because of the danger of a cave-in, we began enlarging it. Nancy was the smallest of the group, so she had the honor of probing around in the bottom of the hole. When she came up with several pieces of obsidian, a type of volcanic glass that is found in Mexico and Central America, I was sure that we had made the most important marine archaeological discovery ever made to date in the Western Hemisphere.

Even though dark was fast approaching, I decided to see what I could find in the same hole. Besides several more pieces of obsidian, I recovered a number of pieces of Spanish pottery that dated from the period of the two Columbus wrecks. Just as I was about to call it a day our dive came to a rather dramatic end. Stan Judge, who was hovering over me and grabbing the objects I handed up from the hole, was suddenly bitten on the neck by a two-foot sea snake, reportedly often deadly. In twenty years of diving I had never seen one, or knew any other diver who had seen one in the Caribbean; yet, as luck would have it, we encountered our first during the most important dive of my life. Stan was in considerable pain and we quickly rushed him to a hospital, where he was given an injection of serum. The next day he had completely recovered and was laughing about the whole experience.

During the next month, while waiting confirmation from various experts concerning the identity and date of the shards and the origin of the obsidian, I submitted a number of petitions to Seaga requesting permission and funds to do more work in St. Ann's Bay. When confirmation finally came, I took the letters from the experts and confronted Seaga. All he would promise was that sometime in the near future—"Soon come" again—he would send me back up there. I was convinced that I had found one or at least a section of one of the Columbus wrecks, and it was incredibly frustrating not to be able to do anything about it.

Doc Edgerton was excited, as I had been two years before, when we first dived in St. Ann's Bay, at the prospect of discovering these two wrecks, so on the morning after finishing our work at Port Royal we asked to have a meeting with Seaga. He was quite satisfied with our sonar survey of the sunken city, but not very happy when we asked for permission to search for Columbus' wrecks. He argued that I was snowed under with my work at Port Royal and shouldn't bite off more than I could chew by going after the Columbus wrecks. Only after I promised that we would spend no more than several days searching and not undertake any excavation work did he reluctantly give us permission.

I lined up a boat by telephone and we drove up to the north coast the same day and found Cotter, who thought I had already given up my search for the wrecks. The next morning we got off to a rather poor start; it was pouring rain and the boat I had arranged to use was nowhere in sight. Then, after several hours during which I nervously chain-smoked, the rain stopped, the sun came out, and the boat finally appeared.

Doc and his Japanese assistant had the Boomer in action in minutes, and within an hour we had two positive sonar contacts, and from the sonar graphs we knew they were shipwrecks. More important, they were in the right area (where the documents said they should be and where we had located the wooden beam, obsidian, and shards) and about the size that we knew both wrecks should be. To be on the safe side, after marking both sites with buoys we made a complete sonar survey of all the other possible areas in the bay where the wrecks could lie, and when no other sonar contacts were found I knew that we had located the two Columbus wrecks.

We returned to Kingston the following day, as happy as though we had found a million dollars in gold; Doc and his two assistants caught a plane for the States, and I then notified Edward Seaga of our discoveries. Although he had shown no interest in those wrecks before, he now became very excited and wanted to hold a big press conference and announce the finds, but I talked him out of it and convinced him that more work would have to be done before we were positive of the discovery. He ordered me to mount a major expedition to excavate the wrecks. When I informed Mrs. Hart of our discovery and Seaga's orders, she said it was just like the minister to order me to mount an expedition without making any provisions for financing the project. She promised to find the funds somewhere.

Before returning to the north coast there were many things that had to be taken into consideration. First, since these wrecks were of such great historical significance, the most scientific methods of excavation would have to be used, and I had neither the best equipment and personnel nor the funds at the moment to obtain them. Furthermore I knew that every sliver of wood from these wrecks would be of immense importance, and without any proper preservation laboratory on the island, I would end up going down in history as the man who destroyed the Columbus wrecks, because once the wood was exposed to air and not properly treated, it would disintegrate and be lost forever. I finally convinced Seaga that it would take a large amount of money to properly excavate the wrecks and build a good preservation laboratory and that we would have to seek funds from outside sources such as UNESCO or a foundation. I pointed out that before any foundation would provide the necessary funds, we would have to establish beyond any doubt that they were positively the Columbus wrecks. To do this I would have to recover a substantial amount of material from the sites that could be identified and dated scientifically.

On a project of such importance as this, I decided to enlist the assistance of other leading experts in my field. They all agreed with me that we should do as little as possible to disturb the sites. So, rather than excavate a large hole to recover the sample material for testing, which would not only disturb the archaeological context of the wrecks but might expose the wooden timbers to the teredo, from which they had been protected in their muddy grave, another method of recovering sample material should be used. Dr. George Bass of the University of Pennsylvania suggested that we use a coring device, and he located one invented by Dr. John Saunders of Columbia University. Saunders not only offered to loan it to us, but offered to send one of his assistants down to help us use it.

When I got back to Port Royal after our successful trip to the north coast, I was aghast. I had noticed on a number of occasions when we were surveying the sunken city, that work was progressing very slowly: the men were starting late, quitting early, and even stopping for a long break at midday on most days, but I was so busy working with Doc that I didn't get an opportunity to do much about it. I was not expected back for several more days and found that, instead of working, Coral and Alphonso had taken the day off and gone spearfishing. Walter was the only one working, and when he informed me that the only thing they had recovered in ten days was about a bushel of ceramic shards and broken onion bottle fragments, I could have murdered someone. Instead I excavated myself that day and recovered a wealth of artifacts from under a small wall, including a sword with a silver handle and two pewter plates. On one of the plates someone had scratched arithmetical computations, probably with a knife. I found Coral and Alphonso waiting for me when I finished that afternoon, and would have fired them except for the fact that I knew I might not be able to find replacements. It was fortunate I didn't, as things turned out.

FEBRUARY

Daily I expected to leave for St. Ann's Bay, but I never got there at all in February. I was told that no funds could be found to finance the project, and after several weeks I even offered to pay all the expenses myself, but Seaga refused to let me do so. Dr. Saunders' assistant, Bob Judd, had his bags packed and was ready to come on a moment's notice, but I had to telephone him every few days and tell him to wait a bit longer. Somehow news of our discovery leaked out to the press, and world attention focused on the Columbus ships, but even this didn't help produce the necessary funds to do the job. Once again Keble Munn got into the act and was now accusing me of finding treasure on the Columbus wrecks and taking it out of the country. He was beginning to sound like a broken record, but I was used to his foolish accusations and they no longer bothered me.

But two other things that happened early in the month did make me furious: One day I was summoned to appear at police headquarters in Kingston and told that someone had reported that I was working with a ring smuggling ganja off the island and into the United States. I could only laugh at such a preposterous charge, but the fact that the police refused to tell me the source of their report didn't make me too happy. Then, several days later, Bernard Lewis telephoned to say that he had just received a report that two large pewter chargers that had been found at Port Royal were on display and for sale in an antique shop and wanted to know if I knew anything about it—

as if I had sold them to the shop. I was a bit concerned that someone else might have robbed them, so I rushed over to the antique shop and found both were nineteenth-century—dates on them verified this—and they showed no signs of ever having been in salt water. The Institute of Jamaica was only two blocks from the shop, and Lewis could have easily seen the tankards himself and seen that they could not have come from Port Royal. Was there really a drive on to get rid of me, as many of my close friends believed; and if so, why? I knew I had made a number of enemies among the members of the local diving club and the Port Royal Company of Merchants, but I hadn't really believed that anyone would resort to trying to drive me off the island.

During the first ten days of the month everything went well at Port Royal with the exception of my own health. We uncovered a vast array of priceless artifacts including a large pewter tankard with "William Deaven all ye ships Taverne St. Mary Hill" engraved on it (later I learned that a tavern by the same name and at the same address had existed in Bristol, England, until late in the nineteenth century), a brass bowl with a handle in the shape of a deer, two copper Spanish maravedi coins, a brass toothpick with pleasing designs engraved on it, and a large and varied assortment of ceramic ware including a delft-ware teapot with tea leaves still in it.

My health had been gradually deteriorating for months, and in the past three months alone I had lost fifteen pounds, which at the time I could ill afford. Since returning from the north coast I had been experiencing difficulty in breathing at times, both on land and underwater, and for several days I was coughing up a considerable amount of blood from my lungs. Finally, on the morning of the eleventh, after getting Coral and Alphonso started for the day, I went to a doctor, who advised me that if I didn't stop diving for at least a month, he feared that I would permanently impair my health. Besides several minor ailments, I had badly infected lungs, throat, and ears as a result of working so long in the polluted waters of Port Royal. His advice was to go to bed and stay there for a month, but I knew that I couldn't do that, for I had so much work that had to be done.

I managed to keep myself out of the water for two weeks, which wasn't easy. During this period I did a great deal of thinking, a thing I hadn't found much time to do in more than two years—Port Royal had so obsessed me that I thought of little else. I spent several days preparing a lengthy report outlining what we had accomplished and the problems we had been forced to contend with, and made a long list of recommendations on how things could be improved, the main point of which was that I needed more working funds to provide additional personnel, better and more equipment, and higher wages for all the personnel involved in the project. I felt that if a proper preservation laboratory was not going to be built and qualified personnel to run it weren't employed, it was not only foolish but also criminal to continue recovering artifacts from the sunken city that might never be properly preserved and eventually be lost forever. After sending it to Seaga, I waited several days to be sure he had read it first; then I went to see him.

All I could get out of him were vague promises, and after having heard them all before during the past two years, I realized that I was batting my head against a locked door and nothing would ever be done to improve the situation. I can still remember the shocked look on his face when I told him that mainly because of poor health, which was in fact quite true, I would have to end the project in a few weeks' time. I finally agreed to continue the excavation at Port Royal until the end of March and then spend two additional months doing preservation work and writing archaeological reports, if he promised that I would definitely be given the opportunity to mount a two-week expedition to St. Ann's Bay and be provided with the necessary funds.

Actually, another important factor had also convinced me that the excavation should be stopped (in addition to the government's inability to provide me with the things I needed to continue). Friends of mine had convinced a number of high-ranking officials in UNESCO of the importance of Port Royal as an archaeological site and they had pressured the Jamaican Government into notifying the representatives of the Port Royal Company of Merchants that no dredging operations could ever be undertaken or a deepwater port built in the area of the sunken city and that if their company still proposed to build the deepwater port, it would have to be done elsewhere. It may just be a coincidence, but the Merchants were notified of this matter only a few days before the problems I had concerning the ganja and the two pewter tankards.

I also felt that the government was not really interested in the historical and archaeological aspects of my work, but rather in the publicity value it generated. One of the most important aspects of any archaeological project is to publish reports on the work accomplished and the knowledge gained. Although I had been obtaining and recording all the information possible, I didn't have the time to write as many reports as I would like to have written. In addition to my monthly reports, which I was permitted to distribute only to members of the Jamaican Government, I had been able to write only two large annual reports and one on clay smoking pipes, and funds weren't available even to have them published on the island. I had many offers to have them published elsewhere but was forbidden to do so. In the end the only reason that they ever reached any scholars at all was because I personally had to type them on mimeograph stencils, run them off on the mimeograph machine, staple them together, and then mail them to those I felt would most benefit from the information they contained. This was really ridiculous—especially since I had to do it at night after long and hard days at Port Royal—when a secretary could have been hired for less than fifty dollars a week.

Another important function of an archaeologist is to attend archaeological conventions and present papers and lecture on his work. Until this time, despite being invited to more than two dozen archaeological conventions, I had been permitted to attend only the one in Miami. For months I had been requesting funds to attend one in El Paso in February, which I knew would be the most important marine archaeological convention held that year, but I was told that no funds were available. Only after

I informed Seaga that I was leaving did he find the money to pay for my plane ticket, and then only because he wanted me to find a person to replace me as the director of the Port Royal project. I attended the convention on the twenty-second and twenty-third and found several qualified persons who were interested until they learned what their salary would be.

I waited until I returned from El Paso before informing my whole team that the project, as far as they were concerned, would terminate at the end of March, when I was sure I would not be able to find someone to replace me. During the two weeks that I had not been able to dive, it seemed as if Alphonso and Coral spent their time on the bottom sleeping or playing with the crabs, judging from the small area they had excavated and the pitifully few items they had recovered. I found that when I wasn't around, the only two men I could really count on to do the job right were Walter and Ivan.

Breaking promises to the doctor and my wife, and despite difficulty in breathing, I was back in the water excavating on the twenty-fifth. My time on the sunken city was limited and there was still so much I needed to know. We recovered more that first day that I was back in the water than my two divers had found during the two weeks that I had been out of action, and we continued to make important finds the rest of the week.

MARCH

We were scheduled to leave for St. Ann's Bay on the first of the month, but several days before this date I was informed that we would need a special permit from the Beach Control Commission. Knowing too well the snail-like pace at which governmental bureaucracy functioned on the island, I spent a full day sitting in the Permanent Secretary's office of the Beach Control, until he was so tired of seeing me that he finally issued the permit. He told me to return the following day to pick it up, but of course, as I should have expected, it wasn't signed yet. In fact, it took exactly three weeks just to get the chairman of the Beach Control to sign it. Remember that I was actually working for the government; had I been requesting the permit as a private party, I might have had to wait months or even years for a simple signature.

I had invited Dr. George Bass to come down and work with me on the Columbus wreck site around the beginning of February, but he had to decline the invitation, because he never flies and believed it would take too long to get to Jamaica by ship. As it turned out, he could have sailed completely around the world and still had plenty of time to arrive before we finally got to start. Instead he offered to send one of his assistants, Larry Joline, who like Robert Judd was waiting daily for the word to come down. After almost two months of waiting, when I finally telephoned him that we would be starting the following day, he had a bad bout of the flu and couldn't come.

During the first two weeks of March we excavated at Port Royal every day, including Sundays, but we were able to work underwater only about five hours each day—instead of the usual eight to ten hours—because of the poor state of my health. My doctor had been so upset when he heard that I was diving again that he refused to see me. I could have left the diving to Coral and Alphonso, but knowing that they were out of a job at the end of the month, I knew they wouldn't work very hard on the bottom. At the end of each day's excavation I felt quite sad, despite the fact that we were recovering many interesting artifacts, knowing that I had one less day left on my precious sunken city. I was so reluctant to stop work on the last day of excavation that I spent thirteen continuous hours on the bottom and only stopped when it got dark and the men called me to the surface to say it was so dark that they couldn't see the objects falling on the screen on the barge. It was the longest period I had ever spent underwater and it was really worth it. The day's finds were a pewter plate and spoon; two shoe buckles, one belt buckle, an ornamental drawer handle, a trigger guard for a pistol and one for a musket, and a keyhole plate, all of brass; two pairs of scissors, two knives with wooden handles, a clothes iron, a grappling hook, and two cannon balls, of iron;

three mugs, a plate, two bowls, and three jars, of ceramic; sixty-six bottles and five wineglasses; a silver spoon; a bone button; and twelve shoe heels and five soles of leather. However, the most interesting items—because they caused me to feel somehow close to the people of the old town—were six glass marbles, three wooden toy spinning tops, and a small wooden ball. I could easily picture children playing in the streets with these toys when suddenly disaster struck. I hoped that they were among those who had survived.

Alphonso and Coral had a week's vacation coming to them, so I suspended diving operations during the third week of the month, with every intention of staying out of the water so I would be in good shape when we finally got to the north coast. But after several days of doing preservation work I was back in again. Walter, who was seriously interested in history, had done a lot of prowling around the land portion of Port Royal, and recently he had located a number of old tombstones in dense vegetation about a quarter mile east of the limits of the present town. Using machetes we cleared off the area and discovered that they all dated from before the 1692 earthquake. They were all located right on the edge of the water of Kingston Harbour, and remembering the contemporary accounts that stated that the graveyard had fallen into the sea, I decided to dive and see what I might find in the water. During the sonar survey with Dr. Edgerton we had discovered that small solid objects were buried under the mud in that area and I had supposed that it was some type of modern debris, as they were quite a distance from the eastern extremity of the sunken city. Walter dived with me, and after locating several hard objects with a metal probe, we used the water jet to blow away the mud. Lying about four feet below the surface of the mud we located three more tombstones, and by using the Braille system of reading with our fingers, we were able to read the inscriptions on each of them. All three dated from before 1687, and they belonged to two men and a young woman. At first I considered raising them, but then, remembering the problem I had had several months before with the bones, I decided to leave them in their muddy grave for the time being. Somewhere in the same area I knew that the tombstone and lead casket of Henry Morgan also lay—which I had been accused of finding and spiriting out of the country.

Walter was just full of surprises. The following day he asked me if I had ever dived in the brackish lagoon, also located to the east of the present-day town, and in the general area where Fort Rupert had once stood. Walter said that as a boy he had swum a lot in there and believed he could see the remains of brick buildings on the bottom. That was all I needed to hear. Minutes later we were diving in the lagoon, and although it appeared to be the spawning ground for thousands of small stinging jellyfish, it was really a treat after diving in filthy Kingston Harbour. The water was remarkably clear and we could see at least fifty feet. The lagoon had an average depth of only ten feet, but it was teeming with marine life from the small and inquisitive sergeant major fish to six-foot-long tarpon. I was later told that small alligators are caught there quite often, but we didn't see any that day. Within minutes we spotted a large standing structure, which I later identified as one of the ramparts of Fort Rupert. The northern end ran right into the northern bank of the lagoon, and it appeared that the rest of the fort was buried under land. Digging around the base of the rampart we located several intact onion bottles, cannon balls, and fragments of clay smoking pipes. The top section of the fort was only a few inches below the surface of the water, and I really felt like an idiot for never diving in this lagoon before. I had driven past it twice every day and always made a mental note to dive in it, but just never found the time to do so. Within thirty feet of the fort we located the bases of three other standing buildings, which were probably associated with the fort. Near the western end of the lagoon we located several other standing brick walls, and near them the end of a cobblestone street. Using the water jet we blew off the several inches of silt covering the street and found that it also ran right into the northern bank. This meant that in this area of the land portion of Port Royal the stratigraphical level of old Port Royal was ten feet below the surface—eight feet deeper than the level of salt water under the land—and could be excavated only with the use of water pumps. About a year after I left the island, someone sent me a newsclip stating that members of the local diving club had discovered those buildings and the cobblestone street in the lagoon.

On the twenty-first of the month our permit from the Beach Control was finally signed. I made plans to leave the following day for St. Ann's Bay. I had requested a minimum of at least five hundred dollars to finance the project, which would run from one to two weeks, but instead I was given the sum of only $168. This called for a drastic change in plans, because I certainly could not put up five or six persons in a hotel, feed them, pay for the rental of a boat, and meet all the other expenses with such a paltry sum. Was that all that the memory of Columbus, who had discovered the island, was worth to the Jamaican Government?

Coral and Alphonso were still on their vacations, and when I telephoned Coral that we would be leaving the following day and asked him to find something to sleep in on the beach, he at first refused to go, stating: "In all my years of poverty I've slept between white sheets and with a girl, and I now refuse to sleep on a beach and leave my girl behind in Kingston." It took a great deal of convincing to talk him into going, especially when I refused to permit him to bring his girl along. Alphonso, wearing a patch over his eye like a pirate because of a bee sting, at first gave me an even stranger reason for refusing to go. He said, "I don't like Jamaicans and don't want to live around them, because they are bad people." In all of his seventeen years, like so many other Port Royalists the only place he had even been to on the island was Kingston.

We planned to set up a camp right on the beach near the wreck sites. From the local chapter of the Boy Scouts I obtained the loan of three tents and other camping equipment. When Alphonso learned that Coral refused to sleep in a sleeping bag, he too refused. From a junk pile on the grounds of the Police Training School I obtained six rusty beds and six filthy mattresses, which Ivan covered over with canvas before either of my two divers could see the state they were in.

We were scheduled to leave the following morning at seven, but the Public Works truck that would transport us and our equipment, which included our aluminum skiff, since I couldn't afford to rent the boat I had lined up, caused an unexpected delay. As we were loading the truck, the driver and his two assistants, all of whom appeared to be quite inebriated, disappeared, and it took me two hours to extract them from the Buccaneers Roost, which I was able to do only by convincing the owner not to sell them any more of the potent white rum. None of us ever expected to reach the north coast alive, and Walter, who was also along, jumped off about halfway there and hitchhiked the rest of the way. The driver careened like a lunatic over those narrow, dangerous mountain roads and managed to force at least a dozen other vehicles off the road before we miraculously reached St. Ann's Bay.

We spent the rest of the day setting up a campsite and erecting land markers on the beach. Alphonso had been right about Jamaicans being bad people, or at least one of them. Hundreds of curious persons from the nearby town walked up the beach to see what we were doing, and by the end of the day two of my cameras and a number of tools had disappeared. Charles Cotter found someone to stay with us and serve as a watchman, and he really took the job seriously. Each time people started to approach our campsite, he fired a shotgun over their heads; not surprisingly, nothing else disappeared.

I was delighted when Dr. Saunders' assistant, Robert Judd, arrived, and amazed when I discovered the voracious appetite he had. He stood six feet eight inches tall, weighed 260 pounds, and during his first meal, which was lunch that day, he consumed seven massive sandwiches and four soft drinks. However, he more than made up for the food he ate once he was underwater. We named him the "Jolly Green Giant," and everyone gazed after him when we went into town as if he were the eighth wonder of the world. We had planned to start making the cores that day, but Judd's luggage, which included the coring device, had been lost and didn't turn up until late that night. So instead we took turns using the water jet to blow away several feet of overburden around the area of the two wrecks.

The following morning all the overburden we had removed was right back where it had been before, because of strong winds during the night. My plan was to obtain core samples from both wreck sites, but we were able to work on only one site before the money ran out and we had to head for home. We started off by using ropes, which were easily visible in those waters, where the average underwater visibility fluctuated between ten and thirty feet, depending on how much we had stirred up the muddy bottom, and laid out a grid pattern on the bottom. We also circled the area with buoys rising to the surface. Using this system we would know eactly where we had obtained each core.

The coring device was ingenious and really quite simple, consisting of a four-inch-diameter steel tube made up in four detachable sections, with an over-all length of sixteen feet. After this was forced down by hand into the sea floor, another small section of thicker tubing was placed on top, which had a steel rod projecting upward for three feet. The tube was pounded into the sediment by a fifty-pound two-handled hammer that rode up and down on the steel rod. It sounds easier than it was, since divers are weightless under water, and trying to hover in the water and move that heavy hammer was quite a feat. Once most of the length of the tube had been driven into the sediment, things were a bit easier, because the diver could stand on the bottom, wrap his legs around the tube, and have more leverage to manipulate the hammer. After driving all but about a foot of the tube into the bottom, the heavier section of tubing and the hammer were removed, a rubber plug was screwed into the top of the tube to maintain suction (otherwise everything would drop out of the tube as it was being pulled up), and then the hardest work of all took place. Generally it took about one to one and a half hours to pound the corer down into the sediment, but sometimes it took twice that amount of time to pull it back out. During the first few days, Judd and I worked on the bottom twisting and pulling on the tube, while the other two divers and Walter worked from the skiff pulling on lines. The task became easier when Stan Judge brought up one of my small portable lifting bags. By attaching it to the top of the tube and filling it with air, it exerted an additional pulling force and helped a great deal.

Once the tube had been extracted, another plug was placed on its bottom and we swam it ashore on top of an inner tube. On the beach both plugs were then pulled out and the contents of the tube were carefully shaken out on a piece of canvas. We would then gingerly separate the sediment, searching for objects from the wreck, and those found were placed in water in plastic containers with tags denoting the location and the stratigraphical depth at which we had found them. During the first day, we made seven cores. Five of them produced a number of pieces of wood, several of which were two to three inches thick and the diameter of the coring tube, having been cut from larger pieces of wood by the sharp edge of the tube bottom. The other two cores we had started had struck solid objects at a depth of four feet and couldn't penetrate any farther. Using the water jet we found ballast rock to be the solid objects that had stopped the corer.

That night we dined on fried fish we had speared during the day and beans and rice—delicious, nourishing, and repeated every day. The mosquitoes and sand fleas were so thick after sunset that we had to sleep with our rubber diving suits on to keep from being devoured alive by the insects. During the day the local people had gone to work on Alphonso and Coral, scaring them with tales of man-eating sharks in the bay, and twice during the night Alphonso woke us all up screaming from shark nightmares. Unfortunately, early the following morning we sighted a large tiger shark hovering near us, and both Alphonso and Coral shot out of the water like a Polaris missile and refused to dive again. From then on, Judd and I had to dive alone, except for several days when my wife and Stan Judge came up to lend a hand.

The second day we made eight good cores, and in addition

to more pieces of wood—which I later discovered were oak and pine—we found fragments of animal bones (pig and chicken), pieces of charcoal, a striking flint (either for a weapon or for starting a fire), and a small coral-encrusted nail. During the day, several more inquisitive sharks appeared, and one suddenly began butting me with his snout while I was trying to measure the distance between the last core hole and the one we were then making. I smashed him on the head with a crowbar and he took off as if the devil were after him.

Our problems were not confined to the water that day. Sometime before we arrived, a rumor had started that we were after a large amount of gold on those wrecks, and the mayor of the town and four police officers appeared that afternoon and tried to arrest us, until I produced the permit from the Beach Control and letters from Seaga. When they realized their mistake and lost face in front of a number of townsfolk who had come with them, they decided to arrest Coral and Alphonso, who had been brazenly smoking ganja cigarettes right in front of them. It took some fast talking to keep them out of jail. It was really strange that both Coral and Alphonso considered the people from the north coast to be foreigners and would have nothing to do with them. Several evenings when they went into town for a few beers, they returned with cuts and bruises from fights they had had with the locals.

On the third day we struck solid objects at a depth of about nine feet, and on three occasions forced our way through them and came up with samples of ballast rock that were different from those we had found close to the surface. In addition to recovering more wood, bone, and charcoal, we found several coral-encrusted tacks, a few ceramic shards, a fragment of green glass, and a black bean—the type called *frijol* in Spain. Although we lost time whenever we had to cut our way through ballast rock, because we had to resharpen the cutting edge of the bottom of the tube, we managed to make nine good cores that day.

During the next four days we made thirty-four more cores, and every single one yielded wood and other material. We had enough samples to properly identify and date the wreck and I didn't want to disturb it any more, so we stopped using the coring device. Almost all the material we had recovered in the cores came up from a depth between eight and ten feet beneath the sea floor, and only a few pieces of wood came up from several feet deeper. These might have actually been pushed deeper into the sediment by the coring tube before it cut through them. Judd came up with a better system to define the exact limits of the wreck than my method of using a metal rod as a probe. With a twenty-foot-long piece of one-inch galvanized water pipe, we attached one of the hoses from an Aquanaut unit, and it worked fabulously. The air rushing down the length of pipe enabled the pipe to go down rapidly and without much force, and it was also easy to extract. Once solid objects were reached we turned off the air, and by tapping the object we could determine if it was wood or ballast rock by both feel and sound.

Before heading back to Kingston we spent another day diving on the site. All the evidence indicated that the wreck lay at a depth of eight to ten feet below the sea floor, so I was curious about the ballast rock we had located at a depth of only four feet in a small area of the wreck site. The question was answered by blowing away a large area of mud covering these ballast rocks. Artifacts we found among them, including clay pipestems and bottle fragments, I was able to date around the middle of the seventeenth century. The absence of wood or any type of ships' fittings indicated that a ship had probably been anchored in this spot, and before taking on a heavy cargo of sugar, rum, or molasses, had jettisoned some of the ship's ballast, a common practice in the old days.

An amusing incident occurred our last evening on the north coast. Judd announced that he refused to eat fish, rice, and beans again and offered to take everyone out for a good meal. The two divers and Walter had dates for the night with some local girls and declined the invitation, so Judd and I went alone. Barefooted and attired in dirty shorts and jerseys, we went to one of the fanciest restaurants in nearby Ocho Rios. The headwaiter refused to let us in because we didn't have jackets and ties on, so we asked to see the manager, who was apologetic when we explained our situation. He produced two ties and dinner jackets and we brought all talk to a stop as we walked into the packed dining room. The dinner jackets hung lower than the shorts and it looked as if we had forgotten to put our pants on. A number of tourists broke into such hysterical laughter that we both fled for the exit with stomachs growling after seeing the fantastic food being served. We then went to the Playboy Club, where things were a bit more informal and they were serving a smörgåsbord, which we attacked voraciously. Judd went through eleven heaping platefuls of delicious food before tackling the dessert.

Next morning we left for Kingston. At a certain point, Judd leaped from the truck cabin, after forcing the driver to come to an abrupt stop. His shorts were on fire. His great weight had forced the seat to touch the batteries stored beneath and the seat had caught fire. After applying first aid to his rear end, we continued our trip back to Kingston.

Then the waiting game began, and it turned out to be longer than I had expected. All the material we had recovered had to be sent to experts in England, Spain, and the United States, and it took almost three months until all the expected results were in. Most of the ballast rocks had come from Central America, and a few were from Spain, which I had expected, because I knew that Columbus had careened his vessels several times during his voyage along the coast of Central America. The Spaniards, according to many documents written by persons of other nationalities who had sailed aboard Spanish ships, were very messy and cared little for sanitation. Rather than throw trash, and sometimes even human waste, overboard, they would toss it into the hold among the ballast. Consequently, when Spanish ships, and also many ships of other nationalities, were careened, the old ballast was replaced with clean ballast.

According to experts at the Corning Glass Museum, the fragment of colored glass had been made in Venice and was probably from an hourglass and definitely dated from the time of Columbus. I knew that the pottery we had found was Spanish, and other experts confirmed this fact, but it was a type commonly in use for several centuries and not easy to date. A new method of dating ceramic or any other material that has been fired in a kiln had recently been developed, called thermoluminescence. Actually this new method wasn't as useful as it purported to be: I sent two shards to the Museum of Applied Science Center for Archaeology at the University of Pennsylvania and they dated the pieces as circa 1637, plus or minus a hundred fifty years. Shards sent to Oxford University in England were dated at 1475, plus or minus a hundred years. Both the striking flint and the black bean were reported to have come from Spain.

The fragments of wood were identified as coming from Spain, but the date I received for the first piece of wood that had been dated by the carbon-14 process presented a real problem. It was dated as twelve hundred years old, plus or minus a hundred years. I figured that the piece of wood might be a piece of firewood they found on land and thus furnish the reason for such an old date. So I sent several more for carbon-14 dating and again received the same date. Was there a Viking ship lying beneath the Columbus wreck? I knew that carbon-14 dating produced more accurate results for organic material dating in the thousands, rather than the hundreds, of years, but even so, the date shouldn't be off that much. The mystery was unraveled after I consulted several dendrologists. It isn't unusual for an oak tree to reach the age of one thousand years or even more, so it is perfectly conceivable that an oak tree seven hundred years old had been cut down and was used in building one of the two vessels lost in St. Ann's Bay.

As a final test of the authenticity of our discovery, I submitted all my findings to Admiral Samuel Eliot Morison and three other experts on Columbus in Spain and Colombia, and they were all convinced that we had discovered one of Columbus' wrecks.

APRIL–MAY

After returning from St. Ann's Bay I closed down my operation at Port Royal—returning the large compressor to the Public Works Department and dismantling the old barge and other equipment—keeping only Ivan and Walter on the payroll. I had enough work left to keep me busy for years, but really only two months left to do what I could, because I had planned to leave on June 1 for Florida, where I would start working as the Director of Salvage and Research for the Real Eight Company, the firm that had been successfully salvaging a number of the Spanish ships lost on the east coast of Florida in 1715. During these two months I divided my efforts between diving to identify the sonar contacts and making the charts containing this information, doing preservation work, and producing a number of archaeological reports on the excavation.

It would probably take a year to excavate and inspect each of the more than four thousand sonar contacts we had obtained during our survey in January, so I was forced to the speedier method of using my metal probe. The Survey Department had already plotted each of these contacts on four large charts, so it wasn't difficult to relocate them. Ivan and Walter worked from the skiff establishing the locations and buoying the positions of the contacts and recording the data I gave them on each one, while I dived and investigated them. Those protruding above the surface in most cases turned out to be either coral heads or the walls of old buildings and were easy to identify. The majority of those buried beneath the sediment, by both feel and sound I was able to identify as wood, metal, brick, or coral. Using this method I was also able to establish the approximate size and depth of the object and corroborate these findings with the same information obtained from the sonar graphs. My health was still quite poor, so I limited my diving to only four hours each day—but seven days a week—and it required six weeks to complete the task. Then I turned all the information over to the Survey Department. Each sonar contact was identified and they produced and published four detailed charts showing what was on and under the bottom of the area covering the sunken city. I made it quite easy for anyone who planned to work on the sunken city in the future.

Before my time ran out I managed to clean and preserve all the artifacts I had recovered, with the exception of those made of wood, glass, and iron. I figured that it would require a team of several preservation experts years to clean and preserve just the iron objects—providing that they could develop a good method. About a week before I left, I was quite surprised to find an Englishman named Jeven Bailey appear and announce that he was employed to take over the preservation work at Port Royal. I had been begging for such a person for two and a half years and I hadn't even been told he had been hired. He had no experience in preservation work, but he was a chemist by profession, which was a good start. I taught him everything I knew and turned over all the information I had on preservation techniques before wishing him good luck and leaving. When I returned for a brief visit to the island seven months later, Bailey was still there and it was as if I had just left the day before. Although he was receiving a salary, no funds at all had been provided for the equipment or supplies he needed, so he hadn't even started cleaning or preserving the first artifacts. Several months later he quit and left the island thoroughly disgusted.

Before leaving, I managed to write four more archaeological reports. The main one covered the complete excavation and was more a book than a report. Three others covered copper and brass, wineglasses, and the more than twelve thousand clay smoking pipes we had recovered. After returning to the United States I completed three others on the bottles, pewter, and silver recovered. After sending them to Jamaica to be published, where they collected dust for more than a year, I lost patience and had them published by the Caribbean Research Institute in the Virgin Islands. It was really heartbreaking after all the hard work of excavating the sunken city that the Jamaican Government wasn't even interested in publishing the results of our findings.

During my last few days on the island Seaga tried in every way possible to convince me to change my mind and stay. He wasn't interested in Port Royal any longer, but in the two Columbus wrecks in St. Ann's Bay. He wanted them excavated even though he was aware that the proper equipment, personnel, and preservation facilities were not available, and threatened that if I didn't stay to do the job, he would find someone who would. He already had several men from the Town Planning Division of the Survey Department designing a hotel and other tourist attractions he planned to have constructed close to the site of the wrecks. Soon after my departure the Jamaican representative to the United Nations approached UNESCO to provide a vast sum of money, supposedly for the excavation of the two wrecks, but I think that more of the funds would have gone into Seaga's tourism-development scheme. Fortunately UNESCO refused to provide the funds and the scheme was shelved, like so many other grandiose schemes created by publicity-hungry politicians all over the world. If the hotel and other tourist attractions had been developed according to plan, the whole archaeological site of New Seville, the site of the first settlement on the island, would have been completely destroyed and lost to mankind forever. This would have been as criminal as the dredging operation planned at Port Royal when I first arrived on the island.

On my last day on Jamaica I made one final nostalgic dive on the sunken city and was really disheartened to find that the hole that I had spent so long in digging and had suffered so many accidents in, was so filled in with silt that it was impossible to even locate the edges. That afternoon the many friends I had made at Port Royal threw a rip-roaring farewell party at the Buccaneers Roost for me. Everyone who had ever worked on the project, including all the persons I had had to fire, showed up, and we drank the place dry. I had tears in my eyes when my plane took off and passed over Port Royal, and my thoughts hurtled back many years as the stewardess announced we were passing over the sunken city of Port Royal. A similar announcement when I first flew over Port Royal fourteen years before had engendered wild visions of my finding and someday excavating the city intact beneath the sea.

Chapter Ten

EPILOGUE

Since my departure five years ago a number of underwater archaeologists and explorers have applied for permission to work on the sunken city of Port Royal—and in several cases those applying have even offered to finance the whole project and turn over every single item recovered to the Jamaican Government —but none of them has been successful. The National Geographic Society has shown a great interest in the sunken city and has approached me about returning to direct another excavation project of the site—this time with sufficient funds to do the project properly, which the society would supply. After more than two years of waiting to get either a "yes" or a "no" answer from Seaga about returning and working under the auspices of the National Geographic Society, I gave up in disgust and decided to see if someone else would have better luck in obtaining the permission.

Seaga had been determined to find someone to excavate the two Columbus shipwrecks in St. Ann's Bay, and he tried to entice everyone from the famous French explorer Jacques Cousteau to Dr. George Bass of the University of Pennsylvania. Fortunately they all declined the invitation for the same reasons I had refused to excavate. Then, early in 1969 I received a letter from Frédéric Dumas, the French archaeologist who had worked with Cousteau for many years and for the past few years has devoted most of his efforts to underwater archaeology. He represented a group of wealthy Frenchmen who had offered to put up all the money required to excavate the Columbus wrecks and already had a contract with Seaga to do so. They had hired Dumas to make a preliminary survey of the site, and he came to Jamaica in February of 1969. The day he arrived I received a frantic telephone call from him. He said that all my reports and charts of the wreck site had been misplaced and he didn't have the foggiest idea where the wrecks were or where to start. I flew down the following day and was able to spend only several hours with him, because I was then conducting an excavation of a shipwreck off the coast of Florida. I gave him copies of what reports I still had and placed a buoy over the site. As I had expected, he received very little assistance from the Jamaican Government, and five days later he left without having accomplished much. That was the last I heard about anyone showing further interest in excavating the wrecks.

The Jamaican Government finally accepted the advice of Dr. Ivor Noel Hume of Colonial Williamsburg and other archaeologists concerning the importance of land excavations at Port Royal. A substantial amount of funds was obtained from UNESCO and the British Ministry of Overseas Development. Four months after my departure, in September of 1968, the services of an archaeologist from the University of Leeds, in England, a Mr. Philip Mayes, were obtained, and he was given a three-year contract to carry on a program of land excavation at Port Royal. Although Mayes worked directly under the Jamaican National Trust Commission and Seaga, he had more control and fewer problems than I had had in getting started, because his salary and most of the financing for the project came from the British ministry.

During the first year he spent on the island he managed to

spend over $110,000 (more than four times the whole amount spent for my complete project), and since that time an additional $350,000 has been spent on the land-excavation project at Port Royal, which has produced very little in terms of archaeological information and the recovery of artifacts from the old town, when compared with my own underwater excavation. More than a year passed after Mayes's arrival before any serious land excavations were even started.

He decided to use the old Naval Hospital as his project center, as I had done, and a great deal of the almost half million dollars that has been spent (and more is still being spent) was utilized in renovating the rooms in the hospital and converting them into offices, storage rooms, and laboratories. The six rooms on the ground floor of the hospital were all air-conditioned and furnished with the most advanced equipment available. Considering that I had to wait two years to have electricity and fresh water connected to just one of the rooms I used, I was bug-eyed when I saw the transformation done to the old hospital. One room, boasting a dehumidifying system, with floor-to-ceiling shelves, is used to store artifacts before they are cleaned and preserved. A second room is used as a conservation laboratory and is equipped with the latest in preservation equipment, including a large X-ray machine; it also contains a photographic studio and a darkroom. A third room is a laboratory primarily devoted to artifact washing and is equipped with sinks and storage tanks. A fourth room is another storage room for artifacts that have already been cleaned and preserved. A fifth room is divided into several different rooms: bathrooms, a kitchenette and dining facilities, and offices for the artists and artifacts' officers. The last room is utilized as the administrative offices, a drafting room, and a library. The second floor of the hospital building is currently being renovated to contain a museum, a lecture hall, and more offices. Presently more than twenty persons are employed to work as assistants to the land archaeologist in the old hospital handling the tasks of recording, drawing, photographing, cleaning, preserving, and storing the items recovered on land.

Finally, late in 1969 Mayes began making various test-hole excavations in areas on land, and he found, as I had previously, that the water table was only two feet below the surface of the ground. Before carrying out any further excavations, he purchased four large well-point water pumps capable of removing six thousand gallons of water per minute and obtained the services of several civil engineers. He had originally planned to excavate in the area of the old hospital, but he then learned that plans were underway with the Port Royal Company of Merchants to build a large hotel in the area that had been used as the Royal Naval Shipyard until 1905. Since this was on the property for which Jenkinson held a 99-year lease from the British Government, the Jamaican Government could not stop construction of a hotel there. Through the British Ministry of Overseas Development, Mayes was able to convince the developers to delay construction until he had thoroughly excavated the area.

A large hole, three hundred feet long by eighty feet wide, was laid out in the threatened area, and then horizontal stripping of the post-1692 levels of occupation was carried out to a depth of two feet, where they reached the water level. It was found that there were, in all, six main occupations, showing as superimposed surfaces, between 1735, the date of the first naval occupation in this area, and the present day. A number of structures, as diverse in form as the dockyard wall and a blacksmith's shop (1735), a sea defense wall (circa 1740), and the base of a watchtower and a ceremonial flagpole base dating around 1840, were revealed.

Once the pumps were put into use and they began to dig deeper, Mayes's group located the rectangular outline of a large brick structure, the walls of which projected to a maximum height of six inches above sea level. Probing along the inside of the wall, they found that plaster still adhered to the walls, which stood vertically to a depth of more than six feet below sea level. Their first attempts to lower the water level were not quite successful; they could lower it only about three feet six inches. But it did allow Mayes the opportunity to conjecture from the shape that the building appeared to be a church. Additional pumps were installed, and by using a closer spacing of the well points and restricting their activities to a hole thirty by forty feet in extent, they successfully lowered the water table to a depth greater than ten feet and the pumps were able to remove water faster than it came into the hole.

The church measured sixty by ninety-six feet in extent, and from contemporary documents and maps Mayes was able to identify it as being St. Paul's Church. The wall tops that had first been located were buried in relatively clean gray sand, and the removal of this material proceeded rapidly to a depth of six feet below sea level. At this depth, quantities of timber appeared, and to protect these waterlogged timbers from rapid deterioration in the sun, a section of the structure was roofed with black polythene. Beneath this roof a system of atomized sprays was used to provide a fine water mist to further protect the timbers. As the timber was very soft, hung scaffolding and planking were arranged so that undue pressure on the unexcavated levels was avoided. Again, because of the softness of the wood, adjustable water sprays were arranged to allow the excavators to gently wash away the sand and silt around the surviving woodwork; the use of metal tools was precluded, and hands alone were used to excavate the fragile wood. Most of the wood consisted of roof beams and fragments of four cedarwood pews. At a depth of nine feet below sea level they reached the planked wooden floor of the building, which was covering a layer of large ceramic tiles. The only artifacts of any note discovered were an iron padlock, a wooden carpenter's mallet, a rat's skull, and fragments of five leather buckets—one bearing very clear red letters three inches high: P.R. 1685.

Adjacent to the church they located a wooden longboat, forty feet in length with a twelve-foot beam, which had probably been thrown up against the church by the tidal wave during the 1692 earthquake. While Mayes and his team were excavating the longboat and plans were being studied to build a wall around the area to make it into a permanent display, the whole excavation project in that area was suddenly brought to a dramatic stop.

In March of 1971, about a year and half after Mayes had begun excavating in the area of the proposed hotel, the Port Royal Company of Merchants, either unhappy about the long delay in their plans for building the hotel or simply because of other factors, attacked the Jamaican Government viciously in the press, accusing them of having stalled and hindered their development plans for six years, and threatening to bring the matter to court. The developers had a court injunction issued against any further excavations on the property leased to Jenkinson, and Mayes was ordered to stop work in the area. Rather than have the developers benefit from the church and other things that had been uncovered, Seaga had the whole area filled in again with the use of bulldozers. A big battle between the government and the developers ensued, and it is still in progress at the time of this writing. The government retaliated to the injunction of the land excavation by having twelve of the sixteen rooms of Jenkinson's hotel declared unfit for use by tourists and consequently leveled to the ground.

Mayes then spent several months making minor excavations in other areas in Port Royal, but his finds were very discouraging. With the exception of one two-escudo Spanish gold coin and a pewter spoon, all his finds consisted of broken bottles, ceramic shards, and badly corroded iron objects. In June of 1971, two months before his contract was due to expire, he unexpectedly left the island and returned home. He had been unpopular with the people at Port Royal and those who worked under him, much in the same way that the Englishwoman Gloria Gilchrist, who had worked for me, had been. Basically the Jamaicans, who were under British rule for more than three centuries, have little sympathy for British subjects, and many Englishmen, I found, aggravate this situation by acting arrogant and treating the Jamaicans as if they were still British subjects. The main reason for Mayes's untimely departure was that Ivan the Terrible, one of the best men who had worked on my project, and who had also worked for Mayes as a watchman, almost choked Mayes to death in an argument of unknown origin, before he was pulled off the terrified Englishman. Ivan became a hero at Port Royal, but he paid for his indiscretion by spending a brief period in jail.

The British Ministry of Overseas Development then sent a replacement for Mayes, another Englishman, by the name of Richard Priddy, who had spent several years working as an archaeologist in England and West Africa. During the year that Priddy has been in charge of the Port Royal land excavation he has supervised the excavation of several buildings near the old hospital, but like Mayes, his excavators have recovered very few artifacts of interest. I was unable to understand why they were recovering so few artifacts until I returned to Port Royal.

In April of 1971, after a long absence from the island, I made a brief visit and found the answer. Both Mayes and Priddy had spent the majority of their time in the air-conditioned rooms of the project center, leaving the actual supervision of the excavation in the hands of others, with only periodic inspection trips to the various sites. At the first site I visited I found all the excavators happily drinking beer in the shade of some trees, and since none of them knew me, they thought I was a tourist and asked me if I wanted to buy any souvenirs of old Port Royal. I said I did, just to see what they had to sell, and they produced eight Spanish silver coins, two British gold coins, and a gold religious medallion, also stating that they had plenty more for sale in their homes. Apparently they were robbing the project blind, and I passed this information on to Priddy and others.

I was also dismayed to find that with the exception of only a few onion bottles and about two dozen iron objects, no preservation had been done, was being done, or was planned for the near future on the thousands of artifacts we had recovered from the underwater excavation. Many of the larger items, such as the cannon, mortar balls, and large iron conglomerates, had been thrown back into the sea, and one of the laboratory assistants confidentially informed me that all the rest of the iron and wood we had recovered were also going to be thrown into the sea. I managed to put a stop to this outrage, but was too late to save the tons of bricks we had so laboriously brought up, one by one, for they had already been thrown back into the sea.

If what I saw at Port Royal made me sad, what I learned later that same day was enough to put me in a state of acute depression for weeks. Several months previously, thieves were reported to have broken into the silver house, or Port Royal Museum, at Devon House, the major tourist attraction in Kingston, and had cleaned the place out. Many people I talked to believed it was an inside job, but there was no proof of this except that someone had neglected to lock the door of the museum the night it was broken into. All the most important items we had recovered—the Chinese porcelain figurine, the silver pocket watch, all the gold items, a large number of coins, and hundreds of other priceless and irreplaceable items—were gone. The government somehow managed to keep the news of the robbery a secret from the unsuspecting public, and the culprits were never found.

I had planned to spend several days on the island but I was so brokenhearted from what I had seen on the first day, that I left the following morning, hoping I would never have to return to Jamaica again. It was almost as if I had wasted three years of my life and had nothing more to show for it than a bad back that will cause me pain for the rest of my life.

Bibliography

No author. *Voyages, Adventures and Escapes of Capt. R. Falconer*. London, 1720.

No author. *The Present State of Jamaica with Life of the Great Columbus*. London, 1683.

No author. *The Importance of Jamaica to Great Britian Considered with Some Accounts of the Island*. London, c. 1740.

No author. *The Laws of Jamaica*. London, 1695.

No author. *A Trip to Jamaica with a True Character of the People and Island*. London, 1700.

No author. *The Truest and Largest Account of the Late Earthquake in Jamaica, Written by a Reverend Divine There to a Friend in London*. London, 1693.

No author. *Ampel en Breed Verhaal van de Jongft-Gewefene Aardbevinge tot Port Royal in Jamaica op den 7 Juny 1692*. Rotterdam, 1692.

Various authors, "Port Royal Anthology," *The Jamaican Historical Society Bulletin*, Vol. II, No. 8, December, 1958.

Various authors. *Underwater Archaeology: A Nascent Discipline*. Published by UNESCO, Paris, 1972.

There are hundreds of documents concerning Port Royal published in the Calendar of State Papers, Colonial Series, America and the West Indies. Volumes one through seven cover the period from the founding of the city until the 1692 earthquake.

Real Estate Transactions Before the 1692 Earthquake: City of Port Royal, Jamaica. Original compilation by the Institute of Jamaica. Indexed and carded by the National Geographic Society.

Aitkins, M. J. *Physics and Archaeology.* New York, 1961

Bass, George F. *Underwater Archaeology.* New York, 1966.

Beer, G. L. *The Old Colonial System, 1660–1754.* New York, 1933.

Black, Clinton. *Port Royal.* Kingston, Jamaica, 1970.

Blome, Richard. *A Description of the Island of Jamaica.* London, 1672.

Bridges, G. W. *The Annals of Jamaica.* London, 1828.

Burgess, Robert F. *Sinkings, Salvages and Shipwrecks.* New York, 1970.

Carse, Robert. *The Age of Piracy.* New York, 1957.

Coke, T. *A History of the West Indies.* Liverpool, 1808.

Cotter, Charles S, "The Aborigenes of Jamaica," *The Jamaican Historical Review,* Vol. 1, No. 2 (Dec. 1946), pp. 137–41.

Cundall, Frank. *Historic Jamaica.* London, 1915.

———. *The Governors of Jamaica in the Seventeenth Century.* London, 1937.

———. *The Governors of Jamaica in the First Half of the Eighteenth Century.* London, 1937.

Cundall, Frank & Pietersz, J. *Jamaica Under the Spaniards.* Kingston, Jamaica, 1919.

Davies, J. *The History of the Caribby-Islands.* London, 1666.

Edwards, Bryan. *The History, Civil and Commercial, of the British Colonies in the West Indies.* London, 1793.

Esquemeling, J. *History of the Buccaneers in America.* Amsterdam, 1678.

Flemming, N. C. *Cities in the Sea.* Garden City, N.Y., 1971.

Gardiner, W. J. *History of Jamaica, from Its Discovery by Christopher Columbus to the Year 1872.* London, 1909.

Goreau, T. & Burke, K., "Pleistocene and Holocene Geology of the Island Shelf near Kingston, Jamaica," *Marine Geology*, Vol 4, pp. 207–25.

Gores, Joseph N. *Marine Salvage*. Garden City, N.Y., 1971.

Haring, C. H. *The Buccaneers in the West Indies in the Seventeenth Century*. London, 1910.

——. *Trade and Navigation Between Spain and the Indies in the Time of the Hapsburgs*. Cambridge, Mass., 1918.

Johnson, Charles. *A History of the Robberies and Murders of the Most Notorious Pirates*. London, 1724.

——. *A General History of the Pirates*. London, 1726.

Leard, John. *Sailing Directions for the Island of Jamaica*. London, 1792.

Leslie, Charles. *A New and Exact Account of Jamaica*. London, 1739.

Link, Marion C., "Exploring the Drowned City of Port Royal," *National Geographic*, February 1960, pp. 151–82.

Long, Edward. *History of Jamaica*. 3 vols., London, 1774.

McKee, Alexander. *History Under the Sea*. London, 1968.

Martínez-Hidalgo, José María. *Columbus' Ships*. Barre, Mass., 1966.

Marx, Robert F. *The Treasure Fleets of the Spanish Main*. Cleveland and New York, 1968.

——. *Pirate Port: The Story of the Sunken City of Port Royal*. Cleveland and New York, 1967.

——. *They Dared the Deep: A History of Diving*. Cleveland and New York, 1967.

——. *Always Another Adventure*. Cleveland and New York, 1967.

——. *Shipwrecks of the Western Hemisphere*. Cleveland and New York, 1971.

——. *Sea Fever*. Garden City, N.Y., 1972.

——, "The Drowned City of Port Royal," *UNESCO Courier*, May 1972, pp. 28–38.

——, "Discovery of Two Ships of Columbus," *Jamaica Journal*, Dec. 1968, pp. 13–17.

———, "The Last Day of Port Royal," *Jamaica Journal,* December 1967, pp. 16–20.

———, "Divers of Port Royal," *Jamaica Journal,* March 1968, pp. 15–23.

———, "Excavating the Sunken City of Port Royal: 1966 The First Year," *Jamaica Journal,* June 1968, pp. 12–18.

———, "Port Royal," *Oceans Magazine,* June 1969, pp. 66–77.

The following are archaeological reports written on the project by me:

Excavation of the Sunken City of Port Royal: December 1965–December 1966, published by the Institute of Jamaica, Kingston, Jamaica, March 1967, 73 pages.

Excavation of the Sunken City of Port Royal: January 1967–March 1968, published by Jamaica National Trust Commission, Kingston, Jamaica, May 1968, 122 pages.

Clay Smoking Pipes Recovered from the Sunken City of Port Royal: May 1, 1966–September 30, 1967, published by Jamaica National Trust Commission, Kingston, Jamaica, March 1968, 123 pages.

Clay Smoking Pipes Recovered from the Sunken City of Port Royal: October 1, 1967–March 31, 1968, published by Jamaica National Trust Commission, Kingston, Jamaica, August 1968, 75 pages.

Brass and Copper Items Recovered from the Sunken City of Port Royal: May 1, 1966–March 31, 1968, published by the Jamaica National Trust Commission, Kingston, Jamaica, May 1968, 103 pages.

Wine Glasses Recovered from the Sunken City of Port Royal: May 1, 1966–March 31, 1968, published by the Jamaica National Trust Commission, May 1968, 35 pages.

Glass Bottles Recovered from the Sunken City of Port Royal: May 1, 1966–March 31, 1968, published by the Caribbean Research Institute, St. Thomas, Virgin Islands, January 1969, 38 pages.

Silver and Pewter Items Recovered from the Sunken City of Port Royal: May 1, 1966–March 31, 1968, published by the

Caribbean Research Institute, St. Thomas, Virgin Islands, August 1971, 93 pages.

Mayes, Philip, "Port Royal, Jamaica: The Archaeological Problems and Potential," *Journal of Nautical Archaeology*, Vol. 1, March 1972, pp. 97–112.

Morales Padrón, Francisco. *Jamaica Española*. Seville, Spain, 1952.

Morison, Samuel Eliot. *Admiral of the Ocean Sea*. Boston, 1942.

Newton, A. P. *The European Nations in the West Indies, 1493–1688*. London, 1933.

Noël-Hume, Ivor. *Historical Archaeology*. New York, 1969.

——. *Here Lies Virginia*. New York, 1963.

——. *A Guide to Artifacts of Colonial America*. New York, 1970.

——, "A Collection of Glass from Port Royal, Jamaica, with Some Observations on the Site, Its History and Archaeology," *Journal of Historical Archaeology*, Vol. 1, 1968, pp. 5–34.

Oldmixon, J. *The British Empire in America*. 2 vols., London, 1708.

Peterson, Mendel. *History Under the Sea*. Smithsonian Inst., Washington, D.C., 1965.

Potter, John S., Jr. *The Treasure Diver's Guide*. Rev. ed., Garden City, N.Y., 1972.

Pyddoke, Edward (ed.). *The Scientist and Archaeology*. London, 1963.

Sloane, Sir Hans. *A Voyage to the Islands of Madeira, Barbados, Nieves, St. Christopher and Jamaica*. 3 vols., London, 1707.

St. John Wilkes, Bill. *Nautical Archaeology*. Bristol, England, 1971.

Taylor, Joan du Plat (ed.). *Marine Archaeology*. London, 1965.

Taylor, John. Second part of the historie of his life and travels in America. This unpublished manuscript is preserved in the Institute of Jamaica and contains the most important description of life in Port Royal prior to the 1692 earthquake.

Throckmorton, Peter. *Shipwrecks and Archaeology*. Boston, 1969.

NOTE: A large amount of original research was done by the author from documents in the following places: Archivo General de las Indias, Seville, Spain; Archivo de Simancas, Simancas, Spain; Museo Naval, Madrid, Spain; Jamaican Archives, Spanish Town, Jamaica; Institute of Jamaica, Kingston, Jamaica; British Museum, London, England; Public Records Office, London, England; and National Maritime Museum, Greenwich, England.

INDEX

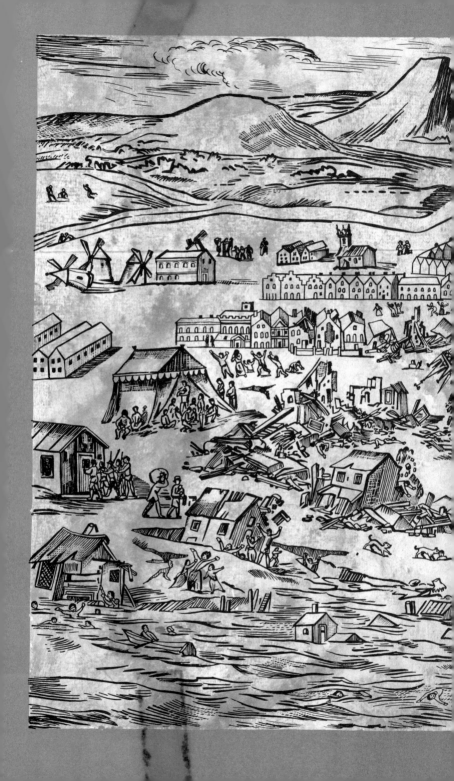